Ratbag, Soldier, Saint

The real story of Sergeant Issy Smith VC

Lian Knight was born in Sydney at a time of prosperous growth for the country's busiest city. She almost missed her start in life, being dangerously ill at birth, resulting in family urgently congregating from interstate and her father rushing the birth details, changing the spelling of her name on her birth certificate. Following a miraculous recovery through the quick thinking of talented Sydney doctors, her family moved closer to their origins in Melbourne where she was raised in the eastern suburbs. For 30 years she forged a satisfying career with numerous senior roles in major corporates before fulfilling her lifelong dream to write. This is her second book, and first nonfiction.

Also by Lian Knight

Idle Lies (Hybrid Publishers 2019)

Praise for *Ratbag, Soldier, Saint*

'From page 1 of 'Ratbag, Soldier, Saint', I entered the magnificent maze of the life of Issy Smith, wonderfully led through that life by Issy's granddaughter, Lian Knight. In her affectionate and uplifting words we learn of his extraordinary odyssey which brought him from Europe to the Middle East to the British Isles and to Australia, from a hand to mouth subsistence to a military career, from the routine of peacetime to the horrors of war, from anonymity to great fame as a war hero, accorded the highest accolade. He was always a battler, against the trials of war, against economic hardship, ill health and prejudice but he never stopped striving. A legendary figure, Issy's story is pared back from the earlier wealth of conjecture by Lian's wry and attractive biography but we finish this account of his life knowing him still to be a legend, an ordinary man making his way around the world and its history, a hero and a remarkable Australian.'

– General the Hon Sir **Peter Cosgrove** AK AC(Mil) CVO MC (RETD)

'The real story of Sergeant Issy Smith is an extraordinarily well researched book on the life of the first living Jewish soldier to win the Victoria Cross. In the process, we are exposed to a detailed documentary on the First World War, the Great Depression, antisemitism and, most significantly, the incandescent life of Issy Smith. It's also a reminder of the hard years during the first half of the 20th century and how Australia tackled them.'

– **Bob Ansett**, entrepreneur

'In this riveting book, written by Issy's own granddaughter, lies a story of courage and caring, of leadership and of life for a man who stood apart from most others. Issy was a patriot, a family man, a man of the community, a VC recipient - but he was also a man who struggled with the repercussions of war. With how it left so many of his fellow veterans.

In this book, Lian Knight captures the soul of her grandfather and yet some of the mystery still remains for unless you read the story and think of it in the context of its time, you will miss its import

– **Ange Kenos** FRVAHJ, Essendon RSL President

'*Ratbag, Soldier, Saint* by Lian Knight brilliantly recounts the unusual life of Sergeant Issy Smith VC, a Jewish war hero of WWI, revealing the many challenges he and his family faced in Australia and England during the war and in the post-war years. A captivating read!

– MAJGEN (Ret'd), Emeritus Professor **Jeffrey V Rosenfeld** AC, OBE

RATBAG SOLDIER SAINT

The real story of
Sergeant Issy Smith VC

LIAN KNIGHT

HYBRID
PUBLISHERS

Published by Hybrid Publishers

Melbourne Victoria Australia

© Lian Knight 2021

This publication is copyright. Apart from any use
as permitted under the Copyright Act 1968, no part may be reproduced
by any process without prior written permission from the publisher.
Requests and inquiries concerning reproduction should be addressed to
the Publisher, Hybrid Publishers,
PO Box 52, Ormond, Victoria, Australia 3204.

www.hybridpublishers.com.au

First published 2022

 A catalogue record for this book is available from the National Library of Australia

ISBN: 9781925736830 (p)
9781925736847 (e)

Cover design: Gittus Graphics

Cover photo of Issy Smith in India circa 1906, from author's collection

In loving memory of my father
(Issy's son)
Maurice Smith OAM
who encouraged and helped me record Issy's life story
8.11.1932–21.10.2020
Order of Australia awarded 26.1.2021
NSW Justice of the Peace (JP) 1963–2020

Contents

Foreword by Issy Smith's Son, Maurice	ix
Introduction: In the Beginning …	1
1: Issy's Parents	4
2: Escape from Russia	11
3: Refuge in Constantinople	17
4: Safety in Egypt	22
5: Stowaway to London	29
6: Detention	36
7: Alf and Boxing Fame	41
8: Issy Meets Elsie	48
9: War Breaks Out	56
10: Neuve Chapelle	62
11: Lost Cigarettes and the Battle at Ypres …	69
12: The BIG News	81
13: On the Road	92
14: Prejudice and Faceless Fraud	104
15: Tales Down Under	110
16: Pressure Mounts	116
17: Disaster and Splendour	121
18: The Ill-fated Campaign	125
19: End of the Fight	139

20: Joys and Challenges of Returning Home	150
21: Postwar Slide	156
22: The Royal Smack and Other Noble Events	167
23: Desperation	173
24: Lights! Camera! Action!	178
25: The Lure Down Under	185
26: Things Don't Always Go to Plan	195
27: Britain vs. Hollywood	198
28: Chaos and Despair	206
29: Racecourses and Picture Houses	213
30: The Politics of Elections	220
31: Life in the Public Eye	230
32: The Punishing Depression	239
33: Dark Clouds Loom	248
34: The Appeals	252
35: Into the Airways	258
36: Grim Resolve	265
37: The Final Salute	274
38: In Memoriam	281
Addendum 1	285
Addendum 2	287
Acknowledgements	289
Endnotes	293

Foreword

by Issy Smith's Son, Maurice

Issy Smith was a war hero. He was also my hero, and my father.

Regrettably, the opportunity for us to spend time together was cut short; he died before my eighth birthday. Consequently my memories of him are limited, though there a few that have remained over the more than eighty years since his passing.

I knew him as a quiet, easygoing individual, kind and generous. He liked to spend time with me and took me to interesting and varying places. I spent time at his workplace and he showed me a development that would change many manufacturing processes – Bakelite, the forerunner to plastic. It transformed the way many products, particularly in the electricity industry, were produced.

He took me to 'The Lane' (Flinders Lane), centre of the rag trade and home to many Jewish businesses, including one belonging to his friend, Henry Lubransky. Issy had a Harris Tweed overcoat made to measure for me, just to match his own. I was about five at the time and I remember wearing it, proudly holding his hand as we walked down the street together.

Issy liked his garden, and on summer evenings we would sit on the front steps and hose the plants, the garden being small enough that the whole garden could be covered without having to move. He named the plants for me but, looking back, I don't think he knew much about gardening or plant names, other than what he had read on their labels!

He taught me about boxing and how to defend myself, a skill that

I only ever used once. At State school, just like everywhere else in the community, there was a fairly strong undercurrent of antisemitism. My school was no different. Generally, I got along fairly well with all of my peers but there was one individual, a boy named Clemson, who constantly gave me a hard time. He always referred to me as the 'little Jew boy'. His group of mates sometimes joined in but Clemson was the leader and he encouraged the others.

One day, in the schoolground, he started to abuse me and for extra attention from his group gave me a hearty shove, sending me down on my knees. They all thought it was very funny. Clemson was standing with his face up close to mine, shouting insults. Completely out of character for me, I hit him. Right on the chin! He went down flat on his back and I thought I was in for a hiding. Not so: he stood up, rubbed the dirt off his clothes and walked away. He never came near me again! I didn't tell Issy about it.

We owned a car – not the norm for most families. Issy taught me to drive. I was too young to reach the pedals so I would sit on his lap and steer. We spent a lot of time driving the streets of Moonee Ponds and occasionally he would take me 'off road' and make me negotiate rough terrain and creek crossings, turning the wheel to ease the car across. Some of the things he taught me remain with me to this day.

I never saw him angry or excited. He was always remarkably placid and there was no greater example than when he resolved an antisemitic incident at Café Florentino restaurant, an incident that Lian explains in more detail within the book.

Just as I was proud of my father, I am immensely proud of my daughter. She has taken on a virtually impossible task to recreate the history of my father and his family. It has been a long and time-consuming project, but one truly worthwhile!

Introduction

In the Beginning …

I hope to be back all right, but if I die on the battlefield, well, greater love hath no man than to die for his friends. If I die, I will be remembered by them and their children.

– Corporal Issy Smith V.C.[1]

It's 1969. Or maybe early 1970. In any case, I am about seven years old and I've just had a huge fight with my best friend at primary school. She just won't listen and it's infuriating.

You have ONE set of grandparents, not TWO.

There are your parents, and your parents' parents, I tell her. Who the heck are this other set she is talking about? I have never heard of them. I storm home and unleash my frustrations on my father, Maurice, who listens and then quietly sits me down for an education on the facts of life and an explanation. The next day I have to eat humble pie.

Apparently, I do have another set of grandparents, I begrudgingly admit to her. There is my grandfather on my father's side, who I have just learned about.

I am over the fight already. Suddenly I know a little about a unique and truly special man who died nearly 30 years earlier.

Instantly I am incredibly proud of him. He was a war hero who saved many lives. At the same time, I am angry that we have wars in which lives need to be saved. If we didn't argue, then we wouldn't have wars. And I would have a grandfather I could have met and loved in person.

Yet I have met him, through his legacy.

They say a cat has nine lives. If this fallacy was indeed true and could apply to people too, then my grandfather used at least that many more lives than his allotted one. Had just one of these near misses been a direct hit, then neither my father nor I would have been here to grace this earth and tell his story.

But this isn't just a combat tale about escaping death multiple times through fortuitous and sometimes fluky survival. This is also about a man with as many different livelihoods and experiences as escapes, each interwoven with a fabric of compassion, perplexity and intrigue.

So who was this man, Issy Smith VC?

What is published about him is extraordinary. Aside from the books and websites in which he features, I found close to 2000 newspaper articles about him, most printed more than a century ago, and likely just a hint of the true number that could be amassed from all over the world if every country's archives and every newspaper's pay service was utilised. Yet almost nothing written about him is consistent. The media varies his name, his age, his place of birth, where he lived and what he did. The man himself added to the mystery, being whimsical with his personal details and remaining modest about his deeds.

The only fact that remains the same is the award of the Victoria Cross – the highest award for military valour that can be bestowed by the British Armed Forces. Presented to him for one of his incredible acts of bravery at the Second Battle of Ypres in 1915, it became the story of the times in Great Britain, France, Ireland, and as far across the world as the Americas and Australia. After its announcement, the media went to town with both real and unsubstantiated stories of his life and exploits. According to the press reports, he became one of the world's greatest heroes, having participated (it would appear) in the capture of German New Guinea and the wreck of the SS *Emden* in Cocos islands, as well as fighting in the battles of Givenchy, Neuve Chapelle, the First Battle of Ypres, the Dardanelles Campaign and Hill 60. Then, after the Second Battle of Ypres and gallant rescues which led to the award of his VC, he was apparently engaged in the battle of Loos and later, sometime after his ship was torpedoed, personally volunteered to row out and save Russian soldiers from their blazing and sinking ship. It would appear that he was involved in the Siege of Kut, the fall of Baghdad and the fall of Jerusalem, and he was purported to be the youngest, the first and the only Jew to ever receive the highest honour Britain could bestow. He became a film star with journalists claiming he featured in more than 20 films, was embroiled in a political drama and scandal, and in the course of this notoriety, the secret identity of the famous English boxer, Jack Daniels, was revealed with great excitement as his alias.

Which of these stories was real? Issy made no attempt to dispel the myths or to separate facts from fiction, and as a result, a mixture of truth and fantasy continues to be reported in the history books to this day.

This makes the mystery about the man himself all the more puzzling. Who was he really and what made him tick? Was he a ratbag, a rebel or a saint? It is obvious from the events that unfold that he wasn't a coward, a wise-guy or a misfit. Nor, from these tales, was he a slacker or a snob. Although inborn with a strong spirit and a wild streak, he bore no racist views, held no radical ideals and carried no grudges.

As I dug into his life and times, what I found underneath the hype was a battler, a fighter, a saviour, a good Samaritan and a man deeply proud of his faith.

All rolled into one.

Chapter 1

Issy's Parents

Issy's parents were Moses Shmeilowitz (spelt multiple ways) and Eva Tchukov (also Choudnovsky), but this is as far back as anyone can trace. The uncovering of their incredible struggle helps explain the battles Issy faced throughout his life, even after such acts of valour were recognised.

Both were referred to, in various documents, as being either of Polish or Russian Jewish heritage, or more simply as 'Polish or Russian Jews'. In order to sort this out, it quickly became clear that it was necessary to dig someway into the depths of Eastern European history. Over the centuries, borders moved in all directions with various invasions, wars and annexations, and ownership passed through different hands; their 'heritage' could best be determined by working out who occupied the area at the time. The term 'heritage' used as nationality was not generally granted to Jews. Issy's parents were therefore not Polish or Russian Jews, but rather Jews in Poland or Russia.

As Eva's birthplace in Berdichev was certain, I began there.

Centuries ago, Berdichev was part of the Kiev *voivodeship* (an area administered by a governor within the Grand Duchy of Lithuania). The Kiev *voivodeship* fell either side of the Dnieper River, from 100 kilometres to the north, near Chernobyl (the site of Russia's nuclear disaster in 1986), to just short of the Black Sea in the south. From 1569 until 1793 it fell under the Polish–Lithuanian Commonwealth, though the city of Kiev was given to imperial Russia by the Treaty of Andrusovo in 1667. In 1793 the ownership changed when Prussia signed a treaty with Russia, and the Kiev *voivodeship*, along with a number of others, was transferred to the Russian Empire.

Eva was born in the city in 1845, therefore her heritage must be considered as 'Russian', as it was at the time.

Things became a little messy with respect to possession of Berdichev in the aftermath of the Great War, which could explain the further confusion about Issy's heritage.[1] The city became part of the Republic of Poland when the state was re-established in 1918.[2] Then, during a period of civil war which ran from 1917 to 1923, ownership changed again as the Ukrainian Soviet Socialist Republic was formed and became one of the constituent republics of the Soviet Union after its inception in 1922. The small town remained under this umbrella until the breakup of the Soviet Union in 1991, at which time Ukraine gained its independence.

There were many articles written about Issy after his investiture of the VC in 1915. Many of those in the family's possession are clippings from the original newspapers and are undated. If they were written shortly after his VC was awarded, then the town of Berdichev belonged to Russia. If they were written immediately after WWI and before 1923, the town was part of Poland. After this time the town was part of the Soviet Union. If the writers of these articles did not give the history of the land any further thought, the confusion about Polish and Russian heritage can be explained.

By 1860, when Eva was fifteen, Berdichev had become the city with the largest share of the Jewish population in the Russian Empire. Nothing is known about her life at that time, and how long she lived there can only be guessed – it was at least until she married in the mid-1860s. Luckily, she and her subsequent family were gone before the following century, when the town suffered one of the worst atrocities in modern times, the murder of more than 30,000 people.

> ## The massacre at Berdichev
>
> In the lead-up to WWII, conditions changed when the Soviet authorities closed most of the town's synagogues and the use of Yiddish, which had become officially recognised and used in the local Courts of Law, was restricted. All Jewish cultural activities were then suspended.
>
> When the Nazis began their invasion of Berdichev on 22 June 1941 there was little chance to leave. The German Army took over the town and occupied it until 5 January 1944. An 'extermination' unit was established in early July 1941 and a Jewish ghetto was set up. On 5 October 1941 the ghetto was liquidated by a 25-member shooting squad, supported by Ukrainian auxiliary police. According to eyewitnesses, pits were dug for the bodies and filled in by prisoners of war who were executed shortly after. In 1973, a Ukrainian article about the history of Berdichev stated that the Nazis killed 38,536 people. By June 1942, the Jewish population of Berdichev had been annihilated.

It is believed Moses was born in 1822 in an area south of Berdichev, known as Bessarabia. This was a large region bounded by the Prut River to the west, the Dniester River to the north-east, the Black Sea to the south-east and the Danube River delta to the south. Its ownership passed progressively between the fifteenth century and the twentieth century to Moldavia, the Ottoman Empire, Russia, Romania, the Soviet Union and Ukraine.[3]

The borders of Bessarabia were fluid. Between the sixteenth and nineteenth centuries, part of the area was under the Ottoman Empire. In 1812, the Treaty of Bucharest was signed between the Ottoman Empire and Imperial Russia. The terms of the treaty allowed Russia to acquire Bessarabia and half of Moldavia, after which the name Bessarabia was applied to the whole region. Control, with the exception of a strip of southern Bessarabia which was in Moldavia's (then Moldova's) possession from 1856 to 1878, remained with Russia until WWI. Between 1818 and 1828 (during which time Moses was born) Russia granted Bessarabia autonomy, which meant it had a local governor and archbishop. Based on this timeline, Moses would therefore be of 'Russian' heritage.

Not long before Moses' birth, Bessarabia underwent 'Russification'. The term, which was first coined in the previous century, describes the process that was designed to reform Russia and bind all the people to one person – the Czar.[4] Essentially, non-Russian communities, nationalities or ethnic groups, voluntarily or otherwise, were to give up their culture and language for the Russian one. At around the same time, an area known as the 'Pale of Settlement' was established, specifically for Jews, which included Moldova and parts of present-day Ukraine. Permanent residency was allowed within it, although some major cities were excluded. Living beyond it was mostly forbidden.[5]

Moses was given the Hebrew name of 'Mordechai', meaning 'Warrior'. His young life, already restricted, now seemed to take a new and alarming turn in this direction with the accession of a new leader.

Czar Nicholas I was a man obsessed with order and the military. Upon his accession, Russian military officers immediately staged a coup in December 1825 in favour of a representative democracy. The Czar quickly crushed this defiance and, using his army as an instrument of deterrence and intimidation, his 'Nicholaevan' system became known as the most oppressive in Europe.[6]

To make matters worse, Nicholas had a bitter dislike for Poles and Jews. In particular, he regarded the Jews as a harmful alien group whose unity should be destroyed. To achieve this, he adopted several measures. Under his rule the Pale of Settlement shrank. Jews were expelled from major cities (for example Kiev, from which Moses' family would have been barred) and hundreds of anti-Jewish laws were passed, including a severe censorship of Jewish books. Yet by far the worst measure was the compulsory conscription, from 1827, of all male Jews into the military. The intention of this law was not just to aid the military, but also to remove Jews from their families and religion in support of Russification.

This had significant ramifications for the young Moses, now just five years old.

It was no ordinary conscription. The age of the draft was eighteen years, with service being for 25 years; yet the 1827 statute also provided that 'Jewish minors under eighteen years of age shall be placed in preparatory training establishments for military training'. The years before the adult age of eighteen did not count.

Officers were required to provide a certain quota of army recruits and were authorised to make up the numbers with children. Wealthy families and those who had taken up agricultural settlement in southern Russia were exempted, so children from the poorest homes became the easiest targets. Special officers, known as *khapers* ('kidnappers'), were personally responsible for seizing the children and handing them over to the military authorities.[7] The *khapers*, whose quotas were a priority, were not concerned with adhering to the minimum age of twelve and took children as young as seven. They lured them with stories or lies, and sometimes snatched them from homes by knocking on doors in the middle of the night. If the doors did not open immediately, they broke the locks with special tools they carried with them and dragged the babes out.

Alexander Herzen, a Russian author who wrote his memoirs in the nineteenth century, described his meeting in 1835 with a convoy of these children:

> The officer who escorted them said, 'They have collected a crowd of cursed little Jew boys of eight or nine years old. Whether they are taking them for the navy or what, I can't say. At first the orders were to drive them to Perm; then there was a change and we are driving them to Kazan. I took them over a hundred versts farther back.'[8] The officer who handed them over said, 'It's dreadful, and that's all about it; a third were left on the way' (and the officer pointed to the earth). 'Not half will reach their destination,' he said.

'Have there been epidemics, or what?' I asked, deeply moved.

'No, not epidemics, but they just die off like flies. A Jew boy, you know, is such a frail, weakly creature, like a skinned cat; he is not used to tramping in the mud for ten hours a day and eating biscuit – then again, being among strangers, no father nor mother nor petting; well, they cough and cough until they cough themselves into their graves. And I ask you, what use is it to them? What can they do with little boys?

They brought the children and formed them into regular ranks: it was one of the most awful sights I have ever seen, those poor, poor children! Boys of twelve or thirteen might somehow have survived it, but little fellows of eight and ten … Not even a brush full of black paint could put such horror on canvas. Pale, exhausted, with frightened faces, they stood in thick, clumsy, soldiers' overcoats, with stand-up collars, fixing helpless, pitiful eyes on the garrison soldiers who were roughly getting them into ranks. The white lips, the blue rings under their eyes, bore witness to fever or chill. And these sick children, without care or kindness, exposed to the icy wind that blows unobstructed from the Arctic Ocean, were going to their graves.[9]

Children who survived the journey to the army barracks were handed over to the supervision of Russian soldiers whose responsibility was to provide military training and to 'influence' the children to become baptised. All Jewish garments were removed and the children were forbidden to pray or even speak in their own language. They were then forced to undertake Christian religious instruction. Disobedience meant starvation, sleep deprivation or lashings, as well as other forms of physical torture. Sometimes they were sent to Russian farmsteads in remote villages where they were used as child labour.

Conscription in the military, at whatever age, also meant

permanent separation from families. The fear of incarceration and loss was so great, parents did whatever it took to evade the law. Jews were supposed to register the birth of children with the rabbi of the synagogue to which they were assigned; however, it is not surprising that few records exist. Registering a child's birth, especially a son, was avoided at all costs. Child weddings were common, where desperate parents married off boys as young as six in the hope this would spare them. Some even went to the extreme of cutting off their son's trigger fingers to render their service useless.

Moses' parents grew his hair long, dressed him as a girl and hid him by taking him across the Prut River into Romania.

Chapter 2

Escape from Russia

Nothing is known of Moses' life in Romania, or of his journey into adulthood. What is general knowledge is that he became a fisherman, presumably as a young man in the 1840s, catching herring to take to market. We know he lived in Odessa, on the Black Sea, and as most species of herring are ocean-dwelling, it is presumed that this is where he fished.

At some stage he developed gangrene, a condition caused by a loss of blood supply that results in tissue death. Various forms of the disease exist, which may progress quickly or slowly, and if unchecked can result in rotting skin and infection that eventually becomes fatal. Moses was forced to have part of his leg amputated.

Moses' gangrene could have been from an accident at sea, or through diabetes, where he unknowingly injured himself (often people with diabetes lose the feeling in their limbs, making complications from injuries more likely). If Moses had diabetes, which is possible as one of his children died from the condition, he may or may not have known that he had it, nor understood its potential risks. If this occurred as a young man, his risk of complications was much higher.[1]

If it wasn't injury, the gangrene may have occurred later in his life through a long and progressive combination of health issues such as old age, a poor immune system, diabetes (again) and vascular problems.

In the nineteenth century, gangrene in any form would have been a dreadful and terrifying prognosis. From the story told, the urgency and brutality of the solution implies some form of damage with a rapid onset, occurring when medical assistance was limited. Worse still, anaesthetics weren't used in surgery until 1846 and would not have been available on a vessel.

Apparently, the captain ordered that his leg be removed, which was done with a hand saw and probably copious quantities of vodka. If this is indeed true, then it is unfathomable to imagine what Moses went through and how he survived.

There are no eyewitness accounts of the event, and therefore it is possible that this was a merely a legendary tale and Moses did lose his leg later in life, possibly in Turkey, under far better conditions. We will never know.

In any case, he survived the ordeal and lived the remainder of his life with a wooden leg. In the only family photograph that exists, he hides his peg leg under the skirt of his youngest daughter, Fanny, who is sitting next to him.

Aside from gangrene, Moses had other things to worry about. Following the Russo-Turkish war of 1828–29, the area of the Black Sea remained under tension with the continuation of the Caucasian War, making it not the most ideal location to run a fishing boat.[2] In 1853 the Crimean War broke out, a conflict between the Russian Empire and an alliance of Britain, France, the Ottoman Empire and the Italian island of Sardinia.[3] For Moses, getting out of the area would have been a priority, and moving inland to Berdichev a safer bet.

It was in Berdichev, sometime in the early 1860s, that the older Moses met a young Eva. We do not have a record of a marriage and there could be various reasons why. Due to the precarious situation, it may never have been recorded. Alternatively, one may have been written but lost in the destruction of Berdichev during WWII. Then again, there is a possibility that it still exists, buried somewhere in the archives of a synagogue.

Olga, the first of eleven children, was born in 1865 when Eva was 20 and Moses was 43. Then came a boy called Mayer, whose birth date is unknown. A son Jacob was born, possibly in 1874, followed by a girl Rosa (with her Hebrew name of Raisel, meaning Rose), then a girl called Rachel. The birth of one more baby (believed to be a girl, born after Mayer) is known but their name and story are lost. Severe epidemics occurred in 1877 and 1878 after another Russo-Turkish war, and perhaps the missing child died as a result. A quarantine had prevented infected soldiers from spreading typhus to Odessa in 1878 but this was a rare success and was not implemented widely – certainly not inland in Berdichev. Death from disease was highly likely.

Moses, Eva and the children moved to Odessa and then, in the late 1870s, to Rostov-on-Don, a port city within the Pale of Settlement, 32 kilometres east of the Sea of Azov. The town of 70,000 people was renowned for the largest number of fish markets in Russia. Moses probably continued to trade in herring, but not at sea. If he was without a fully functioning leg, his boat days would have been over – handicapped people were an encumbrance that no one had the time or inclination to carry.

Eva initially made and sold sauerkraut, a mixture of cabbage and salt fermented in a barrel, although that would hardly have been enough to support a growing family. Either to supplement this or as an alternative occupation, she became a seamstress.

The couple had two more sons – Joseph in 1879 and Morris in 1881, and then another girl Jeannette (with her Yiddish name of Shaindl, meaning beautiful) in 1882. In the midst of all the births, Olga married at fourteen and had her own child shortly after. The baby did not survive.

If times were difficult before, they were even more difficult now. There were more mouths to feed in the Shmeilowitz household and the world was in the midst of the Long Depression.[4] Russia's manufacturing and agriculture, which were already lagging behind developments in the west, suffered considerably. People struggled to find work and competition was high for the little that was available.

In addition, the death of Nicholas I many years before had not made life easier. Although his son Alexander II implemented many reforms, some of which included major improvements such as emancipation of the serfs, support for higher education, changes in the judiciary system and banking measures that furthered economic development, none of these directly assisted Moses and Eva. Nor did increasing the rights of wealthy and educated Jews to live beyond the Pale of Settlement which was one of his hallmarks – the family was poor.

But more critically, the region remained fraught with uprisings. Alexander II became the target of revolutionaries and managed to survive four assassination attempts – two shootings in the Summer Garden and the Palace Square, a bombing in the Winter Palace and an attack on a train line. One of these was blamed on a young Jewish girl, and many believed this to be an excuse to blame all of the Jews. With the final attempt and successful assassination in 1881, fear peaked and antisemitism soared. The glimmer of hope Moses and others had that the Pale would be abolished and the laws relaxed quickly vanished.

After Alexander II's death, son Alexander III ascended to the throne and a wave of pogroms, or anti-Jewish riots, broke out. The new Czar appeared to be hard and unsympathetic. He immediately made it clear he would not reduce the autocratic power he had inherited, and that the internal reforms made by his father were too liberal. In one of his many actions, he tightened the principles of Russification. Now, ethnic groups were no longer accepted in their own right merely by an allegiance to Russia. Instead, he endorsed the view that all minority cultures and nationalities should be expelled. All the people within the empire were to become 'Great Russians', that is, loyal to Russia first; other customs were no longer tolerated. In May 1882, he implemented temporary regulations regarding the Jews, known as the May Laws.

The new laws further significantly restricted their rights.

Specifically, Jews were forbidden to settle outside towns and boroughs, could not be issued with mortgages, could not own property or have power of attorney to manage and dispose of property, and were not permitted to do business on Sundays and Christian holidays. Later other laws were added, such as the application of quotas to the number who could be admitted to high schools and universities, and how many could work as doctors or lawyers. All were excluded from government jobs. These 'temporary' laws, with various additional and harsher limitations, remained in place for more than 30 years.

Neither Moses nor Eva was in a position to own real estate or educate themselves or their children to a high standard, so this probably didn't affect them greatly. However, work which they were dependent on for survival was becoming more difficult to find and the rules more oppressive.

Sometime in 1887 or early 1888, Rostov-on-Don was included in the military area of the Don Cossacks, a group of trained horsemen and warriors who sold their military services to various powers in Eastern Europe. Only certain categories of Jews could live in the area of these fighters and only those Jews who lived in the city before May 1887 were allowed to stay.

Moses and Eva left by boat in 1888 with at least eight children plus one-week-old Fanny in a bread basket. Fanny received the Yiddish name of Vögele, meaning 'Little Bird', perhaps because the family flew away.[5]

It was lucky they departed – the town was not a place to settle. Like Berdichev, Rostov-on-Don became the place of a terrible atrocity, where later more than 27,000 Jews were murdered.

The massacre at Rostov-on-Don

After the two Russian revolutions of 1917, the Russian Civil War broke out. Having grown to a considerable size and now the most heavily industrialised city of South Russia, it became the battlefield for the White and Red Armies. Then, towards the end of WWI, Germany and Austria invaded. In late 1920 nearly 1.5 million refugees rushed to the port, fleeing south from the Red Army. Thousands died there from another typhus outbreak.

Yet still the strife continued. Later, during WWII, German forces occupied the town twice more. In 1942 and 1943, another dreadful atrocity similar to Berdichev occurred. Some 27,000 Jews and a number of Russian civilians were massacred by the German military. The site of Zmievskaya Balka in Rostov-on-Don is considered to be the largest single mass murder site of Jews on Russian territory during that war.

Chapter 3

Refuge in Constantinople

Like Moses and Eva, hundreds of thousands of Jews escaped from the towns of the Pale of Settlement in Russia after 1882. Fleeing east provided a new refuge in a place where there were greater opportunities.

The family moved to Constantinople. Although not a great distance away, the city was at least outside the grip of Russia.[1]

There were limited alternatives to travel elsewhere. Migration to the US was desired by many, but taking passage by ship further east was out of reach for a large family (eleven or twelve in total now) that included a tiny baby. If amputation did indeed occur early, then any travel would have been compromised by the problem of Moses' leg. While millions had arrived successfully from all over Europe, and the new screening station on Ellis Island in New York was not yet operational, a large family with a handicapped provider would have met with rejection.[2] That left countries near Russia to choose from, where the options were rather dire.

Bulgaria had suffered a terrible uprising in 1876, resulting in somewhere between 15,000 and 30,000 deaths. Its newly appointed prince, Alexander of Battenberg, also had close ties to the Russian Czar.

Farther south was little better. The Palestine region, through which the family had to transit, had been in a period of turmoil. Egypt too was now under threat. In August 1882 British forces invaded and occupied Alexandria, defeating the Egyptian Army.

Constantinople, on the other hand, was relatively stable. The largest city and main seaport of the Ottoman Empire, it was undergoing a modernisation with the development of a proper water system, new bridges, electric lights, trams and telephones. The locality afforded the family a degree of protection. Compared to what they had previously endured, it probably felt like a safe haven.

How long and where exactly they stayed is difficult to establish. A 'General Population Administration' had just been set up in 1881 and the first official census commenced, though this was largely designed to gather demographic data such as numbers of males and females by ethno-religious categories and not residences and names of households, like the census records of the United Kingdom and the United States. The process took ten years to complete and, given the transiency of much of the population, very little detail would have been nailed down.

Records were not kept as they are today. The use of surnames, for example, did not come into law until 1935. Until that time, they were used only when necessary. In the nineteenth century, Ottoman Turkish was written using a form of Arabic script and wasn't changed to the modern Turkish alphabet until 1928. The script was difficult to read and names were frequently written down as they were heard, which changed the spelling. Sometimes they weren't bothered with at all.[3]

We don't know where they lived, but we do know that to support the household, Eva continued her work as a seamstress, acquiring an impressive list of clientele. Moses also worked a sewing machine, driving the pedal with his wooden leg as seen in a photograph. Precisely what other work he obtained isn't clear.

Newcomers to Constantinople generally spoke their own native tongue up until the time that the Turkish language became compulsory, many years later. Moses and Eva spoke Yiddish at home, Russian and some Turkish. By the end of the nineteenth century, French had become dominant as a 'bridge' language, namely for trade between groups, which would seem to make the role of interpreter an attractive prospect for him. Many history books report that Moses was an interpreter and worked for the French Consulate. He may have added French to his toolkit … except that we know from family that he didn't. Indeed, the couple's understanding of this language was limited. Years later Eva, looking at the newspaper one day for the cinema, questioned how stupid the title of this film could be, having become confused between 'Pour qui sonne le glas' (Hemingway's *For Whom the Bell Tolls*) and '*Pour qui sont les glaces?*' ('for whom are the ice creams?')!

Despite various books and websites quoting a variety of other places, it follows that this is where the last child, Ishroulch, was born on 18 September 1890. Known as Issy, he was a handful as a small child, which was perhaps somewhat fitting, as the roots of his Hebrew name of Israel mean 'to contend, or fight'.

Being the youngest, he got away with a lot. His older sister Jeannette used to spoil him, and he ran and hid behind her skirts whenever Eva wanted to scold him or put him to bed. Moses was 68 years old at Issy's birth and was not only incapable of running after a little boy, but past the point at which he wished to. Eva, considerably more youthful at 45, was equally disinclined, having a household to run and nine (or ten) other children to deal with. Issy would have been left to do as he pleased – which he did.

He possessed a devilish streak. As a young boy, his many pranks included pinching toffees off the tray of the one-legged beggar and tipping his sister head-first into a barrel of pickled cucumbers. He was frequently in trouble, to the frustration and embarrassment of Moses and Eva who were strict Orthodox Jews. Issy constantly broke the rules.

But there were limits.

As a place to live, Constantinople was not safe – particularly for skylarking. Against a backdrop of perceived calm, the country was destabilising. Armenian revolutionaries were pushing back against oppression by the Ottoman authorities and specifically Sultan Abdul

Hamid II, who was attempting to maintain imperial control over the collapsing empire. In response to their demands for reforms, the Sultan gave Hamidiye and Kurdish troops free rein to attack.[4]

Sometimes the troops would go door to door in search of Armenians. On one occasion they arrived at the family home, wanting to search it. Moses said, 'I tell you there is no Armenian here! Would you question the word of an old man with a white beard?' The soldiers left without searching.

But soon the situation worsened and tensions boiled over. Various skirmishes occurred in the provinces, and in 1895 a protest in the city turned into a massacre, followed by another more brutal one in 1896, in which 5000 Armenians were killed.

In one of those attacks young Fanny, now seven or eight years old, was out getting food for the family when the shooting started. Mistaken for an Armenian child, she got caught in the crossfire. Through luck or good fortune she escaped the bullets, lying among the dead until it was safe to escape and dash home.

In the midst of this turmoil, Issy grew into a handsome young boy: muscular, strong and full of vitality. Despite the danger – or perhaps simply ignorant of it – his misdemeanours grew more adventurous. He took delight in baiting those in authority, taunting the police on several occasions and then dashing away when they gave chase.

One day Issy spotted a group of Turkish men squatting in a circle to chat and drink their coffee, as they liked to do. Quickly and quietly, he crept up and kicked each man in the backside so that they all fell in a pile in the middle, covered in coffee. This was a great humiliation and would not be without consequences, but knowing his own speed and agility, Issy cheekily sprinted off, expecting to escape. Unfortunately, he chose the bridge over the Golden Horn as his exit, where a group of police were coming directly towards him. Having no choice, he leapt many metres into the water below where fishermen later rescued him. How bruised and battered he was isn't known, but in any case, he returned home three days later to whatever punishment Moses dished out.

Whether this was pure wilfulness or resistance to autocracy is anyone's guess. What is known is that he didn't hold much respect for authorities and the law.

But this was not a time when either could be ignored. Towards the end of the century, with the threat of revolts and the fall of the Ottoman Empire looming, the oldest child Olga chose to relocate to Egypt. She was followed later by Fanny in 1902 or 1903, and then Moses and Eva. Jeannette stayed, having met a young man who became her husband.

By the time an assassination attempt was made on the Sultan's life in 1905 and the empire collapsed in 1908, most of the family were gone from Constantinople.

Chapter 4

Safety in Egypt

Life was relatively more settled in Alexandria, Egypt. Prior to their arrival, there had been a period of war in 1882, when British and French forces had sent warships and the British had begun a naval bombardment of the city in order to regain control of the de facto protectorate they had in place.[1] A battle at Tel el-Kebir had ensued, resulting in the defeat of the Egyptian Army. However, from that time on, while there was indignation and discontent there was no further fighting.

This wasn't Issy's first visit to Egypt. Being such a handful, at one point he had been sent to stay with his sister Olga, probably to give his parents a rest. This may explain some of the confusion around his place of birth.

A number of historical records state that his father Moses took a job in Alexandria, working for the French Consulate as a clerk, and that he and Eva were French citizens. This *has* to be completely false. Moses would have been nearly 80 years of age by the time he took the job – and he spoke no French.

Although it wasn't necessary to be born in France or to live there to get French nationality (neither of them ever went there), it wouldn't make sense for it to be granted. Moses, Eva and the children had no papers at all and were stateless – not recognised as citizens of any country. They would not have become citizens in Egypt either. The laws surrounding nationality in Egypt, as was the case in many other countries, were not fully defined until much later. Interestingly, Issy used this lack of stringency to his advantage when he enlisted in the army in London in 1904 (where he was both under-age and claimed to be a British subject).

Moses lived quietly and passed away in Alexandria around 1907 or 1908 at roughly 86 years of age, a remarkable feat at the time. After enduring a lifetime of wars, persecution, disease, personal trauma and hardship, he had truly earned his Hebrew name of 'Warrior'.

Eva lived on in Alexandria with some of her children. After the volatile times in the previous century, life for the family in Alexandria was, for a period of time, untroubled. Following the invasion of 1882, the British remained for 40 years and many new municipal projects were embarked upon. The city flourished and grew, keeping its position as the second city and summer capital of Egypt, and under British patronage the foreign community prospered. This period of relative serenity was shattered when a world war broke out in 1914.

While the Ottoman Sultan had remained the official ruler of the country, overall power and control was under the British Consul-General – a difficult position at the best of times and an untenable position when the parties announced war.

In November 1914 Britain proclaimed a protectorate over Egypt, but this did not shelter the country from battle. Britain brought in masses of foreign troops and set up a base for operations, conscripted 1.5 million Egyptians to assist, and took over buildings, animals and crops for army use. The war invaded the Middle Eastern lands so the Egyptian people, especially the peasants, suffered.

With little place else to go, Eva did her best to hide from the fighting until it was over. She died there in 1934 at the age of 89. If she had a Hebrew name, it is intriguing to contemplate what it might have been. Like Moses, she had resiliently lived through some of the most testing times imaginable.

The following is what is known about the remaining family members.

Olga (the first born) divorced her first husband and married a photographer in 1895 or 1896. That union did not work either and the photographer was succeeded by a printer. However, the love of her life was a Greek man named Stellio to whom she was never married. Although she travelled a lot, she lived in Alexandria until her death in 1965, aged 100. A tiny, thin woman with white hair, she smoked cigarettes endlessly and would have been a fabulous advertisement for British American Tobacco, not only for her longevity but also her use of the butts to keep bugs and beetles away – however that worked! She also trapped mice and set them on fire with alcohol and a match, which sounds horrendous but perhaps it was the way rodents were dealt with at the time. She would visit the local market, buying a cup of oil or rice, and read tarot cards for people. For many years she kept an enormous portrait of Moses above her bed and a trunk nearby. She told her great-nephews it was full of treasures which they would inherit on her death. When they eventually opened the trunk, they found it full of *schmates*, worthless pieces of fabric, textile cuttings and moths that blew a heavy cloud of dust into the air! Needless to say, they shut the trunk more quickly than they opened it and forgot about the inheritance.

Mayer (first son) is believed to have gone to Brooklyn, although no trace of him can be found.

Rosa (third daughter, born after the unknown girl), also known as Rosette, settled in Brazil. She had no children. When she passed away, she offered the house to the family in her will. Government regulations stipulated it had to be lived in but no one took it up.

Jeannette (fourth daughter) remained in Constantinople, although details of her early life are sketchy. She married a man by the name of David Rothman. As Issy would later be, David Rothman was rebellious as a young boy and ran away from his home town of Brailia, Romania, after a number of devilish stunts, the last of which was to glue the long beard of his rabbi to the table while the poor man was dozing (had there been a bell handy, I'm sure he would have rung it!). After receiving a thrashing at home for the trouble, he stowed away on the first ship to leave town. He managed to hide among the lifeboats but was discovered and put to work, becoming part of the crew.

Arriving in Constantinople, David worked in the shipping trade, ending up as a ship chandler. In attempting to woo the blonde, blue-eyed Jeannette, he encountered stiff opposition from Moses, who did not trust a man who flaunted his money and prospects to impress. He tried every form of persuasion he could think of, but Moses was unmoved. In the end he brought baskets of beer bottles and threw them at the prospective in-laws' windows – a sure remedy! To Moses' dismay, the marriage proceeded anyway. David's business prospered and the family lived comfortably; however, he would often be delivered home drunk by the local constabulary, either in a trunk or, later, when his expanded girth meant he could not fit, face down on a donkey. (When seeing him return on the beast, Jeannette would announce: 'Children, the Master has arrived, in company!') One night he became the victim of his own inebriation, fell into the river and drowned.

Jeannette suffered from diabetes, which she may have inherited from her father. Over time her eyesight began to fail, but no one could help. Although the use of insulin was making progress, it wasn't until 1935 that it was learned that there were two types of diabetes which responded differently. Jeannette died in 1936 before treatments were developed. She left behind four daughters and a son.

Rachel (fifth daughter) initially ran a hat shop in Heliopolis near Cairo, where she met a Lieutenant Colonel George Wall, CMG CBE.

George was born in in Australia in 1870. He moved to England and, after training at Aldershot, served as an officer in the Nile Expedition in 1898 and the South African War in 1900, before being placed on the retired list. He returned to Australia and married Ruby Cutbush in 1902. They had four children.

At the outbreak of WWI, George was appointed to the AIF and posted abroad to Egypt. Over the years, his wife received various letters telling her of his promotions through the ranks. In 1917, he came to the notice of the Secretary of State for War for distinguished services rendered, receiving promotion to major (temporary lieutenant colonel) plus the decoration of Commander of the Order of St Michael and St George (CMG) third class. He was subsequently mentioned for valuable services rendered and made Commander of the Military Division; finally in 1919 he was awarded the Commander of the British Empire (CBE).

Granted 75 days long service leave in 1917, George chose to take this abroad rather than return to Australia. Further leave was granted in September 1919, February 1920 and March 1920, the latter two months of which he took in London. By early February, Ruby began making enquiries with the Department regarding her husband's return, with further investigations in March being to no avail. Eventually George did arrive back, but not to his home address. In September 1920, he ended his military appointment and his previous family life, and married Rachel in 1922.

Apparently, the new marriage did not meet with family approval and her husband's parents gave the couple a piece of real estate in Sydney on the condition that they disassociate with them. This they did for the most part, although Rachel was the only relative my father, Issy's son Maurice, claimed he ever met.[2] She died after her husband in 1965 and did not leave a will. The property was acquired by the government.

For decades it was rumoured that George had led a failed expedition to Lasseter's Reef, a rich gold deposit (purported to be hidden in a remote corner of central Australia) that has claimed many lives during fruitless searches. Convinced of its whereabouts, the story goes that he spent much of the family's fortune to no avail. No records of his journey, or any secret treasure discovery, exist.

Fanny (sixth daughter) stayed in Alexandria where in 1904, aged sixteen, she married Isaac Walberg. The couple had six children. In 1942, suffering from a heart condition, she was told by her doctor she would live just six months more. He proved to be right. She died of a cardiac arrest on Christmas day, not one week past the doctor's prediction.

Isaac Walberg has a story of his own, with a number of versions. Born in 1878, his name was purportedly not Walberg; instead, he was supposedly the son of a jeweller named Feldman. In one of the riots in Egypt in 1882 his father was killed, and his mother and sister disappeared. The orphaned child, then four years old, was adopted by a wealthy professor named Alfred Walberg Dzierzanowki. This man was of German or Polish lineage, and was made '*bey*' (the governor of a district or province in the Ottoman Empire) by the Sultan. Alfred in turn was killed in a later riot, in front of the university where he worked.

In a second version of this story, Isaac was never adopted. He was the son of Alfred Bey Zierzanowski Walberg, who was Austro-Hungarian. He and his wife were murdered during a riot, and Isaac and a second son Alexander grew up in an orphanage. Later in life, Isaac was a member of the Wafd Party, a nationalist group that was instrumental in gaining Egypt's independence from Britain.

Fanny was Isaac's second wife. Nothing is known of his first wife, other than she was English. When Fanny died, he married for the third time.

Jacob (second son) possibly led the way to East London. His further whereabouts have become difficult to conclusively trace.

Joseph (third son) moved to East London, becoming a skilled gas fitter and plumber. He met a girl called Hilda Isbitski, a tailoress from Leczyca, a town briefly part of the Russian Empire until WWI, before it was reclaimed by Poland. According to the 1911 census, they lived at the same address in Mile End, London, and had supposedly been married for three years, but records show the marriage didn't actually take place until 1918. This would have been scandalous in the Victorian era, if it was revealed. They had no children.

Morris (fourth son) also went to East London, beginning there as a boarder with his brother Joseph and picking up the same trades.

He married a Polish or Austrian girl named Sarah Berger. In 1905 the young woman, aged nineteen, travelled ahead of her husband to Winnipeg, Canada, where the couple lived and raised five children after Morris joined her in 1906. In 1914, Morris moved the family to Detroit, USA, in the hope of getting work with the Ford Company. Henry Ford had become an overnight sensation when he announced a $5 per day wage, more than double the normal daily pay, and a reduction in the working day from 9 hours to 8. Being at a time of industrial depression, thousands flocked to the company in search of work. Morris was not hired, as Ford was an antisemite. The family then relocated to Brooklyn, New York, where two more children were born.

During the Great Depression of the early 1930s, Morris was chronically unemployed, relying on support from his family, and by 1940 he was widowed. He sent to his nephew, Issy's son Maurice, one of the very first Reynolds ballpoint pens. Advertised as being capable of writing underwater, this incredible writing instrument mesmerised young Maurice's classmates for the entire day; no one had seen anything like it.

Morris exceeded his father Moses in the gift of languages and spoke seven, although the family complained in later years that he said very little in any of them! He told the story that the original family name was Vasser-Treger, which descendants believed for decades, until it was finally realised that this means 'Water Carrier' in Yiddish. He was a plumber! He remained in Brooklyn until his death in 1962.

And then there was **Issy** (fifth son, and last child). His incredible story follows.

Of all the children, Morris and Issy had a special bond. Each named their first sons after each other, even though the Jewish rule was to reserve this for family members who had passed.[3] At the tender age of eleven, Issy followed Morris to London.

Chapter 5

Stowaway to London

Issy's older brother Morris was a striking young man, with a full head of dark hair. He drank Turkish coffee with a sugar cube between his teeth, smoked Turkish cigarettes and ate loads of baklava. He spoke Russian, Hebrew, Yiddish, Turkish, French and also Greek, owing to the many Greek friends that he liked to associate with.[1] Issy, being nine years younger, would have been an annoying hindrance.

We don't know why but Morris hated Egypt, even though it is believed he had never been there, and when the family relocated to Alexandria he refused to go. Instead, at around sixteen years of age, he left for London.

It is possible that his older brother Jacob was already in Mile End, London, arriving and living as a boarder at the age of seventeen.[2] This may have paved the way for the others to follow suit, as ten years later in 1901, both Joseph and Morris resided as boarders in the neighbouring parish of St George's in the East.[3] They were 22 and 20 years of age respectively.

How the boys got there is a mystery. Some believe Morris stowed away rather than take a paid passage on one of the many ships that travelled from Constantinople. Joseph may have proceeded ahead of Morris, adopting whatever way Jacob took first. Or the two may have absconded together – travelling legally or illegally. Searching every ship record, if these could even be located, wouldn't necessarily prove anything one way or the other. While there were penalties for both ship masters and stowaways, the practice was not uncommon, and far more entered new countries, initially as stowaways and then as part of the crew, than were registered – such as Jeannette's husband David did.

There could be as many as 20 stowaways on board each ship. Some were considered adventurous, some irresponsible and others criminal, but many were described as 'youths of humble origin desperately anxious to leave their war-stricken homelands.'[4]

One such youth – aged just eleven – did stow away, in search of his brother Morris. Issy was of humble origins and his homeland was indeed war-torn, but the question of his 'desperate anxiousness' might be answered in the affirmative, with a slightly comical twist.

Prior to his hasty departure, Issy had been made to take violin lessons and took a great dislike to his teacher, who belted him on the back of his hands whenever he played the wrong note. One day, perhaps in an act of defiance, he returned fire in spades, hitting his teacher over the head with his violin. Deciding it was best not to return home, he took off on the next available ship. He never saw his father again.

At the time, organised syndicates operated journeys to London where, for the tidy sum of six to eight pounds, they would provide assistance to stowaways, allowing them on board and supplying them with food during the voyage. Of course, Issy hadn't that kind of money – nor, if the incident was spontaneous, the time to raise the funds. His only option was to hide, which he did, and there were plenty of places to do it.

There were ship holds, containers and barrels; mail rooms, food stores, engine rooms, paint lockers and endless cupboards and storage facilities, just to name a few. But not all were perfect for remaining undetected. Sometimes these were hazardous, with would-be escapists crushed by rolling baggage, baked in boiler rooms, frozen in cool rooms and lifeboats, or as with the famous case of the Greenock stowaways in 1868, treated brutally by the crew until two died. For the most part, however, a safe hiding place could be located with the primary difficulty being the ability to lay low.

While ship's officers were often lax in searching the ship prior to departure, stowaways were frequently caught during the journey when out in search of food or amenities. It is believed that Issy was found by one of the crew on his first attempt – at Port Said, on the Suez Canal (it is possible he did not know where the ship was going, and it was fortuitous that he was caught!). He stayed with the Harbour Master for five days before a suitable ship was available to take him home. On the return journey, he was made to work for his passage.

He arrived back in Constantinople and, learning from the experience, wasted no time in boarding a new ship on which he made it successfully to London.

If stowing away was difficult, finding his brothers was even more challenging. Not even a teenager yet, he needed to find out where they lived. How he managed the entire adventure was quite remarkable. He had no worldly knowledge, had not travelled and had never seen England before. To top it off, although he spoke three languages, English was not one of them.[5]

On arrival and before he could get far, Issy was gathered up, probably as a waif, and placed in temporary accommodation at Sigdon Road School in Dalston Lane, Hackney. One of many institutions managed by the London School Board (LSB), its primary aim was to provide elementary places for all poor children in London. It was also largely attended by Jewish children.[6] As an unaccompanied minor, it served to provide a roof over his head.

In 1901, attendance at school was compulsory for all children between the ages of five and thirteen, and the board paid the fees for the poorest. When, not long after he arrived, the LSB was abolished by the Education Act of 1902, Issy found himself in need of new lodgings. He eventually found his brothers in the East End of London – most likely through the help of the Jewish community.

Over centuries the East End had absorbed waves of immigrants, most notably the rural poor: Huguenots in the seventeenth century, Irish in the eighteenth century and Eastern Europeans in the nineteenth century, a large number of whom were Russian Jews like Issy's family, escaping pogroms after the death of the Czar in 1881. The area was appealing for religious reasons owing to the good reports regarding religious tolerance. It was also in close proximity to the city and the cost of living was cheap. Yet it was one of the poorest areas of London, with a seedy reputation and a high crime rate. Work from the docks and factories paid low wages, scarcely sufficient to meet the population influx, but poor immigrants had little choice in where to settle. Parts of the districts were overcrowded and dirty from the foul-smelling fumes and smoke that travelled east across the city.[7] The parishes of Spitalfields, Whitechapel and St George were the least affluent of all.

By the time of Issy's arrival in 1901, the reputation of East End was at its lowest after years of unfavourable incidents and attention. In particular, a series of eleven killings known as the Whitechapel murders, which included the Jack the Ripper killing spree, had given the area a dreadful reputation.

Morris set Issy up in the boarding house where he was living in Providence Street, St George's in the East, and sent him to the nearby Berner Street School, in Whitechapel, which had just opened a wing for boys aged twelve to sixteen. The school was originally a special one for children with 'physical or mental health needs' who were to be taught cookery, laundering and manual tasks along with the more traditional subjects. When it was expanded to include the boys' facility in 1902, the cookery and laundry classes continued on the first floor.[8]

At the turn of the twentieth century, many young boys had left school by twelve and were in trades, so the classes were designed as additional training. These may have been additional for Issy or a significant part of his education. What is known is that in between his schooling he took a job at the nearby Spitalfields market, delivering fish on a bicycle from three to seven in the morning. In return, he received a meagre wage, board and clothing. He slept in the corner of the shop and, while he was supposed to receive meals, he often went hungry.

Both Berner Street and the area of Spitalfields were infamous as sites of three of Jack the Ripper's murders. All of the murders were committed within a mile of each other, but Elizabeth Stride, the third victim, was killed in Dutfields Yard directly opposite Issy's school, and Annie Chapman and Mary Jane Kelly, the second and fifth victims, were killed in Spitalfields, where Issy worked. Although the murders had occurred ten years earlier and appeared to have stopped, the area was unsafe at night, especially for a child doing delivery rounds.

Speculation and theories as to who did the murders still abounded. Many people were convinced the killer belonged to the Jewish community, and the Assistant Police Commissioner, Sir Robert Anderson, even stated on record that the murderer was 'a low-born Polish Jew living in the heart of the area.' This merely served to increase the level of antisemitism.

A group calling themselves 'The British Brothers League (BBL)' decided to take the matter of the influx of foreigners to the East End into their own hands. They formed in 1901, just as Issy arrived. Initially the group's objective was merely anti-immigration – that is, keeping out the poorest, regardless of background – and they campaigned for restricted immigration with the slogan *England for the English*. Over time, however, Jews became their primary focus.

The BBL organised large rallies and marches through the streets, and eventually collected sufficient signatures on a petition to initiate a royal commission, which took place in 1903. This led to the passing of the 1905 *Aliens Act*, where migrants could be categorised as 'undesirable'. The Act included anyone who could not show they had means to 'decently support themselves, was an idiot or a lunatic, or had a disease that could put a burden on the rates or the public'. Subsequent expulsion from the country could result, and that in itself also included anyone who, within twelve months of arriving, was found 'wandering without ostensible means of subsistence or living under insanitary conditions due to overcrowding.' That gave officers plenty of wriggle room to deport almost any person they wished.

In the lead-up to the new law, immigrants did their best to hide their true identities – after all, there was a critical need to find accommodation and employment, and no one wanted to be expelled. Issy and his brothers were no exception.

A large number of the books and internet references that mention Issy's change of name refer to his recruiting sergeant anglicising his name to Smith. This *has* to be false. If his brother Jacob arrived in the East End first, it was he who was the catalyst for the name change. If it wasn't Jacob, then Joseph and Morris were the initiators, as they established themselves in London before Issy. Joseph and Morris even distanced themselves further by recording their country of birth on the census as Turkey, where they certainly weren't born. When Issy arrived he copied the name – and listed his place of birth as London. (A century later, a cousin of mine observed that this was a miracle greater than Jesus, as neither of his parents ever went to England!)

Changing from the family name of Shmeilowitz was probably not an issue or a loss for the boys. In Constantinople, their last place of residence, surnames weren't enforced (until much later, in 1936). In the nineteenth century, a considerable number of people were illiterate and names were written or translated as best they could be, so spellings often changed. Most Russian names, which were initially written in Cyrillic letters, were also frequently shortened for convenience or translated into Latin names with the nearest possible conversion in sound or root to the Russian originals – so again, the concept of correct spelling was lost. The family name, which incidentally means 'Son of Samuel', was referred to over time as Schmulovitch, Schmulevitch, Shmilovitch, Shmeilovitz, Smilovich, Shimlovits, Shimlovitz, Smylovich, Smulewitz and even Chmielowiez. According to family, the use of S or SH and the letters following depended on the level of ignorance of the listener and the quality of their dentist! Needless to say, on arrival in England, any version of this name would have drawn attention – anglicising it to something simple and common made sense.

Issy also got a tattoo.

Tattooing was fashionable in England in the nineteenth century and even approved of and encouraged by the British Army as a matter of pride as well as for the identification of casualties. Tattoos were also very popular with sailors, and although it is possible Issy got his during his sea voyage it is more likely he acquired it in London. His choice of tattoo sheds more light on his personality – symbols of 'clasped hands and flags'. In the Victorian era, clasped hands represented 'a farewell to earthly existence and God's welcome into heaven'. This seems to align with his view on life *(que sera sera – whatever will be, will be)* which enabled him to undertake such extraordinary acts of bravery later. The identity of one of the flags isn't known but the other was British, probably adopted as a further step towards blending in.

But Issy only blended in to a certain extent – the larrikin in him still prevailed. A story told is that he would eat or drink at a tavern or coffeehouse, run up a tab and then leave his cap on the bar as if he was going to the toilet. Except that he would abscond. Apparently, this required him to hold quite a number of spare caps.

It is unlikely he had criminal intentions – it was probably a combination of devilishness and hunger. He did have work – after delivering fish, he worked for a time at a second-hand furniture dealer in Commercial Road. In a further attempt to make ends meet, he helped Morris on some of his plumbing jobs, gaining skills as a plumber's mate and gas fitter. However, judging by the conditions at the time, it wasn't enough. He needed to improve his position and in 1904, probably because it offered secure paid employment, he joined the army.

Chapter 6

Detention

At the turn of the twentieth century participation in the British Army was voluntary. Across the water, in the neighbouring countries of France, Belgium and the Netherlands, it was a different story, with various forms of conscription in place.

In the Netherlands, conscription was used for all men over the age of eighteen, with essentially only temporary postponement or an alternative role in some form of civilian service capacity for conscientious objectors. In France, limited conscription was applied by lot, also with some exemptions allowed. Belgium had a similar system, although it was possible to escape service by paying for substitutes, which generally benefited the wealthy. In 1905, France implemented universal military service for a period of two years with exceptions only on medical grounds. Later, Belgium followed suit, first abolishing the lot system in 1909 and then introducing compulsory service in 1913.

For Britain, voluntary service had its challenges in recruiting and retaining men. But for those looking to escape poor living conditions such as those in East London, it was an attractive proposition, given that it offered solid pay, regular meals, training and prospects for promotion. This would easily have made sense for Issy.

Nearly all of the published facts about Issy state that he enlisted in the Manchester Regiment on 2 September 1904. There was much speculation about his age at the time, which has been variously described as fourteen, sixteen and eighteen, depending on the date chosen for his birth (anywhere from 1886, birthplace Russia, to 1888 in Egypt, to 1890 in England). It is clear now that the date could only be the last one as he was the final child, arriving after Fanny who was born in 1888. From that information, the location must be Constantinople (now Istanbul, Turkey) where the family was residing at the time.

The enlistment date is true. But there is one very important detail, and an associated extraordinary fact, that has largely been missed.

He actually joined the 6th Militia nearly five months earlier on 21 April 1904. Although he listed his age as seventeen years and eight months, he was actually just over *thirteen-and-a-half years old*!

This seems astounding, and poses the question of how such a variance from the minimum age could pass undetected. The answer is – it probably didn't. It was likely noted and ignored.

The Militia was a territorial voluntary defence force organised by county, with units raised and disbanded as required. Units had a form of military training, and could be called up for military service. The 6th Militia had returned to England after campaigning in South Africa for the Boer War.[1]

Issy gave his address as 5 Mazeppa Street, Bury New Road, Manchester, and his occupation as a plumber, working for a Mr Glasser at 57 Morton Street. He stated that he was a British subject. The medical officer recorded 'fresh complexion with brown eyes and black hair', and noting the tattoo on his left forearm, wrote: '17 years 8 months' in the 'Apparent Age' section. According to the army medical service regulations of the time, if a recruit did not bring with him any satisfactory proof of his age, it was the responsibility of the officer who examined him to compare his height, weight, general development and appearance, decide his age and record this as 'physically equivalent to' on the enlistment papers. Issy's height was recorded as 5 feet, 2⅛ inches (158cm), which was just above the minimum, his chest measurement as 33 inches at maximum expansion (83cm) and his weight at 112 pounds (just over 50kg). This meant one of three things: he was a small young man; he was behind in his development or he was younger than the age he declared. Whatever the officer deduced will never be known – regardless, Issy was accepted, and his 'official' year of birth on his military records, by calculation, was 1886. From here on it had to stay that way, for changing it would reveal a false declaration.[2]

On 2 September, he was discharged from the Militia. That same day he joined the Manchester Regiment at Ashton-under-Lyne – a detail that was not carried over to his army records. In the case of the British Army, a recruit had to be aged between eighteen and 38 years, be taller than 5 feet 3 inches and pass certain physical tests. This was more formal than the Militia; however, leading up to WWI (and indeed after the war began when resources were desperately needed) some criteria – if they meant exclusion – were overlooked. Standards were progressively lowered to ensure more men were eligible.

Various stories existed about enlistment generally during that period. Many young men looked nowhere near the age they claimed to be. Some were quickly exposed and readily admitted they were underage – they might be turned away. Others bluffed their way through and their false age was accepted with the turn of a blind eye. The recruiting sergeant would knowingly look a boy up and down and say, 'Son, go outside and think about your birthday. Then come in and tell me again.' Miraculously, with a change of birth date, they passed.

Parental or guardian approval was required at times. In Australia at the time of WWI, volunteers under 21 needed the permission of one parent, although many managed to enlist without it. One great example is the story of Percy Smith, born in Victoria, who pestered his father and was not granted it. In the end, he presented a note which read: 'Percy's mother is dead and he as [sic] his father's consent to join.' Someone signed the note, but apparently not his father.[3]

How Issy managed to join the Militia at the age he was is an enigma, but he probably considered his chances with the local force likely to be more successful than with the army. The fact that he had no papers probably worked to his advantage. Similarly, his parents being in another country would have helped. Being difficult to reach, the officers would not bother seeking consent – it was too much trouble. Indeed, on his next application – for the army – he put his mother's name as 'Eva Smith' and her address as 'unknown'. He did not mention his father – possibly for fear of the punishment over the violin and decamping incidents that might still be awaiting him.

There are no photos to show how old he looked, but at the time of his enlistment in the Manchester Regiment he was now just two weeks shy of his fourteenth birthday. The medical officer recorded '18 years' in the Apparent Age section and also noted, as had the previous officer, 'fresh complexion with brown eyes and black hair'. His height was recorded at 5 feet, 3½ inches (only marginally more), and he had grown a further inch across his chest to 34 inches. Tipping the scales now at 118 pounds (just over 53kg) he was still a featherweight.

The officer also recorded a few distinctive marks on his body, namely a scar on his left knee and above his eyebrow. Mysteriously, his tattoo was now on his right arm.[4] When the details were later typed up onto a medical history sheet, Issy was eighteen years and two months old as at 2 September 1904.

After the particulars were completed, his place of birth noted as 'St George [sic] in the East, London' and the form duly signed, Issy was told to wait. Nearby was a storeroom and, starving, he took an onion. When the sergeant returned, he was caught eating it. Charged with stealing, he spent his first few days in the 'Glasshouse' – the military gaol at Aldershot (later referred to as the Detention Barracks).[5]

Issy settled in and, now being somewhat better fed, there were no more opportunistic thefts. After six months and a 'gymnastics course', he was measured again. By now he had grown to 5 feet 4¾ inches and his chest had expanded 2½ inches (over 6cm). He'd also put on 16 pounds (7.25kg), despite all the exercise. There were no comments recorded, but it must have been obvious this was a young boy still developing, and not a grown man as claimed!

Issy was placed in the 2nd Battalion of the Manchester Regiment in Aldershot as a private.[6] No sooner had he joined than the battalion, which comprised many draft recruits, was split and moved to the Channel Isles: Guernsey stationed at Fort George, and Alderney, stationed at both Fort Albert and Fort Château à l'Etoc. There are unverified stories that he served initially as a drummer boy – a role typically held by young boys up to the beginning of the twentieth century. Drums were used not only for soldiers to march in step, but also on the battlefield as a communications system – various drum rudiments, or patterns, signalled different commands from officers to the troops. The Boer War was over and the 2nd Battalion was at home, so the role as a drummer was likely for training and official duties.

Strictly following orders took some getting used to, and within six months Issy found himself in trouble again. On 17 April 1905 he received a blow to his left rib in a fight and was tried that day by the district court-martial 'for using insubordinate language etc.' After five days confinement, he found himself sentenced to a further 42 days hard labour, which he served.[7]

The Manchester Regiments travelled extensively, protecting colonies of the British Empire and it is possible, in view of his misbehaviour, that the battalion considered moving him elsewhere as advisable. On 15 March 1906 he was drafted to the 3rd Battalion and sent to South Africa for Foreign Service. Not long afterwards the unit was disbanded, and on 28 October 1906 he was moved to the 1st Battalion in India where he remained until the end of 1912.

Chapter 7

Alf and Boxing Fame

During his service in India, Issy met Alfred Burley, another army recruit, who became his closest friend. Just one year older, Alf had joined the 1st Regiment on 4 October 1902, immediately upon leaving the Andover Children's Home.

Alf's father George, a hairdresser, had struggled to cope following the death of his wife Elizabeth in 1898. Alf was the seventh of ten children, although only nine remained – a sister, Jessie, had died at birth in 1892. Times would have been tough financially so in January 1899 George admitted himself into the Islington Workhouse, along with the three youngest children – Alf aged nine, Lily aged eight and Willie aged four. The family was never to be together again.

The workhouses of Britain were a last resort. Their purpose was to provide relief for the poor, elderly and sick who could not support themselves, but they were deliberately harsh with minimum comfort in order to deter others who did not need to rely on them. Once admitted, families were split up and most adults were required to work to ensure the 'able-bodied were not "idle" and a burden on the system'.

George and the youngest two only stayed a week. Alf remained until the end of the month but was deposited back again on multiple occasions throughout the year, sometimes on his own and other times along with Willie, Lily and an older sister Rose. In October 1899 he was admitted to the Andover children's home, separate from his siblings. This stay was to last a full three years, with the reason 'deserted' marked on the records. It's not known whether 'deserted' meant that Alfred was an orphan at this time (with the remainder of his siblings elsewhere) or his father never returned for him.[1] What is known is that by the end of 1904, the time of his sister Nelly's marriage, George was dead.

For Alfred, it made no difference either way. He was under the care of a Board of Guardians, who could detain him up to the age of sixteen if they felt he might suffer 'injurious consequences' by leaving. During his stay his oldest brother Frank, who would have been out making a living for himself, died – aged 24.

Children were generally held in the workhouse until they were old enough to enter employment. When Alf was discharged, the records noted his entry into the army and his age as fourteen and a half. Based on earlier workhouse records, his age was closer to thirteen. Both the navy and the army were typical destinations for boys (girls frequently went into domestic service) and therefore it would appear that this acceptance of underage children was common practice.

Alf began as a bandsman in the Manchester Regiment and was transferred to India with the 1st Battalion. When Issy arrived in 1906, Alf had been there for almost two years. The two became close friends.

The 1st Battalion was initially stationed in Secunderabad, as part of the British Indian Army, and consisted of both British and Indian soldiers. Training, which took place every morning and night, included practice following orders, improving the speed of reflexes and hand-to-hand combat. In February 1907 Issy ended up in the base hospital with a fractured left hand – either some of the drills took a little while to accomplish and he was accidently injured, or he was involved in an affray. If it was the latter, there were no immediate penalties for it.

But authority did not gel with Issy. The following year, on 20 March 1907, he couldn't help himself and was once again tried for 'using insubordinate language to his superior officer'. He was sent to confinement and sentenced to 35 days in the detention barracks – as a stern reprimand, or possibly with days added for the last altercation. It was later reduced to 33 days and was his last incarceration. After several stints interned – a total of 90 days which was docked from his future pension – it would appear Issy had finally learnt his lesson. By now he really was seventeen years of age, and from this time on there were no more blemishes on his conduct record.

After serving his detention he returned to duty, but within a month spent two weeks in the Station Hospital in Secunderabad, where the battalion had moved, this time going down with ague – a fever, chills and sweating. The cause was determined to be malaria, which was prevalent in India at the time.[2]

Treatment for malaria was rudimentary and there was limited availability of vaccines for viruses and infections. It was two-and-a-half years before Issy received his inoculations against typhoid. In the meantime, he had another hospital spell, suffering an abrasion. Being pre-penicillin, he required four days in the infirmary to reduce the risk of a serious infection.[3]

Issy quickly recovered and, aside from training, he and Alf undertook their education. At that time there were four levels for promotion within the ranks, the fourth-class being the lowest. In August 1909, Issy obtained his third-class certificate, the level required to draw his full pay.[4]

There was also sport.

Sport was a major drawcard for the British Army. For recruits, it offered amusement and enjoyment. For the army, it lifted fitness levels, relieved boredom, created a sense of cohesion and identity, improved morale and provided a distraction from the reality and horrors of war.

During peacetime, army sports included competition with foreign teams. Belgium and France, being countries enforcing conscription, had their best players serving time in the military and went about developing their games professionally. As a result, their teams were far superior so Britain, lacking conscription, struggled to compete. This did not go unnoticed by British Army authorities, and by 1916 sport had been made an official part of the army system.

Alf and Issy, suitably encouraged, played soccer and rugby in India for their battalion, and may also have boxed together. Issy decided to take up boxing competitively; Alf may have done so too, but we don't know.

Issy contested 133 bouts, with a total of 1095 rounds.

In the early twentieth century boxing was making a name for itself as a path to riches and fame. Prior to this time, it was considered by many as a sport of dubious legitimacy and questionable social acceptability. The introduction of the Queensberry rules, which incorporated a new code of conduct and adopted the use of gloves in place of bare-knuckle fighting, helped to change the perception of boxing as a savage brawl. The changes made the sport more entertaining and gave it greater commercial appeal, leading to a notable shift in attitudes and the inclusion of boxing as an Olympic sport in 1908. All the same, while gloves made boxing less brutal (to an extent), it also made it more dangerous and deadly. Previously, bare knuckle fighters had to be mindful of where and how hard they hit for fear of breaking their hands – as a result, more punches were directed to the body, a softer target. Padded gloves, although far lighter than today, allowed fighters to aim for the head. The padding did little to protect the hands and even less to protect the face. Instead, they served to help the 'hitter' and hurt the 'hittee'. This raised the excitement of the game and the frequency of knockouts. Unfortunately, it also accelerated long-term head injuries and increased the number of deaths.

There were no rules that covered what happened in the event that a competitor did not survive. One boxer with the stage name or, if not, unfortunate name of Johnny Basham, found himself in a difficult position when his opponent, Harry Price, died in the ring. Basham was arrested on manslaughter charges and forced to stand trial. Fortunately for him, he was acquitted when the magistrate ruled that the fight had been fair and sporting. A different verdict may have changed the sport.

Britain, a country steeped in class consciousness, began to take a keen interest in the new sport across all levels. Aristocracy – administrators and organisers – enjoyed the art of a good duel, while the middle classes – promoters and managers – saw the hero-making potential and its profitability. The working class – boxers and trainers – frequently came from Britain's enormous pool of labourers hoping to escape their circumstances. Many were drawn from the factories and docks of London's East End. For some, boxing gave them a chance to rise above their peers and make a name for themselves. For others, the sport provided a little more cash to feed large families and ward off poverty or the dreaded workhouse. Some men fought from sheer necessity.

Issy was no longer in this desperate situation and had the security of the army to fall back on, so he may have taken it up purely through the army's encouragement. He boxed under the name 'Jack Daniels': an ironic choice given that he did not drink. Perhaps it was because the whiskey had a surge in popularity – it won a gold medal in 1904 at the World's Fair in St Louis, USA. Maybe he wished to be associated with its success. Alternatively, it may have enabled him to compete under a veil of anonymity, hidden by such a well-known name.

If the answer was limited to these options, I would take a punt with option two. In 1915 Arty Powell, one of Victoria's most prominent theatrical and sporting writers, saw a story in a local newspaper of the winning of a VC by one Sergeant Issy Smith. A photograph accompanied the story, and after studying the picture for a few seconds, he declared that this was none other than the English boxer Jack Daniels, who had beaten Alf Morey on points in Melbourne the previous year.[5] This announcement hit the news in both Australia and the UK.

Of course, it may have been neither whiskey nor anonymity, but instead simply a reflection of the 'contending' nature of his birth name Israel. He chose a life as a boxer and a soldier.

Jack Daniels began as a welter, that is, a competitor weighing more than a lightweight and less than a middleweight. According to the records, he debuted on 10 February 1906 at Wonderland, a renowned East End hall that staged concerts, freak shows and major boxing events until it burnt down in 1911.

The punishment that could be inflicted would never be allowed today. While the referees were there to ensure the rules were followed, it was also their role to ensure the patrons were entertained. As such, scandalous and dangerous moves often 'slipped' through.

From the fight reports printed in the papers of the day, Jack Daniels' skill at the game was evident. He progressed smoothly from novice to amateur to professional, winning the majority of his bouts and honing his talent against more and more serious competitors. Indeed, it wasn't long before his tournaments were advertised as the main attraction, with up to 5000 rowdy patrons packing the stadiums. In 1910, at the King's Hall in Blackfriars, England, he fought Freddie Welsh, the world lightweight boxing champion from Wales. From that day on, he was billed as 'Jack Daniels of St George's in the East, who fought Freddie Welsh'. This drew big crowds.

As more of this illustrious career was uncovered, my father and I learned, with great excitement, that some film of the fight with Freddie existed – now more than one hundred years old. We looked forward to watching the film with some trepidation as Freddie Welsh was regarded by many as a cruel fighter for his use of kidney and rabbit punches as well as shoulder and head butts which, although not outlawed, were seen as callous and unsporting.[6] The tournament was reported as a warm-up for Freddie, who took an easy win and finished Jack off with a knockout in round seven. We watched the short film with bated breath.

Jack was nimble on his feet and put up a good contest, but there was something clearly wrong.

It wasn't Issy.

It took several moments to register the implications – that all the famous boxing records that have been attributed to Issy over the past century were in doubt.

Aside from the Regimental Middleweight Championship in India, where he got through to the second round, the elite career of Jack Daniels of St George's in the East belonged to someone else.[7]

Chapter 8

Issy Meets Elsie

On 22 March 1911 a royal proclamation was announced in India. The 'Delhi Durbar' (Court of Delhi) would be held in December that year to commemorate the British coronation, and recognise George V and Mary of Teck as the Emperor and Empress of India. The king would be attending, along with almost every ruling prince and nobleman in the country, plus thousands of others from high society. Many official ceremonies would take place over the course of two weeks and tight security was required.

After five years in Secunderbad, the 1st Battalion Manchester Regiment had transferred to Kamptee in 1908. Now in 1911, the battalion's E Company were to move to Jullundur, 360 kilometres north of Delhi, to form a new depot where the rest of the regiment would join them.[1] In the meantime, however, the other companies, including Issy's, were to go to Delhi first, in readiness for the Durbar. Alf and his band were already there, having gone ahead in mid-October to form part of massed bands assembling and practising for the event.

On arrival, a significant transformation took place. Three battalions from different parts of the world were placed together. They were the 1st Manchesters, the 47th Sikhs and the 59th Scinde Rifles, who consisted of Pathans, Sikhs, Dogras and Punjabi Muslims.[2] The group became known as the Jullundur Brigade, forming part of the Lahore Division (3rd India War Division) of the Indian Army.

The combination of British and Indian soldiers had not always been harmonious. In 1857, Indian soldiers rose up against their British commanders in a mutiny that grew to include civilians and spanned over two years, resulting in hundreds of thousands of deaths. The Jullundur Brigade, with its mix of different cultures, religions and beliefs, had to learn to work together.

On 14 December, the Brigade joined a consortium of 50,000 troops in a military parade held for the King-Emperor. The 1st Manchester Regiment was required to form many guards of honour, from the arrival of dignitaries on 2 December to their departure on 16 December. On 8, 9 and 15 December, guards of honour were provided by C, B and D Company respectively; on 11 December, the function was provided by A Company under Second Lieutenant Shipster – a man whose life Issy would later save.[3]

In recognition of this event, 26,800 Delhi Durbar medals struck in silver were awarded to soldiers. Of these, the Jullundur Brigade was allocated 26. Four were given to officers, six to members of the band and sixteen to warrant officers, non-commissioned officers and men. Alf received one, the 1st Manchester Regiment having won a silver cup competition for the best band present – presumably he was the best bandsman.

Surprisingly Issy, a private, also received one. I wondered if this was an acknowledgment of his boxing achievements (he represented the regiment in the Delhi Durbar Middleweight Boxing Competition) or to encourage his improved behaviour as a disciplined and obedient soldier. Alternatively, it may have been for his prowess at sport. The 1st Manchesters had also won the only other silver cup offered – for soccer. Maybe he was the best player.

Decades later, it was widely reported that Issy had been a member of the late King's personal bodyguard. Whether indeed he received the medal for this function, we will likely never know. The record for the award has since been lost.

Whatever the reason, the Delhi Durbar medal now sat proudly

alongside Issy's General Service Medal, awarded earlier for the Indian campaign.

✢

After the Durbar concluded, the battalion reassembled at the new depot at Jullundur. In October 1912, Alf and Issy had completed their service: Alf decided to stay on and was promoted to lance corporal, while Issy transferred to the Army Reserve with payment of a £20 bounty. According to the records, he was now 26 years old (not 22 as he should have been), 5 foot 7¼ inches tall, was brandishing the tattoos as previously noted and had not one but two scars over his left eyebrow. He had served eight years and 44 days, of which six years and 211 days had been abroad.[4]

During that month the two boys went to London, with Issy in search of work and Alf on leave. For a time Issy worked as a gasfitter, his occupation listed as 'Plumbers Mate'.

In family memoirs written by Issy's daughter Olive, the story is told that while in England, Alf met a girl named Flora McKechnie and, wishing to make a foursome, asked her if she would bring a friend. She brought her young sister Elsie.

This contradicts some of the history books which claim that Issy's brother Morris, waiting with crowds of other wellwishers at Charing Cross Station, introduced them.

Yet in a letter found by accident and written by Elsie herself, there was a different account again: coming home one night from a tailoring job, she was introduced to a young soldier who had just arrived from India the day before. As this comes from 'the horse's mouth', we must assume it to be the definitive version of events.

Who introduced them, however, remains an enigma to this day.

✢

Elsie was born on 5 June 1892 in Westminster, England, to Scottish parents, John McKechnie and Isabella Porteous. While Issy came from poor and war-torn beginnings, Elsie's upbringing had been quite the opposite. John's father William, who was married to a Dame of the British Empire, was a taskmaster at Hooper and Co., a successful maker of luxury horse-drawn carriages. The company held a royal warrant from 1830 and concentrated on the very top tier of the market, building decadent coaches without consideration of cost for such nobility as King William IV, Queen Victoria, King Edward VII, the Marquis of Londonderry and the Marquis of Crewe.

William specialised in painting the heraldic work on the doors of the coaches, with their elaborate coats of arms and delicate gold leafing. John followed in his father's footsteps and perhaps this is where he met Isabella, whose father David Porteous was also a coach painter.

The tradition continued with John and Isabella's first-born William joining the trade. Together, John and young William worked together on the finishes of the coach used for King Edward VII's coronation. Later, with the decline of the horse-drawn vehicle and the introduction of the motor car, William Junior painted the first horseless carriage for Hooper's and watched it proceed up the road behind a man with a red flag.

While the McKechnies circulated on the fringe of high society, life for the family was more middle class. They lived in a three-storey brick terrace in Horse and Groom Yard, Westminster, just a stone's throw from the River Thames. Elsie was the last of ten children, and an interesting story is that one of her siblings was given away. Isabella told one of her older sisters, who was childless, that she could have one and to pick the child with the dirtiest face. The dirty-faced Agnes apparently grew up in Canada with her aunt and uncle.

Compared to the turmoil of Eastern Europe, life was comfortable. In typical Victorian style, Elsie's father John ruled the household with an iron fist and the children were brought up to respect and obey. Elsie's memories of her father were of an austere man who insisted that his clothes be fresh and neatly pressed, and his meals be served to him hot and at set times. It was her job to go to the pub every morning to get his billy filled with scotch whisky and, along with her brothers and sisters, to wait on him at meal times. He dined on the third floor in lone splendour at the head of the table while the rest of the family ate theirs in the basement kitchen. Elsie was not allowed to have her own meal until she had worked out the time in roman numerals on the grandfather clock and sometimes, if she could not do it, she missed out completely.

But behind this autocratic demeanour her father hid a secret. In his younger years he had been a soldier in the 74th Foot at Aldershot. Averse to authority, he had absconded on 3 February 1871, aged 24. His details were published weekly in the *Police Gazette* for the next five weeks under the title 'Deserters from Her Majesty's Service' while they searched for him. Eventually he was caught and court-martialled on 9 August 1873; he was charged with desertion and making away with kit, and was sentenced to 84 days detention plus eight lashes and stoppages of pay. On return, he deserted again and was charged on 18 September 1874 with 112 days detention plus eight lashes and stoppages of pay. After serving his sentence he parted ways with the army, perhaps by mutual agreement – either that, or they had had enough of him and kicked him out.

Yet not everything from his military days wore off. Elsie remembered her father barking orders to the household on a regular basis, with everyone taking heed. Her mother Isabella spent her time dutifully overseeing piano lessons and instructing children to race upstairs, as required, to respond to their father's demands. Later, with five women each wearing a full-length dress and four starched petticoats, it was oddly Isabella, and not the servants, who managed the laundry. Elsie doubted if her mother was permitted to move far from the iron.

Over time, her father managed to throw all of the children out of the house for trifling reasons. At ten every night he would do a round of the bedrooms, and if a bed was empty, he packed a case with that child's clothes and put it outside the door. A couple of the older children who had married took in the evicted ones until alternative arrangements could be made. Unusually, her sister Isabella, who had married a Charles Wilson in 1900, moved back in with her own daughter Mabel after unsuccessfully filing for divorce. Although the grounds of the petition were that her husband 'rendezvoused' with another woman and gave his wife a venereal disease, the case was struck out. Three more siblings for Mabel later joined the household, their heritage unknown.

When her mother died of cancer in 1904, Elsie took up the family laundering and dressmaking duties, and trained as a tailoress and gentlemen's outfitter. One of her brothers became a Saville Row tailor and she was apprenticed to him. Later, she worked in a tailoring factory near St Paul's Churchyard. In 1911 she was trapped in a 'pea souper' fog, arriving home late due to her bus being involved in an accident. Not surprisingly, her possessions were waiting for her on the front step.

Elsie moved in with her sister Myra, husband Bert and her sister Flora, leaving Isabella to take care of their father. The split was obviously bitter, as she did not see her father again and later claimed to have no parents during her early years. But John was alive and well, living to the ripe age of 88 in 1936. He was not missed.

✢

And so it goes that one night in 1912, Elsie met Issy. The two began seeing each other and it wasn't long before Alf, Flora, Issy and Elsie became good friends. Over the next two years they went out regularly together.

But Elsie was unsettled. 1n 1914 the idea of travelling abroad was exciting and Australia was the top of the list – there, the prospects were bright; the economy was strong, jobs were aplenty and young Brits were encouraged to immigrate. Elsie made arrangements to sail on 2 July on the SS *Geelong* and, according to her, Issy agreed to follow. Securing a free trip at short notice supervising 40 boys from Dr Barnardo's orphanage, he managed to leave before her.[5]

Dr Barnardo's Homes was formally known as The National Incorporated Association for the Reclamation of Destitute Waif

Children. It was founded by Thomas Barnardo in 1866, ostensibly to care for vulnerable children, in particular those who had been left orphaned and destitute after a cholera outbreak. It grew to be both a significant organisation and a major scandal. Specifically, Barnardo was accused of wandering the streets of the East End and kidnapping children, modifying before and after photographs of them so that their rescue and later care was clearly justified and exporting them to the colonies for cheap labour on farms. He was also charged with poor management, cruelty, neglect and even immorality, and there were questions about his title of doctor.

He confessed to the kidnapping, explaining it as 'philanthropic abduction' and using the defence that 'the end justified the means'. This didn't wash with the London community and he was taken to court no fewer than 88 times for a wide range of charges. Incredibly, he managed to dodge any convictions.

Disembarking in Melbourne in June 1914, Issy did no further work for Dr Barnardo's Homes. Arriving one month earlier than Elsie, he got a job almost immediately as a gas fitter with the Metropolitan Gas Company.[6] The Superintendent, Joe Tallents, was a kind man with a large household of eight who lived in Ascot Vale.[7] He offered Issy board at his house. The children, unaccustomed to the name of Issy, rechristened him Jack.

Some of Joe's kindness probably rubbed off on the young Jack/Issy. But even more than this, Issy understood hardship and the plight of others in less fortunate circumstances, having faced these himself. He felt for the people without jobs who struggled to find enough to pay for their lodgings, and it wasn't long before he became well known as the kind and generous young man who stood outside the gates of the gas company every pay day and gave away half his wages. Men queued for hours, waiting for a handout from Issy of a few pennies each.

Apparently, according to later news reports, Issy had sent Elsie letters with 'glowing descriptions of the new land, loved by the sun, in which wages were very good and conditions easy'. At the earliest opportunity, as the papers romanticised, she 'said goodbye to the fogs of London and set out for the land of promise.' But in truth, Elsie was already on the boat, having first come up with the idea.

In any case, much bigger matters were about to unfold. During her voyage, the world erupted into chaos.

Chapter 9

War Breaks Out

On 4 August 1914, following the assassination of Austrian Archduke Franz Ferdinand and a rapidly escalating chain of political events, Great Britain declared war on Germany.

For Australia this was somewhat of a prickly problem, aside from the economic and personal cost of war. The Germans had long been thought of as Anglo-Saxon cousins and desirable immigrants to grow the country's population. Now they had to become the enemy.

The decision could not be challenged. Having already proven its willingness to participate in the motherland's colonial wars, Australia dutifully took note and immediately offered 20,000 troops. Britain's acceptance of this offer became public knowledge on 8 August, but Issy hadn't waited. On the very day the war broke out, he presented himself to Victoria Barracks and the following day, 5 August, he and seven others set up the Broadmeadows Camp in Victoria. The formal call for recruits was made five days later.[1]

Although Broadmeadows had been earmarked as a site for military training in 1913, nothing had been established and the rural area was predominantly a tented camp on a barren landscape. The first Australian Imperial Force (AIF) immediately began recruiting there with the intention of sending servicemen to this European war and Issy hoped to join them. Because of the significant difference between Australian and British rates of pay (six shillings compared to one shilling a day), there was a temptation for Imperial Reservists to join the AIF if they could. Given that many thought the war would be over quickly and sending Australians was a waste of time, the Aussie recruits became known as 'Six Bob a Day Tourists', a label which has stuck to this day.

Initially the Australian authorities did not know what to do with the reservists while they awaited instructions from Great Britain. The Australian Minister for Defence, Edward Millen, made the following call:

> As a considerable amount of uncertainty appears to exist regarding the Imperial Reservists now in Australia, it might be as well to state that these at present are being attached to our local forces, pending further directions from Imperial authorities. These men are, of course, liable for service at the direction of the Imperial War Office, but obviously there is some little difficulty in the way of their immediate return to Great Britain. Their services are at present, and with the sanction of the Imperial authorities, being utilised in connection with our own expeditionary force. It is probable, however, that the Imperial authorities might desire them to proceed to Great Britain, in which case, arrangements for their transport will be made by the Defence Department here.[2]

Britain did indeed want its reservists, and it quickly became clear that Issy had to return to Manchester and rejoin his old regiment. It is here that the facts and the history books get very muddy.[3]

There was some speculation that Issy actually managed to join the AIF and was later embroiled in a court case regarding AIF entitlements. A newspaper clipping and a military record about a journalist's telephone call to investigate make note of this. The attestation paper for service abroad, on which Issy's details were recorded, was titled 'Australian Imperial Force', with the word 'Australian' crossed out by hand.[4]

It is also claimed he travelled with the AIF and when this was discovered in Egypt, he was transferred to the British Manchester

Regiment. It is more likely he merely travelled as a reservist alongside AIF troops in the convoy of the first ships until they reached Egypt, where the AIF disembarked and the Imperial Reservists continued to Great Britain. The 'discovery' was probably more like Chinese whispers, i.e., the story was rewritten by multiple journalists until its original facts became distorted.

The SS *Miltiades* was used for the despatch of the reservists and should have been the ship he boarded. Because of their previous military experience, a number of reservists were held back when their embarkation orders came, and were used to help train the recruits of the fledgling AIF. This may have been the case for Issy.[5]

Yet more theories abound.

Apparently, he departed Australia just as Elsie was arriving. According to the century-old romance story, they missed each other – their ships passing on the Indian Ocean during the night.

If Issy was with the first convoy, then the 'passing ships' tale has to be a fabrication. While it was expected that the troops would depart almost immediately, this did not happen. Transport vessels had to be transformed from merchantmen and gathered at ports of departure.[6] Although many were soon ready to go, they were delayed as there were significant concerns that German warships were lurking off the coast, waiting to sink them. While they lingered, wild stories spread about disasters and the Australian destroyers already scouring the Pacific:

> … so the man in the street said; and he was backed up by the man in the tram, the man in the club, the man in the bar, the man coming home from church … and some who never go to church [but] still hang on to the belief that 'there must be something in it.'[7]

There was, in fact, some legitimacy to these fears, as German Admiral Graf von Spee's squadron *was* circulating, with HMAS *Australia* in search of it. The Australian convoy had to wait for escorts and did not leave Western Australia until 1 November 1914.[8]

This was long after Elsie's arrival. In her memoirs, daughter

Olive claimed that when Elsie landed, the Tallents family was at Port Melbourne to greet her and break the news that her fiancé – they were apparently now engaged – was already on his way back to England. She moved in with the family and took a job as a seamstress with Davies, Doery and Co.

Although many soldiers had said their goodbyes to family and friends in August, there were still some opportunities to circulate – and indeed many soldiers had to be rounded up from local bars and establishments over the course of the next few months for what turned out to be a series of false starts.

When at last they did depart in November, they marched past huge cheering crowds and were sent off with much fanfare, including the boisterous roar of brass bands. Issy and Elsie would have had plenty of time to reunite and bid their farewells.

Unless, ironically, Issy had been on the SS *Geelong*, the same ship Elsie came out on. It was converted to a troopship and left Melbourne with 440 soldiers on 22 September, collecting more from Hobart in late October before arriving in Albany to join the convoy. This would have left them just a few weeks to see each other.[9]

So where was Issy? The 'truth' gets muddier still.

There are many mentions in wartime newspapers that Issy served in the German New Guinea campaign. No evidence can be found to support this. Germany had a colonial empire, like Britain, but on a significantly smaller scale, encompassing parts of Africa as well as the north-eastern section of the island of New Guinea and various West Pacific islands. German wireless stations situated in New Guinea threatened shipping in the region and had to be destroyed or else Australia's convoy would be at great risk.

The capture of German New Guinea took only six weeks and occurred at the start of the war. A small contingent of 2000 men was hastily assembled on 6 August (two days after Issy mustered) to create the Australian Naval and Military Expeditionary Force (AN&MEF) for this purpose. It would seem obvious that, as this needed to happen quickly and early in the war (within days), only trained soldiers would be sent. Issy had served in the regular British Army for eight years and would have made an ideal candidate.

The AN&MEF is reported to have comprised eight companies of infantry men and six companies of naval men. Its nominal roll shows that men were drawn from Queensland, New South Wales, Victoria and South Australia, and a number were recorded with places of birth outside Australia. Issy is not listed, nor can any Australian Army number or service record be traced for him; neither can a special medal be found for this service. NAJEX war historian Jack Epstein believed that it is possible he did in fact serve in the German New Guinea action, thus there remains a chance that Issy did participate but was not included on the 'Australian' list.[10]

The campaign, occurring during September, was over quickly. Issy's records show that he arrived at the Manchester depot in England on 9 December 1914. Many troops who had served in the German New Guinea campaign arrived at the same time, so it was assumed he had been with them.

Yet there was more.

Speculation abounded that Issy had been aboard HMAS *Sydney* and was involved in the wreck of the German cruiser, SS *Emden*, on 9 November 1914.[11] HMAS *Sydney* operated in New Guinea and Pacific waters during August and September 1914, and was part of the AN&MEF contingent in the German New Guinea campaign. After carrying out a number of patrols, she was returning to Australia to form part of the first convoy of troops when she was ordered to investigate a distress call from the British cable and wireless station on the Cocos Islands. After a short battle, the SS *Emden* was run onto the reef with over half its crew killed or wounded.

In a newspaper report from Belfast in January 1916, Issy purportedly said, in answer to a question, that he was a reservist when war broke out and was shipped to England on board HMAS *Sydney*.[12] An account of the sinking of the SS *Emden* was then broadly described with inaccurate details, but the reporter did not indicate if these were Issy's direct words or his own fanciful journalism.[13]

Without substantiation, it would be reasonable to presume that this was simply another story. Yet incredibly, in among Issy's possessions, found a century later, was an original typed account of the battle, written anonymously but clearly by someone who was on the ship and saw the action. Was Issy there and did he detail the event?[14] A search of Australia's National Archives, the War Museum and the Royal Navy Historical Section for the passenger lists of both the HMAS *Sydney* and the SS *Miltiades* (the ship he was believed to be on) was unsuccessful.

And just to muddy the waters one last time, a newspaper article from 1927 reported that Issy was on the RMS *Osterley*. This was a troop ship used by the AIF which apparently managed to avoid the SS *Emden* ... twice!

Issy's introduction to the war will likely remain a mystery forever.[15] The only thing that is known, for sure, is that Issy departed Australia sometime between August and October of 1914. In a letter written by Elsie and discovered in 2020, Issy and Elsie got engaged, not in England before they left, but on the eve of his sailing out. As he boarded to sail away, he asked her, 'How would you like me to bring home the Victoria Cross?'

She thought that was very funny.

Chapter 10

Neuve Chapelle

The SS *Miltiades* sailed to Port Said, Egypt, where it parted with the Australian troopships before continuing on to England, reaching Plymouth on 22 December 1914. Issy's military records state that he had arrived in Ashton-under-Lyne thirteen days earlier.[1]

During the voyage the Ottoman Empire, including Constantinople, his place of birth, entered the war on the side of the Central Powers – the enemy. If Issy did not know of this development while at sea, he would most certainly have learned of it by the time he reached England. Whatever tugs of allegiance he had towards his birthplace, if he had them at all, were never displayed.

On arrival at the barracks, nearly all reservists were immediately promoted to Sergeant so they could bring the new recruits up to speed as quickly as possible.

But not Issy. He was appointed Acting Lance Corporal, Manchester Regiment. I can only assume this was due to his poor conduct record and the belief that his leadership qualities were unsatisfactory. More surprising, however, was that the rank he was given was lower than when he had been demobilised two years previously. I find that hard to explain.

For Issy, there was no time to argue the point. In less than a fortnight he would be equipped and transferred.

It is quite possible that the following incident occurred while waiting to be despatched. According to a family anecdote, he was on the terrace of a café in England talking to a friend in Yiddish when an officer overhead him and, thinking the language was German, mistook him for a spy. Issy retrieved his boxing skills and wasted no time launching a swift uppercut that left the officer's jaw in a sorry state. Issy was a fighter who did not tolerate intimidation.

Where the army sent him first is unclear. Some newspaper stories reported, months later, that he fought in the Battle of Givenchy on 19–20 December 1914, copped a bullet and spent three months in hospital. The 3rd (Lahore) Division, his former unit, *was* fighting at Givenchy during that period and, taking into account the conflicting records, it is not impossible (though it seems unlikely) that Issy could have just made it by that time.

In 1927, Issy gave brief particulars of his service where he apparently told a reporter that he landed at Marseilles on 19 December, went into action at Givenchy five days later and was subsequently wounded there. This places him in the location, but after the main battle – which could be a simple memory loss of the exact dates, or the reporter's shabby journalism. There was also a story that he played soccer with the Germans in the Christmas truce of 1914. This truce occurred along a number of places on the Western Front in that year only and generally (with a few exceptions) was prohibited from happening again. But there is no evidence to confirm he was there at that time.

Instead, in a book written about him in 2014 by a member of the Manchester Regiment, he was believed to have been posted to the Special Reserve at its new base at Cleethorpes on England's east coast.[2] The Special Reserve was established to maintain a supply of additional manpower for the British Army in times of war. Organised into battalions, they provided a third unit for each of the regular army's two-battalion infantry regiments. Issy was assigned to the 3rd Battalion (Special Reserve) Manchester Regiment. In addition to training recruits and providing replacements, his unit's role at Cleethorpes was to guard the coast and, in particular, the River Humber.

Issy's stay there was short. As the fighting in France intensified in early 1915, he was sent to rejoin the 1st Manchesters, still part of the Jullundur Brigade, who were in the trenches between Festubert and Neuve Chapelle. Alf Burley, who had stayed with the 1st Manchesters and seen combat in Givenchy in December 1914, was with them. Two more Indian brigades, the Sirhind and the Ferozepore, also part of the 3rd (Lahore Division), were there too, along with the 7th (Meerut) Division.[3]

The first of the Indian troops to arrive in Marseilles in August 1914 fell victim to the freezing weather. The new winter uniform wasn't ready and they were forced to endure the rain and snow in their summer khaki drill. Marching to their destinations would have been particularly unpleasant, and not just because of the climate. Packs were heavy, initially weighing over 70 pounds (32 kilograms) – about the same as a medieval suit of armour. Later, with the addition of steel helmets, box respirators, wire cutters and extra ammunition, stories abound that they weighed as much as 110 pounds (49 kilograms)! Clothing was often itchy and army boots, too, were frequently uncomfortable. Made to a few standard sizes, they rarely fitted well – a soldier was lucky if he didn't suffer raw and blistered feet.

By February 1915 the troops had warmer clothing, but were dealing with punishing conditions – operating often from shallow and poorly constructed trenches that offered minimum protection from the elements or the enemy. Continuously bombarded with artillery fire or picked off by snipers, they became known, like many other soldiers during that time, as 'cannon fodder'. The fierce combat came as a terrible shock. One soldier wrote home: 'This is not war; it is the ending of the world.'

The lines of opposing trenches now ran all the way from the English Channel to the French–Swiss border. The area between the Allied and enemy lines was referred to as 'No Man's Land' – a barren terrain consisting of craters, endless barbed wire, and broken and abandoned military equipment. Soldiers killed in this space generally could not be retrieved without enormous risk. During heavy battles, trenches could be battered by artillery fire constantly during the day and then subjected to multiple incursions at night. Soldiers who died in the trenches lay or were buried largely where they fell.[4]

With the unrelenting rain, the trenches filled with water. Standing in the water, which could be waist-high, promoted frostbite and trench foot.[5] Corpses, excrement and food scraps that littered the trenches attracted rats. Just one pair of rats could produce 880 offspring in a year and as their food supplies grew, so did their size and numbers. Lice, which accompanied the rats, caused endless itching, typhus and trench fevers.

Altogether the conditions, attacks, vermin and parasites compounded the men's misery, afflicting them day and night.

Issy joined Alf and his original brigade in the trenches near the village of Neuve Chapelle.[6] Since water levels in the area were close to the surface, these trenches were not deep and consisted mostly of parapets made from piles of soil and sandbags. They overlooked fields broken by many small drainage ditches and separated by rows of decapitated willow trees, behind which German snipers had cover and a considerable advantage.

Neuve Chapelle consisted of just a smattering of houses, already ruined and now fortified by the enemy which had broken the trench line in the previous October. The town was neither large nor of significance, but if Allied forces could penetrate and re-seize it and the slightly higher ground of Aubers Ridge, which offered a good observation point, they could move through to the city of Lille and then intercept the roads, railway lines and canals used by the enemy as transport routes. The little town thus became strategic and the site for the first planned large-scale British offensive. A consortium of 40,000 British, Canadian and Indian troops prepared to take part, with their attack approach used as the model on which all future assaults would be based – concentrated bombardment of enemy artillery followed immediately by attack. Efforts would then be concentrated on preventing the enemy reserves from coming up.

On the night of 9 March it was cold, with steady rain and snow flurries that turned, in the early hours, to damp fog. The assault began at daybreak the next morning, with hundreds of guns firing at once. A British supply officer, Herbert Stewart, described the incredible bombardment and destruction:

> As soon as the range had been accurately secured, a tremendous fire was opened on the village of Neuve Chapelle and the neighbouring trenches occupied by the enemy ... Under this hail of flying metal, the village, the neighbouring trenches, and the whole German position selected for attack were blotted from sight under a pall of smoke and dust. The earth shook and the air was filled with the thunderous roar of the exploding shells. To the watching thousands the sight was a terrible one: amidst the clouds of smoke and dust they could see human bodies with earth and rock, portions of houses and fragments of trench hurtling through the air.[7]

Once the line was broken, the infantry advanced. Indian troops provided nearly half the assaulting force and were the first ones sent in. The 1st Manchester Battalion, including Issy and Alf, proceeded as advanced guard with the 47th Sikhs and were attacked by heavy enemy shellfire. The soldiers ducked for cover behind breastworks and, as night fell, slept in ruined houses.

On the morning of 11 March, they again moved forward, but enemy fire killed or injured a number of officers and men, adding to a battlefield already littered with the dead and the wounded. Due to severe losses from the previous day, the 59th Rifles, who were to be the backup, had to be brought up into the front line – now there were no reserves. The troops sheltered behind houses, but the enemy's guns and shells turned and fired into the buildings, forcing them to retreat. At 8 pm, as the shelling eased, they withdrew to the ruins where they had spent the previous night.

At 5 am on 12 March, the Jullundur Brigade, with the Manchesters leading, moved again towards Neuve Chapelle, the road on which they travelled being constantly hit by enemy fire. At 9 am they received orders to attack the Bois du Biez, behind the German line. There were gaps in the line where the trenches were crossed by roads and dykes, and as men scurried across to move into position, they were hit by shells and rifle fire. There were heavy casualties and, when coupled with the previous day's shellfire, resources rapidly diminished. Due to these impacts, the attack was postponed until 1 pm.

Orders were eventually given to commence the assault and soldiers bravely clambered over the parapets into intense enemy fire. Many were killed. In the midst of the fighting, Issy came face to face with a German soldier and was at the point of bayonetting him when something held him back. He didn't bayonet the man, but took him prisoner. On searching him, he found he was wearing a Jewish token. According to Issy, that told him that there was a God, and with his help they would win the war.

The battle was fierce and raged over and around the trenches for hours. It was 4.30 am before the battalion was eventually withdrawn.

Although the history books describe the battle as 'finishing' on the fourth day, 13 March, with the capture of Neuve Chapelle, the fighting did not stop. Over the next three days, Issy's battalion were forced to escape and return several times a day from the church where they were attempting to rest until safer billets could be found. On the night of 18 March, they moved back to the trenches at Bois du Biez and relieved other brigades. For the next four days, despite still being shelled, they strengthened the defences and at night buried the dead. Issy was reported to have been wounded – apparently shot in the arm; but if he was, it went unrecorded and it is not known how he was treated.

The attack at Neuve Chapelle did not go as planned. A breakdown of communications caused confusion and allowed enemy reserves to seal the break in the trench line more quickly than it could be exploited. Only a small area was gained for a huge loss of over 11,500 British and Indian soldiers killed, wounded or who were missing. Of these, 1694 were from the 3rd (Lahore) Division. The Germans also suffered, with around the same number killed or wounded and many taken prisoner.

A Neuve Chapelle epitaph to the Indian soldiers who died there reads:

> Tell them at home,
> There's nothing here to hide:
> We took our orders,
> asked no questions,
> died.[8]

Chapter 11

Lost Cigarettes and the Battle at Ypres ...

Neuve Chapelle was Issy's first experience of battle and it was brutal. How much time he had to recover isn't known, but it couldn't have been more than a few weeks before he was sent to fight again.

For the Allied forces, protecting the Western Front was vital and the town of Ypres critical, as it was a major transport hub that provided a route across Belgium to the French coastal ports of Calais and Dunkirk, which the Germans were keen to secure. In October 1914, British, French, Canadian and Belgian troops had established themselves north of the town to defend it.

Guarding Ypres was difficult. The Allies had been defending roughly 15 square miles (24 square kilometres) of mostly flat landscape with a slight dip in the centre, much like a satellite dish. The town was to the rear of their front line, effectively in the centre of the dish, and the German Army was entrenched on slightly higher ground, around the rim. The area formed a salient – that is, it extended into the enemy's territory and was enveloped on three sides. It was a very dangerous place. If the enemy managed to invade the rear, the defenders would be surrounded and cut off.

Fierce fighting ensued, lasting until late November. This became known as the First Battle of Ypres.[1] A second battle began in April 1915, but this time the warfare – which Issy would experience – would be very different.

On 14 April 1915, British and French headquarters received

reliable information that the Germans planned to use a new weapon – an asphyxiating gas that was a killing agent – at the northern edge of the Ypres Salient at a village called Langemarck.[2] The gas would be discharged from large, pressurised cylinders and carried with the wind, providing an opportunity to break through the defences in the gap created by the gas cloud. The release would occur in the next day or two or when the wind was most favourable, and would move the Allied line back to the west of Ypres.

The Hague Treaty of 1899 specifically prohibited the use of asphyxiating or poisonous gas, and the follow-up convention of 1907 added the banning of 'poison or poisoned weapons'. But neither the French nor the Germans considered tear gas, an irritant, to be a violation, and the French used small quantities of it as soon as the war began. The Germans followed with a single, much larger-scale attack against Russian troops at the end of January 1915, but the chemical froze and failed. During the fighting at Neuve Chapelle, shells filled with tear gas were again released, although the levels were so small that the troops, including Issy's brigade, were hardly affected and most did not notice it.

The various divisions holding the line at Ypres were warned to expect an attack, but the use of gas was not conveyed to the troops. When the gas onslaught occurred on 22 April, it turned out to be the 'killing agent' that headquarters had been warned about. Being much heavier than air, the greenish-yellow poison turned into a blue-white mist as it drifted and sank into the trenches and dugouts. The Allies were taken by surprise; thousands died almost immediately, leaving many others to die slowly and painfully.

Issy and the rest of the 3rd (Lahore) Division, however, were unaware of these developments. Based at L'Epinette near Armentières, roughly 16 miles away as the crow flies, they were resting in billets. On 23 April they were joined by a number of officers, including Lieutenant-Colonel Henry Hitchins, who had been shot in the thigh at the Battle of Givenchy. They were given instructions to move at short notice to an unspecified destination.

Here, for the first time, we are in the fortunate position of having Issy explain what happened next in his own words:[3]

> On the night of the 23rd April, we heard a rumour that our division – the 3rd (Lahore) Division – was to go to the Dardenelles. On the following day we got orders to get ready – no one knew for where. We started off about 11.30 on that morning and marched until 6 o'clock on the following morning, doing a forced march of about thirty miles. No one knew all the time where we were going, and many of the boys were asking how far off the Dardenelles were. This was one of the finest marches I ever remember. General Strickland, who was commanding the Jullundur Brigade, kept us fit and ready for battle. He was never happy except in the trenches with his men, encouraging them. He is, in fact, one of the finest heroes of the war.

According to the battalion's war diary, the troops actually arrived at Boeschepe by 11.30 pm and rested the night, having covered a distance of just over 23 miles. They departed again at 6 am on 25 April and travelled a further 12½ miles to Vlamertinghe, arriving there at 10.30 am the same day. It is not known when Issy provided his account and it is possible with so much action he forgot this minor detail.

> We rested for a night at Vlamertinghe in Belgium, and next morning we resumed our march to the unknown place which some of us thought to be the Dardenelles. Finally, however, we got to Ypres. We were shelled heavily when we were marching through it, and the native troops suffered heavily. About 11 o'clock on the morning of the 26th April we halted in a field for a rest, but we had no time to take our equipment off before shells were rained on us from a German aeroplane, killing a great many. We then got orders to run for cover at once and leave everything behind us. I left my pack behind me, and when we went to look for cover, I suddenly remembered that I had left my cigarettes behind.

> I went back to get the cigarettes out of my pack, and it was lucky I did, for just then a Jack Johnson dropped among my platoon and killed or wounded about 14 of them.[4] No doubt, only I had turned back [sic] to get my cigarettes I would have been amongst the casualties.

Issy scrambled across the field and made it to where the rest of his battalion were setting up. They were immediately ordered to improve the trenches. Now west of Weiltje, not far from St Julien, they worked diligently under a clear, sunny sky while they waited for further instructions. They were not to know that the salient had, over the past few days, been compressed into an area now just six miles across and three miles deep, and all British forces within it would soon come under intensified artillery fire. Issy continued:

> After this, we got orders to dig ourselves in and we got ready our entrenching tools. The day was frighteningly warm, and we perspired at the work.

There was a significant delay with the orders. Although they had been issued from the divisional headquarters just after 2 am, this transmission did not reach the brigades and in turn the battalions until 12.30 pm, nearly 10½ hours later. Eventually they were told to set up in their 'forming up' position – the Jullundur Brigade to the right of the 1st Manchesters, and other troops, including the Ferozepore Brigade, to their left.

The plan that was now received was to attack about 1,500 yards due north, where the Germans were entrenched on the higher ground of Mauser Ridge. The battalions were to move forward at 1.30 pm under cover of an artillery barrage and then, when the artillery lifted at 2 pm, they were to be in an assaulting position close to the trenches.

Between their trench and Mauser Ridge was an open, unfenced field. In front of them the land rose slightly for the next 500 yards to the crest of Hill Top Ridge. It then descended gently for a further 500 yards to a small stream before rising gently on another bare slope for the remaining distance to the German trenches. There was no protection.

As soon as they began, the enemy's return fire was heavy. In the confusion, the Jullundur Brigade veered to the left, squeezing Issy's platoon and crowding the troops next to them. They rushed forward regardless, and when their heads appeared above Hill Top Ridge, they were visible to the enemy. Immediately they came under what was later described as 'a perfect inferno of fire of all kinds – machine-gun, rifle and every kind of shell, many of which were filled with gas'. They ran, dodging shells, as men fell all around them.

Although you might expect the troops would have been told by now about the use of gas over the past few days, it appears they hadn't. The poison surprised and blinded them for several minutes, but they could do little about it amid the mayhem.

Issy explained the events from the beginning of the bombardment as follows:

> Then we got orders to fall in, and word was passed along the line that the artillery would commence a bombardment at 1.20 [pm]. This lasted for 40 minutes, and was followed by 5 minutes of rapid fire. Our platoon was leading, with Lieutenant Robinson in charge. After our long march we were almost breathless with fatigue but just then we got orders to fix bayonets and charge. It was an awful charge that.
>
> The Germans yelled like madmen as they saw the cold steel coming on them like an avalanche. We thrust the bayonets through them without flinching. Our commander [Lieutenant Robinson] was hit and I at once got my field dressing out and bandaged him up. There was heavy machine gun fire at this time. I carried the wounded commander about two or three hundred yards before I got to a first aid post. On the way, I saw Lieutenant Shipster running up and down continuously with ammunition for a machine gun. Lieut. Shipster was a man who knew no fear.

He saw me bending under the weight of another wounded man – Sergeant Rooke, of the 1st Manchester Regiment – and said – 'Don't falter, old chap; I shan't be long, and will give you a lift.' The place was swept by a heavy fire at this time, and Lieut. Shipster had not gone twenty yards until [sic] he was shot in the neck. I said to Sergeant Rooke, 'Lay here a minute while I bandage Lieut. Shipster.'

I rolled down the hill with my hands by my side and reached the officer. I carried him to the spot where Sergeant Rooke lay. I removed [sic] Sergeant Rooke a few yards, and then Lieut. Shipster a few yards, and so on alternately until I reached our trenches, where Lieut. Priestly came out of the trench and took Mr [sic] Shipster in. I brought Sergeant Rooke to safety, and then, dead exhausted, I fell down, not able to move. The officer then gave me his flask and said 'There is brandy in this. Take a drop and it will revive you.' I said I would not, as I was a teetotaller and intended to remain one, no matter what happened.[5] But I was dreadfully weak.

I rested for an hour, and then went back to my Company to hear that Lieut. Robinson was missing. A few hours afterwards I went to look for him, but could not find him. I saw a lot of our wounded lying about. I, with the help of stretcher bearers, managed to take them all out of danger. We were relieved by the Highland Light Infantry about 3 o'clock on the morning of April 27th, and we went back and received a good meal – the first for two days. I was slightly gassed, and was carried to the first aid post. I lay there very sick for about 24 hours but would not leave the battalion as I wanted to see the fight through.[6]

Issy had advanced on his own initiative towards the enemy trenches to save his platoon commander, 2nd Lieutenant Robinson, then Sergeant Rooke (who had taken over from Lieutenant Robinson), then Lieutenant Shipster. After depositing 2nd Lieutenant Robinson at a first aid post, he carried the next two men in turn, a few yards at a time, more than 250 yards. Being only of small stature himself, the tasks must have taken a great deal out of him. After bringing the men in, he rested for an hour, suffering from exhaustion and the effects of the gas. When he recovered, he found what was left of his Company and then, when it was dark, went out in search of others, including Lieutenant Pretty who was now missing. He stumbled about the rough terrain, throwing himself on the ground as the searchlights flashed by, and found many wounded men, bringing them back one by one. Without his help, these men would have died where they lay. Afterwards, Rooke gave his own account:

> During the attack I was shot through the liver and was quite helpless. Smith at once ran out to my rescue, put me on his back and carried me through a terrific hail of shrapnel, rifle and machine-gun fire onto the Ypres road. I was lying only 200 yards from the German trenches and the fact that Smith escaped being hit was a sheer miracle.
>
> Just at that time the Germans turned on the poison gas, and the Algerians, who were on our left, began to retire. We were again in a most exposed position and Lieutenant Shipster, who passed us, told Smith to put me down and said he would send for assistance. The officer had only gone a few yards when he was shot through the neck. Smith went to him, bandaged his wounds – all the time under heavy fire – and carried him, and afterwards me, into the trenches of the 45th Suffolks. He helped to take me on a stretcher to the first aid post of the Suffolks and afterwards returned immediately to fight on with his battalion. Smith behaved with wonderful coolness and presence of mind the whole time and no one ever deserves a VC more thoroughly than he does.[7]

Other comrades gave their version of the event, which puts into perspective how incredible and miraculous the feat was:

> It was after a temporary withdrawal of our line that Smith

was found to be missing. The last heard of him he was inquiring about the position of a wounded man who had been left behind. Nothing more was seen or heard of him for an hour, when something was seen moving towards our trenches. It stopped at intervals, but gradually it came nearer and became more distinct. Then it was seen to be the figure of a man assisting another who was badly wounded. Snipers were firing at the two solitary figures, and the bullets at places were making rings of dust around them.

All the while shell and machine-gun fire was raining down, and every minute we expected to see the two figures blotted out of existence. Once they went down, and we thought it was forever; but soon we saw signs of life again and the figures now became more distinct. Some of us who knew Smith recognised him as he came nearer, and we set up a cheer when we realised what he was up to. The Germans were evidently bent on finishing off the two men, for the nearer they got to safety, the greater became the fire they had to face. We could do little to help them, but what we could we did do. We opened a heavy rifle and machine-gun fire in the direction of where the enemy snipers were, and gradually we silenced the enemy. Under cover of this Smith and the other man were able to crawl the remainder of the distance, and they got a rousing reception when they came in. It was later in the day that Smith went out to help in bringing in the wounded.[8]

During the battle, some of the troops eventually got to within 70 yards of the German trenches; however, faced with heavy fire and chlorine gas, they were unable to advance further and the attack failed. By the time they were relieved by the Highland Infantry on 27 April, the Manchesters had lost their new commanding officer Lieutenant-Colonel Hitchins and fifteen men. In addition, eleven officers and 206 men had been wounded and 56 were missing. Issy explained what happened next:

> We left the reserve trench on the 30th [April], and marched through Ypres, which was still being shelled. We fell over dead bodies which were piled three feet high in places. We had gone about five miles when, as a result of a message received from a despatch rider, we got orders to go back and support the French. Well, you can imagine how we felt. But the motto of a soldier is 'Never Say Die' and we marched back, singing the song 'As We Were Marching Along'.

This would have been a terrifying experience, not just for the fear of the instructions but also the return journey. Although they marched back through Ypres at night, it was the only route through which ammunition and rations could be sent to the front line. The enemy was well aware of the steady stream of troops and transport passing through and they shelled it constantly. Horse-drawn vehicles went through at a canter, but the marching infantry, walking in the dark, had to keep alert and simply hope for the best.

> We found afterwards that we were not required and retired into some huts for a rest. We had hardly gone into them when shells began to fall, and we were moved into an open field.
>
> On the 9th May, we got the order that a bombardment would start at 5 o'clock in the morning. It was a fierce bombardment that – like two hours of hell. Another bombardment, just as fierce, started on May 10th.

The bombardments that Issy referred to here were occurring at Hooge, a village on one of the most eastern parts of the salient. British troops had been forced to retreat closer to Ypres after 6 May, but the village, which had been under siege since the previous year, was now ruined. It was, nonetheless, no less hazardous. The opposing front lines, which were very close together, were battered, under fire and prone to snipers and trench raids. The 1st Manchesters were doing their best to hold their position.

On Tuesday morning the colonel commanding the troops in Ypres was astonished to receive a message from a Lance Corporal

Smith, who informed him that he was holding on to 'the stables at Hooge' with 24 men. These buildings were believed to be empty. Issy, along with another lance corporal, had collected the men and, as there were no officers on the spot, had taken command and held the trenches all day Monday and until Tuesday morning without orders or connection with the remainder of the troops – alone, and on his own responsibility. When he managed to get a message through, he did not ask to be relieved. He simply asked for reinforcements and more bombs. It wasn't until Tuesday evening that he was able to lead his weary team out.

This Second Battle of Ypres continued until 25 May. Gas was used frequently and there was no means of protection from it other than to urinate on handkerchiefs and hold them against their faces to neutralise the chlorine. By now, the troops on both sides were exhausted and ammunition stocks were running low. Issy explained the last few days for his platoon:

> On the night of the 19th May, the Connaught Rangers came to relieve us. Such fighters, these Connaught Rangers. They gave the Germans more than enough, and the heavier the shelling, the more at home they were. I often said after that 'These Irish can fight.' Why, the Connaughts looked like they'd grow fat on it.
>
> I was once gassed so badly this time [sic], and had to be removed to hospital, and I would hardly be so well today only for the constant attention the wounded get at this hospital at Mountjoy Square.[9]

Issy supposedly kept a diary in Yiddish of these battles, but unfortunately it has never been found. One wonders what other details these pages would reveal.

The Aftermath of the battles in Ypres

Issy was sent to hospital to recuperate from the gassing.

Sergeant Rooke recovered from his injury in Dr Steevens' Hospital, Dublin, and later posed for a photograph with Issy at

Ashton-under-Lyne barracks. In all the historical records there is no reference to his first name, but after extensive searching I believe his name was Sergeant James David Rooke, born in Malta in 1887, where his father was part of the British Army Medical Corps at the Malta Garrison. Records show he was serving in India in the 1st Battalion Manchester Regiment in 1911, and later became sergeant of that battalion. In one of his interviews with the newspapers in 1915, he revealed he was a friend of Issy's, and that they fought together in Neuve Chapelle. According to reports, he was wounded again in December 1917 near Tekrit, Iraq when fighting in Mesopotamia.

Lieutenant Walter Neville Shipster recovered from his injury and returned to continue fighting with the 1st Battalion Manchester Regiment. Born in London, it is believed he resided for a short time in South Australia before returning to England and joining the regiment in India in 1909. He would have met Issy there before Issy's transfer to the reserves in 1912. In January 1916 he was a recipient of the Military Cross and was mentioned in despatches. He was promoted to captain, transferring to Mesopotamia in March 1916. He was wounded on 5 April 1916 near Kut and sadly killed in action near Azzun in Palestine on 20 September 1918, just two months before the war ended. He was 28, the same age as Issy. He is buried in Ramleh War Cemetery in Israel.

Despite Issy's best efforts to save him, **Second Lieutenant Arthur Hine Robinson**, also from the 1st Battalion Manchester Regiment, died that day, 26 April 1915, aged 20.

Lieutenant Donald Pretty from the 4th Suffolk Regiment, who Issy had searched for, was located on 26 April, but was seriously wounded two weeks later, fighting with Issy at Hooge. He died from his wounds on 11 May 1915, aged 23.

Lieutenant-Colonel Henry William Ernest Hitchins, who was responsible for mobilising the battalion at the start of the war, was shot through the heart when crossing the ground between the French and British trenches between 9 and 10 pm that evening. He was carried by his men to a ruined farmhouse but was confirmed dead. He was twice mentioned in despatches for gallant and distinguished service at the capture of Givenchy, 20 December 1914 and at Ypres, April 1915.

General (later Sir) Edward Peter Strickland was the commanding officer of the 1st Battalion of the Manchester Regiment and the Jullundur Brigade, and led the troops into the Battle of Neuve Chapelle and the Second Battle of Ypres. He became General Officer Commanding, 6th Division in Ireland, where in September 1920 he survived an assassination attempt by the Irish Republican Army. He received many honours and died in 1951, aged 81.

Second Battle of Ypres

The second battle was costly. The 47th Sikhs, part of the Jullundur Brigade, were the first line of attack. They lost 348 men from a total of 444 (78 per cent of their battalion). Overall, losses during the battle were estimated at 35,000 for the Germans and 69,000 for the Allies. The chlorine gas played a significant part in the toll.

Battles continued in Ypres until the end of the war. By this time, over 1,000,000 soldiers were killed or missing. The town was all but obliterated and deserted – the population having fled, died or been forcibly evacuated. And yet within ten years, it had been rebuilt in a manner resembling the prewar architecture.

Chlorine Gas

The British retaliated with chlorine gas on 25 September 1915 at the Battle of Loos. The total number of casualties during WWI due to gas (all types) is only a broad estimate, due to both the difficulties of gathering details amidst the fighting and the methods of recording of the time. The total estimated (killed and wounded, all sides) was 1.2 million.

Adolf Hitler

On 14 October 1918, a young Adolf Hitler, who had also fought at Neuve Chapelle and the Second Battle of Ypres, was a messenger in the trenches near Ypres and was temporarily blinded during a gas attack. He spent the remainder of WWI recuperating.

Chapter 12

The BIG News

The use of chlorine gas was widely condemned.
For those who did not die from the gas but received a substantial dose of it, the suffering was immeasurable. Once inhaled, it caused tremendous irritation of the nose and throat – coughing, choking and vomiting – as well as severe headache and chest pains. It burned the eyes and blistered the skin, but the build-up of fluid in the lungs was by far the most crippling. There were no simple treatments, certainly no antidote, and it took a long time to recover from.

The frightening experience often affected the nervous system, with ongoing attacks of shortness of breath brought on by apprehension. Indeed, many soldiers, like Issy, suffered from continuous and distressing bronchial problems for life. For those who were heavy smokers (like Issy again) it was worse, despite military authorities believing (or persuading) soldiers that the calming effects of smoking offered protection for the lungs against the effects of the gas. The chemical was never collected for analysis and the long-term effects on the lungs and heart weren't known; gassing became the subject of much debate and controversy for both its cruelty and the lack of compensation for it after the war.[1]

Issy was taken to No. 6 Station Hospital, Le Havre, France, in June to recover. On 8 August he was transferred to the Dublin Volunteer Aid Detachment (VAD) Auxiliary Hospital in Mountjoy Square, Ireland for further recuperation.

With so many men being wounded every day, the existing hospitals in the UK were overwhelmed and could not deal with the incoming wounded, let alone patients needing to convalesce. To cope, large numbers of public and private buildings were converted into auxiliary hospitals and staffed with volunteers. Mountjoy Square was in fact the private residence of Mr and Mrs Picton, who offered their home to the Red Cross free of rent until the end of the war. The hospital had a total of 24 beds and over time came to specialise in shell shock.[2]

Issy recovered there from 8 August 1915 with nine other men – one who had also been gassed – as well as three with bullet wounds, another with shrapnel, one with a fractured leg, one with rheumatic fever, one with neurasthenia (a term that was used broadly for exhaustion) and one rendered deaf and dumb from shell shock.

On 23 August 1915, an announcement was made in the *London Gazette* that Issy had been awarded the Victoria Cross (VC) – the highest award bestowed by the British Empire for valour. The detail read:

> For most conspicuous bravery on 26th April, 1915, near Ypres, when he left his Company on his own initiative and went well forward towards the enemy's position to assist a severely wounded man, whom he carried a distance of 250 yards into safety, while exposed the whole time to heavy machine-gun and rifle fire. Subsequently Corporal Smith displayed great gallantry, when the casualties were very heavy, in voluntarily assisting to bring in many more wounded men throughout the day, and attending to them with the greatest devotion to duty regardless of personal risk.

The news spread quickly throughout the UK, then over to America, Canada, Australia, New Zealand and even China.[3] The following day, the hospital was besieged by Jews from all over Ireland who came to offer their congratulations. They took him from the hospital on their shoulders and carried him through streets lined with cheering crowds to a restaurant where they made a great fuss of him. Indeed, at times he had to be shielded from the rush of people who wanted to shake hands with him but didn't know he was still recovering from the effects of poison gas.[4]

Late that same evening, following the full day of festivities, a news reporter from the *Irish Times* presented himself at the door. Issy appeared in a hospital dressing gown as it was past bedtime, and after introductions, was anxious to express his gratitude for a couple of razors the newspaper had been able to get him. According to the reporter, he seemed 'hardly able to realise the thanks the nation owed him for much greater services'. When asked how he was, Issy replied, 'Yes, I am getting better now, and I hope I shall sleep. Sometimes I can't, for the gas still makes it hard for me to breathe. But I am well looked after here; they make a fuss of you whether you're a VC or not.'

The next day, in the daily news, he was described as both a 'young, good-looking, fresh-complexioned Tommy' and 'a plain, straightforward man, who talked of the action which won him the VC in a matter-of-fact way as he would talk of the incidents of a holiday. Corporal Smith seemed to think that good attention under such circumstances was more than enough reward for being wounded.'[5]

A day later, on 26 August 1915, a supplementary to the *London Gazette* reported that the Czar of Russia (Nicholas II), had conferred rewards for 'gallantry and distinguished service on the field' to hundreds of British soldiers of all ranks. Of these, eleven VCs were included. Issy received The Russian Order of the Cross of St George 4th Class – the first Jew to be decorated by the Czar.[6] Reports immediately circulated that the medal was 3rd class, along with a spurious story that Issy had won it by volunteering to row out and rescue Russian soldiers from a sinking ship – purported to be a bombed oil tanker.[7]

This award to Issy is surprising, given the history of the czars and their treatment of the Jews over the previous century. I wondered, briefly, if perhaps this czar was different.

He wasn't.

Nicholas II blamed the Jewish people for all the woes that preceded and followed his abdication.[8] He did nothing to change the hard-line principles of Russification which his great-grandfather Nicholas I had introduced (and grandfather Alexander II and father Alexander III had continued), and in January 1915 the Russian military were free to publish a statement of charges against the Jews, followed by expulsions in various areas and attempts at mass deportation from the front lines.

In the summer of 1915, at the time of Issy's award, the then Russian Finance Minister, Pyotr Bark, tried to persuade Nicholas II to change his view, advising him that 'we cannot and must not simultaneously wage war against Germany and the Jews. In that case we cannot count on victory.'[9] It is clear that the Russian medal was either a weak endeavour to disguise this unpalatable practice from Western Europe, or Nicholas II didn't realise Issy was Jewish.[10] One newspaper noted that had Issy fought in the Russian Army, his name would not be published in Russian newspapers; had he been wounded, he could not even remain in a Moscow hospital for convalescence.[11]

It would be intriguing to know how Issy felt about receiving a medal for serving the very people and country his family had fled.

Regardless, this didn't seem to dampen the spirits of Britain's general public, who were delighted with the awards. Proclaimed as one of the most gallant heroes the war had yet produced, many believed that this was the very first Jewish soldier to be awarded the VC and this assumption was published around the world.[12] Issy became an overnight sensation and the hospital was flooded with reporters and well-wishers, hoping for a word with their celebrity. The press went wild, with banners such as:

> CORPORAL SMITH DESCRIBES THRILLING MOMENTS ON THE BATTLEFIELD

and:

HOW I WON THE VC, RESCUING WOUNDED, MET BY TERRIFIC SHELL AND MACHINE GUN FIRE.

The public could not get enough. Deprived of a true understanding of the reality of war, they were hungry for detail of his VC and 'these great adventures', as the press called them. It sounded like little more than a wild party. Nothing was mentioned of the horrific nature of trench warfare or the use of poison gas. Stories were published demonising the German enemy and recounting one-sided acts of barbarism. Without any further information available, these claims were accepted as fact, boosting support for the cause.

When asked to describe the events, Issy modestly protested that he hadn't done much and couldn't understand why so much fuss was being made about one man, when every British Army soldier was a hero.[13] Newspaper headlines soon followed, with the words: 'I DID NOTHING MUCH.'

'I was astonished when I heard that the great honour of the VC was bestowed upon me,' he said. 'What I hope is that when I go back, I will be able to bring some of the men from Dublin with me.' The war office, in urgent need of recruits to cover the heavy losses, would have been delighted with these words.

The papers pushed for more. 'Tell us how did it happen?'

'I believe I went out to help some of the lads who lay wounded, and I brought some of them back,' said Issy. 'But it was a surprise to me when they said I had done something out of the ordinary.'

'Where do you get the courage?'

'There are people who think they would not have the courage to do this,' Issy replied. 'But the sad scenes you see on the battlefield impel you on and you simply cannot resist the impulse. Shells burst here and there, making large holes, and bullets whizz by you and over you, giving you a jerky feeling. Then, you see objects fall every now and then – men who have been shot. Then you become desperate and you do not care what happens. So long as I succeeded in taking them out of the danger zone.'

'So what does it feel like to be under fire?'

'You just feel normal, like you would about anything,' Issy said. 'Once you get used to it. You have but once to die. You are there to do or die and if a bullet's going to hit you, it will hit you. Of course, you take any cover you can find.'

'But how did you feel at the beginning?' journalists persisted.

'Oh well, you feel a bit "trembly", but you've just got to get used to it, and the sooner you make up your mind, the better it is. If you die, it is for your country and empire. Then there's good attention for you as soon as you get wounded.'[14]

The public lapped it up. A reporter noted that his accent suggested that he was a Londoner by birth, and this put the British in a further spin. This was somewhat amusing, given Issy had been in England for less than fourteen years. Prior to that time, he had never set foot there and could not speak a word of English when he did.

Nevertheless, he became everyone's hero.

Suddenly he was the 'first Hackney man', the 'first Leeds man', the first 'Balham man', the 'first Manchester man', the 'first English Jew' and even the 'first Smith in the present war' to be awarded the coveted VC. Jewish communities throughout America and Canada claimed him, and the 'land down under' ran stories in every part of the country about the 'VC hero from Australia'. Issy had resided in Melbourne for just a few months.

The boxing industry, too, was not to be outdone, claiming that Issy was 'the first follower of the noble art to gain the coveted Victoria Cross',[15] and touting banners such as 'BOXER WINS THE VC' worldwide. It was also falsely declared that Issy was none other than the English boxer Jack Daniels (as the Melbourne writer Arty Powell had incorrectly stated).[16]

Issy was also apparently 'well-known in Auckland', a city he had never been to, where he was reported to be employed working the toboggan at the Exhibition under his ring name. Apparently, he had been matched to fight Jim Hagerty for the lightweight championship of New Zealand but the arrangements had fallen through.[17]

Even the Women's Christian Temperance Union announced their association, proudly claiming he was a teetotaller.[18]

But it didn't stop there. According to the newspapers, he also became the 'youngest' Jew, the 'only' Jew and the 'first' Jew to be awarded it. For a while, this last point was regurgitated in almost every bulletin.[19] A postcard with a photograph of Issy smiling into the distance also graced the newsstands.[20] Cigarette companies, quick to capitalise on the interest in the Great War, added him to a set of cigarette cards of Victoria Cross heroes. A painted image of him with his regiment and heroic deed printed on the back was circulated widely in Belfast and London.[21]

But Issy was not born in any of the locations which laid claim to him. Nor was he the first Smith in the present war; that accolade went to James Smith for two acts of bravery at Rouges Bancs, France in December 1914.[22]

And Issy certainly wasn't the youngest recipient – he was 24 years old. By 26 April 1915, 86 soldiers had been awarded the VC (including five others who were awarded it on the same day as he); of these, 22 were younger than him. Wilfred St Aubyn Malleson, at eighteen years of age, was awarded the VC for gallant services at Gallipoli on 25 April – the previous day.

By the end of the war the title went, sadly and unenviably, to Jack (Boy) Cornwell who, at the tender age of sixteen, had fought in the Battle of Jutland on 31 May 1916 but died shortly after. He was buried in a simple grave marked by a wooden peg.[23] Incredibly, there was no allowance in the original Royal Warrant to award VCs posthumously, and indeed the official policy was not to award them. Jack Cornwell's medal occurred after a newspaper story and a public outcry, forcing questions to be asked in the House of Commons. Following a second public funeral attended by many Navy personnel, the award was subsequently made in September of that year.

Issy was not the first nor the only Jew either. Lieutenant Frank de Pass, who was both the first Jew and also the first Indian Army officer ever to receive it, was awarded his VC for gallant services on

24 November 1914 at the trenches of Festubert.[24] Frank was unfortunately killed the following day. His medal was granted on 18 February 1915, but his father was too ill to attend the ceremony at Buckingham Palace and it was sent to the family by post.[25] For whatever reason, the great deeds of Lieutenant de Pass weren't widely known and the media assumed Issy was the first Jewish hero. He was even reported to be the very first Jewish recipient since VC awards began, but this honour also belongs to de Pass.

Frank's father, Sir Eliot de Pass, gave Issy a collapsible sterling silver cup enclosed in a leather case, to take with him to battle. On the base of it was engraved 'Corporal Issy Smith VC From Mr & Mrs E.A. de Pass'.[26]

Issy was not the youngest, nor the first, nor the only; but he did have a few special feathers in his cap. At the time of his award, he was the only *living* Jewish VC, and also the *first Jewish non-commissioned officer* to be bestowed the prestigious medal. By the end of the war, he was one of an elite group of less than a half dozen Jewish men to have received it (five, or six – depending on debate). Similarly, in these infinitesimally small statistics, he was one of only 627 VC recipients from the nearly 9 million soldiers who had fought gallantly for the British empire in WWI.[27]

Another Jewish VC was granted not long after. Interestingly, this third Jewish VC winner, British-born Leonard Keysor, arrived in Australia around the same time as Issy, a few months before war broke out. With no former military experience, Keysor joined the AIF on 18 August 1914 and as a lance corporal was awarded his VC during the Battle of Lone Pine on 7 August 1915. Being part of the AIF, he was considered to be Australian, even though he had spent just a few months in Sydney before enlisting and less than five months there again after the war ended, when he returned to England in 1919. Although both men enlisted from Australia, Issy, rejoining as an Imperial Reservist, was not deemed to be Australian.

Captain Albert Jacka, born in Winchelsea, Victoria, became the first official Australian VC recipient, but Issy's deeds preceded those of Jacka by several weeks. Years later, many considered Issy to be the first Australian VC recipient and the first Jewish Australian, by virtue of the date of his award and his long association, remaining residency and burial in Australia.[28]

✧

So why was everyone so excited about a VC?

It was (and still is) the highest honour for most conspicuous bravery 'in the face of the enemy'. It took incredible courage to undertake such an act of valour under heavy fire. Indeed, it was tantamount to a near-death experience if you survived – and many didn't. In WWI, 25 per cent died in the process. People still debate today whether those who performed these deeds simply acted spontaneously, without waiting to consider the consequences, or whether these soldiers were on the edge of the spectrum of madness. Perhaps it was both.

Issy seemed to have a life motto of 'whatever happens, happens'. He didn't think twice. His rescues, which were numerous, must have been exceptional. But it wasn't just the acts of bravery that made the award so special; being granted the award was no simple task.

Recognition of an extraordinary deed relied on several factors. Firstly, it needed someone in authority, along with witnesses, to be in the vicinity and notice it (ironically, the more intense the battle, the less likely it was to be seen amidst the mayhem). Secondly, it needed the authority or at least several of the witnesses to survive the carnage and pass the recommendation on. Thirdly, it required an officer to take the trouble to file a commendation, something that was not always done in the heat of a battle when officers had plenty to worry about. And lastly, the commendation had to pass through a significant amount of bureaucratic red tape to be approved. This final process was not devoid of politics and was not always independent and impartial.

Issy didn't receive any special favours.

For starters, he wasn't a golden child – from all reports, he was a superior's nightmare and spent several periods in detention for insubordinate language. In addition, he'd missed the promotion many others received upon re-enlisting – specifically, his early conduct record showed he lacked discipline and hadn't displayed the leadership desired to train and develop recruits. To top it off, he was part of a minority: both a race and a religion that was not accepted as equal at the time. But VCs were not awarded to make up for past misdemeanours, encourage good behaviour or acknowledge faiths, and therefore his award recognised the extraordinary acts of bravery and the lives he saved while risking his own.

Sometime later, he was also awarded the French Croix de Guerre with bronze palm. Foreign awards from Allied countries were sometimes given as a bulk issue to divisions, who would divide them up between brigades and then battalions. They were handed out at the discretion of commanding officers and, as opposed to the VC, were given for various reasons using criteria such as popularity, dedication or length of service – not necessarily bravery. This was not the case for the Croix de Guerre.

The Croix de Guerre was created in 1915 and again in 1939 in France to reward feats of bravery by their soldiers and citizens, as well as foreigners.[29] It was awarded for, or accompanied, distinguished acts, thereby providing a sense of cohesion for the Allies in their united front against the enemy. The highest degree that could be bestowed was represented by a bronze palm – which Issy received as a result of his VC.[30]

As the number of medals grew, so did his fame. Suddenly, he was the 'Hugo Hercules' of superheros, fighting with great aplomb in almost every major battle since the war began.[31] Many news articles abounded about new locations he had fought at, which it can only be assumed the press drew from speculation and rumour, or took poetic licence to make a good story. The narratives included the story of being a member of the late King's personal bodyguard for the Delhi Durbar in 1911.

There was no time to fact-check. With a war in full swing and a nation delighted with their saviour, the focus was on what he did next. He didn't disappoint.

In among all the excitement, Issy cabled Elsie from Dublin, telling her about his award. He asked her to return so they could be married, and sent her the fare.

A VC celebrity romance was a refreshing change from recapitulations about the doom and gloom of war, and the papers made good use of it. 'Wire me if you wish to come to England', a newspaper printed. The story quickly made the news in Australia, and it wasn't long before reporters presented themselves at Elsie's door in Melbourne, seeking more.

'And will you be going?' she was asked. Elsie gave them a knowing stare, and the paper reported that 'the answer was a look that implied there were no limits to masculine stupidity.'

The Scrapbook

Sometime after he left the Dublin hospital, Issy was presented with a leather-bound scrapbook prepared by one of the residing nurses, a Sister Gertrude P. Wood, who had gone to a lot of trouble. The beautifully bound book contained newspaper clippings about his war campaigns, the story of his VC, and many other invitations, incidents and events in which he featured within the UK. Issy was never far from the public eye and later Elsie continued the scrapbook with more news stories about him, recorded throughout his life.

Sister Gertrude P. Wood

It is interesting to ponder whether Gertrude ever held a flame for Issy. She was of similar age: the following year she married Albert Hayes, an air mechanic with the Navy and then the Royal Airforce. It would appear they had no children. Albert completed his service in WW1 and enlisted for WWII. On 24 Sep 1939 on a flying instruments training combat mission as a student pilot, he lost control in cloud at altitude too low for the instructor to rescue the situation. The aircraft was destroyed and the instructor William Pryde and leading aircraftman Hayes were both killed. Pryde was sadly the first of three sons to die in action. Gertrude passed away in London, 1970, aged 80.

Chapter 13

On the Road

A blistering suite of engagements began for Issy almost immediately.

At the precise time that news of his VC and recovery in hospital hit the Australian newspapers, advertisements graced the Dublin news promoting his visits to not one but three theatre houses on the one night. Recovered or not, he duly arrived at the Empire Theatre on the evening of 25 August where he was well received. He then proceeded to the first amusement house of the Theatre Royal and in the Royal box was given a standing ovation. After a brief speech, he was conveyed on a short detour to a recruitment meeting at Clontarf where he gave a longer address, before motoring to the second house at the Royal.[1]

Getting about to all these engagements in quick succession was an achievement in itself. Cars were a rarity, with mass production to the general public having only come on stream within recent years.[2] Cars were expensive and therefore owned by few – in 1915 just 9,850 were registered in Ireland against a population of roughly 4.3 million people.[3] Although the army used them, they were mostly reserved for the high military command. It is likely this was his first trip in one.

Issy's speech at Clontarf – 'deeds were wanted, not words' – was just what the army was looking for. And it wasn't just the army that was happy – the audience warmed to him immediately. 'I have had a very great honour conferred on me but nevertheless, I have to return to the front and try, if possible, to win something more', he said, to which there was much laughter.

The remainder of the address was short and practical. He did not attend the meeting for show, he explained, but merely to say he had done his humble duty as a soldier, and to ask them to do theirs. It was the clear duty of every man of military age, unless employed in munitions work, to be in the firing line. It was the only place for men of military age, and the sooner they got there, the sooner the war would be over. He had done his bit and was prepared to do more, but the question young fellows had to settle with their consciences was what were they going to do. They should not remain at home to read in the papers that 'Corporal Smith had won the VC or that Billy Wells had knocked out Jim So-and-so.'[4]

A few days later, at a reception at Mansion House in Dublin held by the Lord Mayor in honour of him, Issy paid tribute to the Irish Connaught Rangers who belonged to his brigade. He also outlined his view of the war. They were helping one another to finish a great struggle, he said – not for the possession of any country, but for civilisation and humanity.

At another meeting at Mansion House some weeks later, he extended this view. He had left his home in Australia to fight for freedom and the rights of humanity, and he came now to ask those who were so vitally interested in this great struggle to give him comrades to win freedom for civilisation.

The audience applauded and cheered. 'I am ready,' he declared, 'to lay down my life in that noble cause. I have fought for ten months, and I hope to go back soon, and when I do, I am going to look for that German who sent the gas over.'[5]

✢

As Issy spoke at various events, many were quite surprised by the hero who had burst unexpectedly onto the world stage. He was frequently described as short with a modest, gentle, even shy demeanour. 'Just a scrapper' – not the kind of brawny, hulking man one expected to storm in and whisk the wounded out of danger. The astonishment at a quiet, unassuming man as a dashing hero continued, and in 1926, Issy was woven into a story published in *Truth* in Sydney, an excerpt of which is worth retelling here:

> As the years passed, there was born to Jacob and Rebecca a family of six children, one son, Isadore, and five daughters ...
>
> At school and in the neighbourhood of the shop, Issy Hoozenazarus was known as 'Hawkeye', and though hard in a marbles or cigarette-card deal, the lad was a fair little chap, noted for always managing to side-step challenges to fight.
>
> 'Hawkeye' had just passed into his majority when the big war broke out.
>
> One night, he found his father sitting alone in the living-room. Issy approached him, and boldly declared his intention to enlist. He said that he couldn't any longer bear the sneers of people asking him why he was not going to the war.
>
> Jacob Hoozenazarus gasped, put aside his paper, and for a moment looked away in silence. Then he opened fire:
>
> 'You! There must be something growing in your head,' he said, with a shaking voice. 'You go to the war, ah? Why, why, you want to be a fighter, ah? You, Isadore Hoozenazarus, a fighter. Did you fight little Mossy Cohan the other day, when he tied a tin to your sister's dog, and then punched your nose, ah? You go and see what they will tell you at the Town Hall. They will call you a loafer, ah. You go tomorrow, and see for yourself.'
>
> Isadore did go on the morrow, but he left the recruiting depot with bitter jibes ringing in his huge ears, and a new-born feeling of resentment in his heart, against the parents who were responsible for his pitiful physical make-up.
>
> Time went on, and then the world was told of the glory of little Issy Smith's deed in winning the VC in France.

In the story of it, the little Jew hero's miserable bodily measurements were duly elaborated, so 'Hawkeye' secretly swore to get through.

A year at a boxing gym, and a less strict once-over by recruiting doctors, sufficed to pass the son of Jacob into camp, and on the day he embarked at Woolloomooloo, the proudest man in Sydney waved him adieu. It was his father.[6]

What Issy Smith's own family thought of his award in 1915 and his immediate fame isn't known. Issy's father Moses had passed away seven or eight years earlier and his mother and a few sisters were in Egypt where it is possible the news had not reached them. Joseph still lived in England and could not have missed the headlines, but meeting his hero brother in person to congratulate him was another matter entirely. Issy's busy program had so far taken him along the east coast of Ireland from Belfast to Dublin with little respite. On 4 September he made a brief trip to London, staying just over a week. Perhaps this was the opportunity to celebrate with Joseph and Hilda.[7]

While in London, Issy paid a visit to his old school at Berner Street, where the mayor of Stepney presented him with a gold watch and chain inscribed with the words *To Corporal I. Smith V.C. from Berner-street Old Boys' Club, as a mark of esteem, 1915.*[8] The school headmaster declared that no one at the school was surprised by the award because Issy had always exhibited great coolness in school sports.[9] Issy graciously responded, thanking the school, and noting that this honour was not the first he had won for Berner Street – he had once won a shield for swimming! In raising a toast in the memory of the Club's fallen soldiers and sailors, he said he felt very proud to be able to be present that evening, with so many kind words said about him. He was sure he did not deserve them more than some of the fellows who had done their bit but had not been recognised.[10]

A short stop at the Young Men's Jewish Community in Aldgate on 10 September to celebrate the Jewish New Year, then Issy was once again back in Dublin. He was met and entertained by several prominent co-religionists, was a guest at a friend's wedding and then attended a presentation at Mansion House in his honour. Photographs of him appeared in several papers, including the *Illustrated War News*.[11]

The event, held on 15 September, was a very distinguished affair, commencing with a parade by the City Troops and a guard of honour upon his arrival. Aside from the attendance of the Lord Mayor, the Attorney General, the City High Sheriff and Councillor Joseph Isaacs JP, also present were Sir Matthew Nathan GCMG, Under-Secretary of Ireland and Major General Lovick Friend, Commander-in-Chief of Ireland and formerly an aide to Lord Kitchener (Commander-in-Chief of the British Armed Forces).[12]

Sir Matthew gave the presentation and a liberal sum in the form of a cheque from donations amassed by the local Jewish community. He then spoke of equal advantages with their fellow countrymen and what all could do to help their country in its present need. He was followed by Major General Friend, who explained that Ireland had so far been mercifully spared, and that many did not realise there was a war at all until such people as Corporal Smith had returned with the greatest honour.[13]

The reality behind these words was that both Nathan and Friend were facing longstanding and growing Irish civil unrest, with a divisive fight for both loyalism and independence from Britain. Although a contested Home Rule bill had finally been passed, implementation had been suspended to enable focus on the war effort. Yet there were many unresolved issues.[14] The unionist movement was significantly disenchanted with the bill and broad anti-war sentiment abounded, not helped by heavy losses at Gallipoli. Tensions were mounting and Issy would soon learn that recruiting in Ireland was going to be very difficult.

Not that recruitment was easy anywhere else. Volunteer enlistments were universally declining and insufficient to meet the mounting casualty rates. Returning to England, where the greater number of eligible candidates resided, was made Issy's immediate priority.

After one last reception at the Jury's Hotel and a thank-you wired to the Lord Mayor for his gracious hospitality, Issy left Ireland with great fanfare (and a soldier's cane as a gift) from the Westland Row Station at Dublin.[15] A short film of his departure was shown at the Coliseum Theatre just as announcements graced the papers of his impending arrival in Leeds. There, at the Grand Northern Station on 20 September, he was met with similar panoply, and cheers continued as he was driven through the streets to the Jewish Institute, for his first meeting.[16]

In his opening speech back in England, Issy raised the hotly contested issue of conscription that would form a thread in the forthcoming recruitment rallies. 'I hope it will not be found necessary to bring in conscription,' he said, 'for if it is, we will never again enjoy the same measure of freedom we have enjoyed in the past.'

At a meeting at the Empire Theatre the next evening, recruiting officer Captain Hill, who introduced Issy as 'the only Jew who ever lived to receive the VC', added more: 'For goodness' sake don't wait with that horrid cry, "I will come when I am fetched". We don't want to fetch you if we can avoid it. But if you won't come voluntarily, you have got to come in the end whether you like it or not.'

The topic was particularly sensitive. The crusade for compulsory national service had raised formidable antagonism among the industrial workers throughout the United Kingdom, and both parliament and the general population were deeply divided. In the past week, Lord Kitchener had given the country its first official hint of the possibility of some form of military service. A national registry was being compiled and would soon provide a basis to calculate the resources of the country and the number of men who would be available.

Captain Hill furthered this debate. 'It is no use saying that everything is alright,' he said. 'There are still hundreds of young men walking around the city who are doing nothing, and when the number becomes known in about three weeks' time the public will be astounded.' Issy spoke next, and appealed not only to the men to join, but to the mothers and sweethearts of the men to make it easy for them to join. This would become a pertinent point the very next month.

Issy's steady list of engagements left him little time to ponder the government's plans for a military solution and its associated angst. On 23 September he spoke at the first performance that evening at the Hippodrome, and later that night at the Newtown Picture Palace. The next day he met the Lord Mayor at the Town Hall, attended a service at the Belgrave Synagogue and attended a service at the Leeds Union Infirmary in Beckett Street,[17] where he distributed cigarettes to the wounded soldiers.[18] He then continued to the Queen's Theatre (first house), Palladium Picture House Holbeck (second house) and the Theatre Royal (second house) where he gave speeches.[19] And before the week was out, he made a surprise visit to the city of Manchester while en route to the Ashton barracks, where he had been recalled to assist with recruiting in East Lancashire.[20]

On Saturday evening, 25 September, Issy attempted to have a night off by attending discreetly as a patron at the Manchester New Palace Theatre.[21] It didn't work. He was spotted, and halfway through the performance was persuaded to go before the curtain. The newspapers reported that his appearance was 'secured with some difficulty, for Corporal Smith is as modest as he is brave'. The audience enthusiastically applauded him and his 'turn' was noted as 'quite the most successful of the evening' and 'probably not without its effect on the East Lancashire campaign'.[22]

If Issy's appearance did have such an effect, it was but a small contribution to an epic task of turning the tide of reluctance. In this part of the country the total call-up was for 10,000 men, but after one week of steady work by Issy and other agents, only a little over one-tenth had been enrolled.

'Good news from the front has a bad effect in one way,' one recruiter explained to the local paper. 'It may cheer us up and make us more keen to do our bit, but it seems to make the slackers slacker than ever. 'If the Allies are doing so well,' they say, 'we needn't worry. There's nothing for us out there.'[23]

The onerous task continued, and after two weeks of recruitment drives at various establishments and a visit to Manchester Grammar School, Issy was back in Leeds on 8 October, this time to aid a Jewish recruiting campaign.[24] Heralded incorrectly in the newspapers as the 'HERO OF HILL 60', his arrival and purpose were duly reported; but also announced in the same article were details of the recently wounded, which, for those plagued with indecision, most likely destroyed what little enthusiasm remained.

By this trip Issy was brandishing three stripes on his arm, having been appointed to the 'unpaid' position of Lance Sergeant a few days prior.[25] A committee from the Jewish community quickly formed to raise a purse of gold for presentation to him by the Lord Mayor at the town hall the following week.[26] The upcoming event was widely broadcast and Issy received a personal letter from the renowned Scottish singer and comedian, Harry Lauder, who apologised for being unable to make it.[27]

The pupils at Leeds Boys Modern School were also pleased to receive a visit from the famous soldier. When asked for the story of how he won his VC, Issy confessed that he did not really know. 'Anyway, I have a slight idea,' he began, before giving them a short retelling. He spoke of the fine benefits of sport in life and revealed his acceptance of a challenge from a boy for a 100 yards swimming race. 'I love swimming,' he said, smiling, 'but as I am older than he I shall want him to give me some start now.'[28]

On 11 October, Issy took a trip to nearby Bradford and gave an address on the steps of the town hall. This time he adopted a bold approach, catching many by surprise. Pointing to individual young men in the crowd, he challenged them: 'What is keeping you here? Aren't you fit for service?'

Several of the men produced certificates of rejection. 'I've been six times,' one man exclaimed. 'They won't have me.'

'Well, you come again, we have got a fresh doctor,' Issy replied, amidst much laughter. 'Those of you who have been rejected, hold up your hands,' he called to the crowd, but no one responded.

'Those of you who are eligible are hiding!' he cried. 'Now then, anyone behind there who is 45 and wants to be 40, step forward.'

Still no one moved, so Issy directed his attention to a man near the stage. Pointing his finger at the young man he persuaded him to step up. 'Why haven't you enlisted?' he asked.

'I've lost ten hours' wages waiting at recruitment offices,' the man retorted. 'I'll go again if you will pay my wages while I am there.'

'Lost your wages, have you?' Issy repeated. 'You will lose your life if the Germans come!'

Continuing with his speech, he informed the audience of a picture he could see – the wearing of a large 'C' on either side of the soldier's collar if conscription had to be adopted. One 'C' would denote 'conscript' and the other 'coward'.

'And you will be treated like cowards when you come alongside the voluntary men,' he commented. 'But don't wait to be fetched. We have always been successful in our voluntary system and I hope we should continue to be so.'[29]

A few days later, on Saturday 16 October, Issy was at a large recruitment rally at Hull.

It was not the only event in search of enlistments. Nearby, four battalions forming the second line West Riding Brigade had done a complete tour of all the areas from which it was supposed to draw. Its parade, comprising 430 marching officers and men, included a full transport train of accoutrements and three travelling bands to encourage a fighting spirit. Meetings were held, factories and mills canvassed and thousands of leaflets distributed. Yet after a month of maximum effort, fewer than 300 recruits had been obtained. The situation was looking grim.

For Issy's event at Hull, each of the 26,000 male residents of military age had been sent an invitation to attend an impressive military display with aeroplanes alighting in the fields. At half past one a procession was formed in the city square comprising the 14th Local Reserve battalion East Yorkshire Regiment, the 11th Hull Heavy Battery (with its horses and guns) and three marching bands. The cavalcade strutted through busy streets to the playing fields some two miles away where roughly 5000 had assembled.

But the attendance was disappointing. Those who came to witness the display were largely elderly men, women and youths. In view of the lower-than-expected numbers, the ten platforms that had been arranged for the speakers were reduced to three.

General Sir Eric Swayne, Director of Recruiting, Northern Command, addressed the audience with the recurring question of 'When will the war end?', explaining that three million men were needed by spring to convince the enemy that it was useless to go on. They did not want compulsion, he said, but unless they got the numbers needed, they would not be responsible for the ongoing war.

During the afternoon Issy spoke at all three platforms, receiving an enthusiastic ovation at each. 'Come on lads!' he called, to which men immediately responded. To a young man who refused due to a failed medical, he again proposed the solution he had suggested at Bradford.

'Will you come forward and try another doctor? There is a new doctor out there,' he said, pointing in the direction of where other recruits had been assembled.

'What about you?' he asked another potential candidate.

'I can't. My sweetheart objects,' the man answered.

Issy gave a questioning look to the young lady alongside him.

'Five of my best boys have already gone to the front,' she retorted. 'I do not wish to lose another.'[30]

A small, middle-aged man approached him. 'Will you have me for the bantams?' he asked.[31]

Issy looked the man squarely in the face. 'Will you give up drink for the duration of the war?' he questioned in return.

'Yes,' the man replied.

'Well, then, get up: we'll try you.'

The man climbed onto the recruiting platform and others followed until it was crowded.

'I am getting dry,' Issy said after talking for some time, and there was a burst of laughter. 'I can tell you that I am a staunch teetotaller myself, and I am financial secretary of the Royal Army Temperance Association,' he remarked. The crowd applauded.

He then told the audience that he was sent home for gas poisoning and he still had the effects in his throat. He would be glad when the recruiting was over to return to the hospital again for another week's rest.[32]

But no rest was forthcoming. The recruiting might have finished that day, but that night, as billed in the newspapers, Issy appeared at the comedy revue *Beauty Spot*. On Monday, 18 October he attended the Manchester Jews' School, speaking to the children in each department. The girls' school sang 'See the Conquering Hero Comes' and the infants sang 'Hearts of Oak', 'The Marseillaise' and 'The National Anthem' before presenting him with small gifts. And then it was on to the Manchester Town Hall for another presentation in his honour by the Lord Mayor and a cheque, given to him from the Jewish community. A photo of Issy receiving the cheque graced the papers the next day, just as he attended a patriotic concert in the Ashton pavilion with a Lady Aitken, wife of a local Colonel and MP.[33]

The newspapers reported all of these events, with great detail about the rallies and uplifting words appealing for more recruits to fill the gaps. Despite careful prose and the avoidance of numbers, opposite the articles were half-page spreads listing army casualties – broken down by wounded, missing or dead. The campaigning was falling on deaf ears.

On Tuesday, 19 October 1915, Lord Derby, newly appointed Director-General of Recruitment, announced his new plan. Under the new scheme, men of military age could continue to enlist voluntarily and serve immediately after passing a medical test, or they could be put into age groups and called up for service only when necessary. The public was promised that married men would only be selected when groups of unmarried were exhausted.

This was the last attempt at voluntary recruitment, but it still relied entirely on the loyalty and patriotism of those eligible, and provided extended deferment to men so long as they were married. Single men with sweethearts were left in the cold.

Neither married nor single men were pleased with the scheme and it created considerable debate.

It also didn't turn out quite as planned. It was expected that groups would be drafted later and gradually, one by one. Instead, the call-up happened in just over twelve weeks and nearly all at once, with the last batch called up by March 1916.

The community was angry. The system was deemed a failure and in January 1916 the *Military Service Act* was passed, imposing conscription on all single men of military age with only a few exceptions.

As the new year began, it was becoming glaringly apparent that the war was far more than glory and medals. And it wasn't letting up.

Chapter 14

Prejudice and Faceless Fraud

During the heavy recruitment program in Leeds, Issy accepted an invitation from a non-Jewish friend to adjourn to a café for refreshments. On arrival at the Grand Restaurant, they were informed, firstly by the attendant and then by the restaurateur, that the civilian could be served but Issy could not. He was a Jew.

This caused an uproar across the world, with the story appearing in such places as America, Palestine, France, Australia and even Austria, Slovakia, Hungary and Germany.[1] Many wrote to the papers for months and even years after the incident.[2] One particular article, written under the pseudonym of John Bull, read as follows:[3]

> DEAR SIR, – I have had so many complaints about your attitude towards inoffensive and respectable Jewish citizens who enter your house for refreshment, that I am inclined to advise that your licence shall be opposed when opportunity occurs. I do not believe in Jew-baiting in Leeds any more than I believe in Jew-baiting anywhere else; still less do I believe that the proprietor of a restaurant carrying on his business by special privilege, under licence, as well for the public convenience as for the accumulation of profits, should be permitted to refuse to serve for money in legal hours any member of the community who conducts himself with propriety. Your last refusal to serve a Jew, a teetotaller by-the-way, is an outrage on a hero whom the King himself

has delighted to honour. In company with a non-Jewish friend, Sergeant Issy Smith, V.C., a Jew, entered your restaurant and was refused service by one of your servants on your standing instructions that 'no Jews are to be served', though no objection was made to serving the friend with him. I do not know whether you have equal objections to serving Germans, Austrians, Turks or Bulgarians, but I gather not. In any case, it appears to me that your anti-Semitism is being carried to lengths disagreeable to public interest and contrary to the obligations implied in your licence – to which I recommend opposition, in order that the Magistrates may express their view whether or not you act in the reasonable exercise of your discretion.

JOHN BULL.[4]

A New Zealand newspaper gave another colourful description of their contempt.

> The bigoted biped still lurks about even in this enlightened age. His last address was Leeds, where at the Grand Restaurant on a recent occasion he refused to supply refreshment to a Jew. His bigotry this time is most glaring, because this Jew happened to be an honoured soldier – none less than Sergt. Issy Smith V.C. The being who will offer insult to another purely for sectarian reasons is a bigot of the first water. But he who will insult the wearer of the King's uniform and the winner of a coveted distinction should first of all be tarred and feathered and then locked up to give him time to pluck the feathers off his mean carcass.[5]

This type of offensive insult was nothing new and Issy was not the only person enduring it. Counsellor Joseph Isaacs, who had accompanied Issy throughout his recruiting campaign in Dublin and was also Jewish, was facing indignities in a different form – a series of unfounded and scurrilous allegations by a certain Thomas Dickson, who had begun a scandalous and vitriolic newspaper called *The Eye-Opener*.

In the nine issues of the paper that circulated in Dublin in 1916, Counsellor Isaacs, who was president of the local synagogue and a successful draper, was described in the editorial as 'a Scotch Jew shoddy clothes merchant' and a 'Judas Iscariot' who employed 'sweated labour' while running a gambling den. Isaacs sued for criminal libel but the case only got as far as pre-trial proceedings. Dickson was remanded on bail but before he could produce any more salacious material, was accidently rounded up with another newspaper editor in a case of mistaken identity, taken to local barracks and shot dead by firing squad. The man who ordered the killings, a Captain Bowen-Colthurst, was court-martialled and found guilty but insane.[6]

Sir Matthew Nathan, who had given the presentation to Issy at Leeds, was not immune from such abuse either. His appointment as Under-Secretary of Ireland in 1914 had not been universally welcomed; partly because he was not Irish, but also because he was Jewish. Yet it was in his earlier position of Governor of Natal that he received the worst treatment. It began even before he arrived at Government House when a Mrs Cook, who had been recommended as housekeeper, refused the position. A battering of racist and anti-semitic insults haunted him throughout his two-year tenure there and finally, when a farewell function was arranged in his honour, every single invited official declined to attend.[7]

From time to time, Issy referred to antisemitic articles that were 'disgracing the pages of the press', as he put it. He argued that 'lads [Jewish comrades] went forward to fight for freedom, to show England that Jews were not shirkers. They had been told that they would return to a land fit for heroes. What had been the result? On their return they were met on all sides by a wave of antisemitism. One had only to read in the *Times* of the unwarranted attack on the Jewish people by men of the type of Beamish. The Jewish boys had sacrificed everything for England and the honour of the Jewish race and now they would have to go on fighting very hard their antisemitic enemies at home.'[8]

But he did not feel that all was lost. 'Jews ought to be proud to fight for England,' he said, 'for no other country in the world has been so good to them.'[9]

To this end, he wasn't far from the truth. While in 1915 antisemitism was virulent in parts of Europe such as Russia and Romania and problematic in Germany and France, it was far less of an issue in other places such as Belgium and Britain.

Britain had indeed been far better. To the argument that Jews were treated badly in the British Army, Issy said his experience was the reverse; men of Jewish faith who enlisted as Jews were granted many facilities for the practice of their religion, and they were well treated and appreciated.[10]

But antisemitism still raised its ugly head.

Some soldiers of Jewish heritage enlisted as Christians for fear of being derided. And derision could take the form of more than just taunts and insults. As anti-German feeling rose in Britain, attacks were made on Jewish shops and people with German-sounding names. Jews presenting for recruitment found themselves rejected, often without basis; at one point the Under Secretary of State for War issued an advice to recruiting officers that 'an English-speaking, British-born subject of friendly alien parentage who presents himself for enlistment may, therefore, if otherwise considered suitable, be accepted by the recruiting officer and in the case of a Jew, if there is any reason to doubt the bona-fides of such a candidate, or if he bears a German or Austrian name, a reference should be made to the Secretary of the Jewish Recruiting Committee before he is finally accepted'.[11] Then, to compound matters, there were arguments that English Jews were shirkers not doing their fair share for the war, while reports surfaced that some of the commanding officers at the front were ignoring the bravery of anyone Jewish.

At the height of WWI, Issy did not let this discrimination slide under the carpet. 'Every Jew should take a stand against antisemitism,' he said. He encouraged others to act kindly and fairly and to call out such acts. In March 1916 he took a taxidriver who refused him a fare to court. Issy was due at his barracks and without the taxi, he missed his train at Kings Cross and was arrested as an absentee. The driver presented a feeble case that he was short of petrol, but it did not stick. He was fined 10 shillings and ordered to pay Issy 40 shillings in costs.[12]

Issy experienced this intolerance for the remainder of his days, at times being refused entry to public assemblies, including a hall on one occasion where he was to be the guest speaker. He felt compelled to bring these issues to light, but also did not let them rule his life. Speaking at a presentation in Dublin, he said, 'I am bound by my faith to do all I can for my fellow-man, regardless of race or creed.'[13]

Unfortunately, life was rarely fair. Prejudice and insults fell on one side of the fence, and scams and swindles on the other. With fame came the opportunity for con men to make a quid, and they did. Albert Smith VC, a hero from the Sudan campaign of 1885, got wind in January 1918 that a man who was in his battery at the time was now impersonating him – more than 30 years later – and wearing the ribbon of the VC. The two met in court where the accused, whose real name was Teetham, was sentenced to six months' hard labour.[14]

Issy experienced something a little different. In 1915 a Mr Herbert Cole, an author and publisher from Southsea, established a 'Patriots' League' incorporated with 'The League of Mercy' and began selling pamphlets with stories on the war; the money was supposedly going to war charities for wounded soldiers and sailors. A series of pamphlets, of which several hundred thousand were printed, were distributed via agents to anyone who would buy. Each leaflet contained statements that the League had sent money to hospitals and used the words 'Help us to help others'. The pamphlets comprised various articles, with one titled 'The Life Story of Issy Smith V.C.'

There were several problems with this philanthropy. While The League of Mercy existed and was an old established charity, the Patriots' League was a spurious creation with no relationship to it. The League had no banking account or committee minutes, and no money had ever been paid on its behalf to a charity. Herbert Cole, however, had received considerable proceeds from the sales which, after expenses, he had pocketed. He was found guilty of procuring charitable contributions by false and fraudulent pretences and sentenced to three months prison with an order to pay £25 towards the cost of the prosecution.

What is intriguing about this whole affair, however, is what he could possibly have written about Issy. With no detail of Issy's early life circulating anywhere, the story must have been pure fabrication.

Chapter 15

Tales Down Under

The press was the one constant source of information for the public and in October 1915, just as a third Jewish VC award (to Private Leonard Keysor) was announced, the Australian (and British) newspapers - keen to herald more good news - printed several columns trumpeting Issy's romance.

In among the details of the upcoming nuptials was the information that the War Office had allotted Issy £500 pounds - £250 of which was paid over to him with the remainder to be banked for his benefit 'so that financially, the way to matrimony has been made easy for them'.[1]

This was an unusual act, if true, and an extraordinary amount of money. In 1914–15, the minimum pay for a corporal was 1s 9d per day; as a lance corporal, Issy would have been paid slightly less.[2] The British Army was not known for generous remuneration and it is doubtful the War Office would have forked out such a princely sum - equivalent to roughly sixteen years of pay - as a gift.

In Australia, the Melbourne Gas Company where Issy had worked prior to enlisting did provide money, sending Issy a letter of congratulations and a cheque for £50. The vote of gratuity was announced in every major newspaper across the country.[3]

The Herald devoted several columns with the banner 'WAR'S WEDDING PRESENT, V.C. HERO FOR HUSBAND, FACTORY GIRL TO BE BRIDE' accompanied by a photo of young Elsie and one of a uniformed Issy on a horse.[4] The *Sydney Evening News* followed suit with the same story. The articles went on to say:

> In a Melbourne clothing factory there is a bright-eyed happy girl, who is making arrangements to leave for England, where she is to marry the man from whom she has been separated by the war. The girl is Miss Elsie Porteous, of Lennox-street, Moonee Ponds, who is employed by Messrs Davies, Doery, and Company, 98 Flinders lane, and the lover who waits impatiently at the other end of the world is Corporal Issy Smith, the first Jew to be awarded the Victoria Cross.
>
> Fate, which brought them together has also brought them apart: but the war which separated them a year ago is now to be the means of bringing them together again, for the War Office has allotted Corporal Smith £500 – £250 has been paid over to him, and £250 banked for his benefit – so that, financially, the way to matrimony has been made easy for them.

As a result of this news, much speculation was indulged in as to Elsie's religious denomination. On 5 November 1915, a strange letter purporting to be from her was published. It read as follows:

> Dear Sir,
>
> I would like this letter inserted in the next issue of 'The Jewish Herald'. I am of Jewish descent, and have been brought up in the Jewish faith. I wish in these few lines to express my gratitude to all Jewish people, including especially Mr. Hyman Cohen, who has shown such keen interest in my welfare, and who has proved a good friend to me in my anxious moments. I wish to thank him publicly, but will also do so personally.
>
> My fiancé, Corporal Smith, is the second Jewish boy to win the much-coveted prize, the V.C., and I am sure all of us of the Jewish faith can be very proud of our hero. I am under the impression that Lord Rothschild has invested to

his credit money to the value of £2000, so by his conspicuous bravery he is now a rich man. He very much wants me to share in his good fortune, and has shown his eagerness by sending my fare home to London. So with God's will, I sail on 22 December on the *Omrah*.

I remain, yours sincerely,

E. PORTEOUS.

P.S. – I would like to mention that Mrs de Pass, the mother of the first Jewish holder of the V.C., to show her pleasure and gratitude, asked Corporal Issy Smith to choose anything he liked to mention in the way of a gift in recognition of his good work; so he chose a silver tea service.

E.P.[5]

There were several things wrong with this letter.

Firstly, Elsie was not Jewish. Her parents were Presbyterian, with her mother baptised at birth in Canongate, Edinburgh, in Scotland. Elsie never openly discussed her faith and was not one to suddenly make such a declaration.

Secondly, the paragraphs were also not in a writing style consistent with her personality, which family members could attest to later in life. She was not an anxious person and never sought the spotlight. It is assumed the writer was referring to the joint governing director of Elsie's place of employment (announced in the article), Mr Hyman Cohen. A man well known in the Jewish community and described by his business partner, Mr Doery, as 'a man of high moral character and practical religious ideals', it would appear that Mr Cohen was mentioned in an attempt to add an air of authenticity to the letter.[6]

Thirdly, Elsie did not chase wealth and prosperity and never made claims to any. Raised in a middle-class family, she was managing comfortably under her own means. No reason can be conjured as to why she would publicly announce a personal stake, nor is it certain that Mrs de Pass (whose first name isn't cited as the writer likely didn't know it) would be inclined to give a gift of a tea set – although the family did indeed give Issy the sterling silver cup which would not have been widely known. This fact is likely mere coincidence.

But lastly, what is glaringly obvious as the biggest blunder was the sign off – Porteous was Elsie's middle name. The media had reported this error in their story about the couple's romance.

The letter was not written by her.

The papers were pleased to have a 'resolution' to her religious heritage; however, of greater interest was the offer by Lord Rothschild of the significant fortune.

The story of the fortune is worth a short diversion. Lord Rothschild, or more correctly, Baron Rothschild of Tring, was in fact a title and not a specific individual. The original holder, Nathaniel (Nathan) Mayer Rothschild, was a Jewish banker and politician in the early 1900s who also provided private venture loans to various European governments and the US. The Rothschild family's wealth was believed to be the largest in the world and Nathan, a noted philanthropist, supported a number of charities, including one devoted to improvements to housing for the Jews of Spitalfields and Whitechapel, where Issy had lived.

It is therefore not surprising that a story was circulating in which the Baron intended to handsomely reward the first Jewish soldier to win the coveted VC, and that Issy, the only living recipient of such an award, was the beneficiary. By 1921, during a tour by Issy in Australia, the tale was still circulating and the papers reported both his visit and Lord/Baron Rothschild's gift in every port and town in which he stopped and even those that he didn't. The amount, paid in 1924 war bonds, was £5000 and was supplemented by cash from unknown benefactors to a princely total of £11,000. Issy had supposedly been presented with the bonds personally in recognition of his decoration.[7]

What the papers failed to mention was that Baron Nathan Rothschild died on 31 March 1915, four weeks *before* Issy made the gallant rescues at Ypres that granted him such a distinction. Upon Nathan's death, the title passed to his son, Walter Rothschild. There is no evidence that any instructions were left for such a gift to be conferred to a VC holder, living or dead, and nothing was publicised. Walter, too, was of an entirely different disposition to his father; just a teenager when his father died, he did work reluctantly for a time in the family bank until he was allowed to give it up. His passions, zoology museums and the collection of associated specimens for them, were not the fields his father was renowned for. Instead, Walter amassed millions of bird skins, eggs, butterflies and mammals, and on one occasion drove to Buckingham Palace in a carriage harnessed with four zebras to dispel a prevailing myth that the creatures could not be tamed. A generous gift, left to the British Museum in his will, was an enormous aggregation of exhibits – the largest they had ever received. Nevertheless, the story of the award of war bonds to Issy from the Baron continued to flourish in various forms for many years.

✢

As the news caught on across Canada and the US, Elsie gave her notice in Melbourne and on 2 December 1915, equipped with a wonderful thank-you letter from her employers and a wedding gift from her colleagues, she prepared to depart for England. Although mindful of the danger of torpedoes, she set sail.

When she arrived in England in January the following year, she learned, for the second time, that the plans had changed. Issy was not there – his leave had been cancelled. The British Army, keen to strike while the iron was hot, had wasted no time in sending him on another recruitment drive. He was now in Ireland, and there was no indication of when he would be back.

With the war showing no signs of ending any time soon, new plans had to be made. For Elsie, the options were to give up on the romance or wait it out – for however long that would be. Initially at a loss, she stayed with Issy's brother Joseph and his girlfriend Hilda. She was able to see him when he arrived in London to receive his VC from the King, but the visit was brief and it wasn't long before he was called away again.

After a time, she took another passage to Australia, where employment prospects were brighter, and returned to work.

*Family in Egypt 1906 – (from left) Rachel, Moses,
Fanny with first born Adele on her lap, and Olga*

*Moses in Constantinople in the late 19th
century, working the sewing machine*

Eva, year unknown *Issy ready for leave from India, 1912*

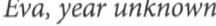

Issy (fourth row back, seventh from left) with the 1st Battalion, Kamptee, India, 1908 (Copyright Tameside Image Archive)

Issy (bottom left) mustering at the Broadmeadows Camp, Australia, 8 August 1914

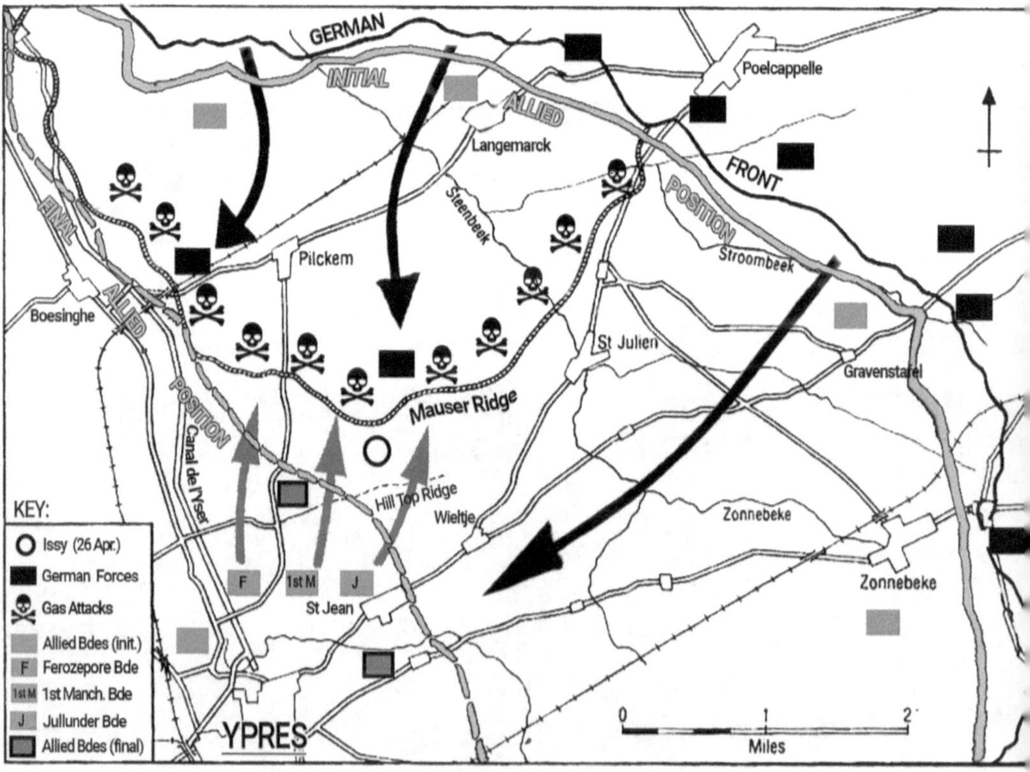

The Second Battle of Ypres on 26 April 1915 where Issy rescued many wounded soldiers, leading to the award of his VC

Recovering from gas poisoning at Mountjoy Hospital, Dublin, Ireland

Issy (right) engaged in a friendly boxing bout on the day he heard he had been awarded the coveted honour

Issy (right) at Mountjoy Hospital. The man on the left is believed to be Sergeant Rooke, who Issy saved. (Copyright Tameside Image Archive)

Chapter 16

Pressure Mounts

Issy had spent a busy second half of 1915 heavily involved in the war efforts. The last months in Britain had been particularly arduous. After many engagements, he had formed the view that the best place to find recruits and raise funds wasn't at mass rallies but rather at entertainment venues, such as theatres and boxing tournaments. The boxing industry was delighted to be associated with him and proudly promoted his upcoming attendances. On the evening of 27 November he appeared at The Ring Boxing Club in London, where he was introduced to a delighted crowd. What he said isn't recorded but perhaps it wasn't much, as it was later noted that 'Issy is a doer of deeds and not a maker of phrases, therefore his speech, as an oratorical effort, did not reach Asquithian standard.' [1]

A few days later on 1 December, tournament holders and a large crowd, along with the mayor and other dignitaries, waited excitedly in poor weather at Coventry Railway Station for Issy and another VC recipient, Lance Corporal Vickers, to alight. The 3rd/7th Battalion Royal Warwickshire Regiment, headed by the drum and fife band, marched to the station with an impressive display to herald the men's arrival – only to discover they weren't on the train. It was later learned that a mishap had occurred to the motor vehicle on which they had relied and they would appear later.

This did not dampen the spirits of those already waiting at the Drill Hall. In the evening, when the VCs finally arrived, £6 was raised from Issy's autograph on a program, along with £21 of donations which he contributed to. Both celebrities addressed the gathering, calling for recruits.

A few weeks later Issy was billed to reappear at Coventry and spar three rounds with Ted Broadribb. Better known as Young Snowball, Ted was admired for having fought the famous Jim Driscoll (Peerless Jim), the British featherweight and Commonwealth champion, and thus the event was eagerly anticipated. The tournament attracted a large audience and Issy, stepping into the arena to a deafening cheer, stripped for the rounds and battled it out with Young Snowball. Later, he acted for other bouts as referee.[2] Local men and wounded soldiers attended and the local reverend spoke, noting that boxing learnt under good conditions was a very good thing, as it taught the competitors to keep their tempers and act fairly, thus making better men of them.

The boxing fraternity proudly reported the event, and even the *El Paso Times* in Texas wrote a paragraph two weeks later about Issy, under the headline: 'Another Highly Honoured Soldier Boxer.'[3]

It was therefore to the great dismay of many in the industry when, in the same month, Sheffield apparently barred boxing until the end of the war.[4] One disappointed fan wrote:

> ... I wonder what they make of a speech from the Jewish VC Issy Smith, who a night or two ago paid a magnificent public tribute to the important part boxing plays in fitting men for the sterner game of war. He said, in effect, that boxing helped materially to inculcate exactly the right spirit for that sterner game, and he was only stating a truism, after all.
> E.A. BLAND
> London, 7 Dec[5]

Issy didn't have time to comment on the merits or otherwise of boxing during world hostilities. He continued on but eventually the busy schedule took its toll, and on 27 December he fell ill. He missed a presentation planned for him at the Cheetham Jewish Working Men's Club, along with the unveiling of a roll of honour.[6]

Yet important duties awaited and it wasn't long before he was back on his feet.

On 5 January 1916 the first military conscription bill was introduced to the House of Commons. There could be no delay in the desperate search for men for the front, so while the bill was debated, Issy was despatched to Belfast to round up as many recruits as he could.

But the mood in Ireland was not the same as in Britain. Although there was initial support for the colours, this view had changed rapidly when it was realised the war would not be over by Christmas as promised. And this was not the only cloud that darkened the horizon.

Protestant and Anglo-Irish landowners held the upper hand through British rule in a country mostly inhabited by Catholics. There was a growing level of disenchantment in the use of the new *Defence of the Realm Act* (DORA), which suppressed freedoms and now saw court martial for such acts as discouraging recruitment. Yet by far the greatest acrimony was over the Home Rule bill. Irish civil unrest was now verging on civil war, with heated debate between the private armies of the Nationalist and the Unionist Volunteer groups. The atmosphere was tense, and for a large proportion of the population there was no room for a visit from representatives of the British Army.[7]

Issy arrived in Belfast on 13 January en route to Dublin and initially things went well. That evening he visited the Great Opera House and occupied a box for the *Humpty Dumpty* pantomime. When Miss Clara Beck (who played the principal part) stated that Issy was in the theatre and that she had been singing to him: 'You were the first one to teach me how to love', the audience gave him a roaring reception. Issy thanked them with a small, modest speech.[8]

The following day, his arrival was noted in the local newspapers with the comment that as war broke out, he had returned to England from Australia 'on board H.M.A.S. *Sydney* [and] during the voyage the *Emden* was hunted down and destroyed.'[9] Whether this was a random remark in reference to success stories or a deliberate mention as a show of imperial muscle is anyone's guess, but no doubt it did not endear him to those already offside.

Recruiting meetings were advertised in various Dublin newspapers, with Issy set to speak on the afternoon of the 15th at nearby Palmerstown and then later outside the Theatre Royal in Hawkins Street.[10]

Although the afternoon session went without hiccup, the evening was an entirely different matter. Hecklers continuously interrupted his speech and sneered at his faith. Frustrated, he remarked that it was disgraceful to see so many men of military age not in khaki. 'Are you going to stay around here until the Germans come to Ireland?' he quizzed the crowd.

'We will,' said a voice.

'Are you an Irishman?' Issy asked.

'I am, but you're not,' the voice retorted.

'I'm not an Irishman,' Issy responded. 'I'm a Jew and I'm proud of it. But the question of Irishman or Jew is not involved in the war; our only concern is the defeat of the common enemy.'

'Of course you are a Jew,' the interrupter proceeded, 'and you've no right to direct Irishmen what they should do in this war.'

Frustrated, Issy told the man it was a good job that he himself was in khaki, or instead of speaking to him, he would do something else.

'Are you ashamed to wear khaki?' Issy asked another who had begun to walk away.

'I was fifteen months in the trenches in France and returned home here disabled, and I've not got a penny since from the military authorities,' the man replied bitterly.

'Any man disabled or invalided from the front is entitled to a pension of 25 shillings a week,' Issy explained – to deaf ears.

There were more interruptions and Issy did his best to continue. As last, exasperated at the many men slurring and staggering about, he delivered his Parthian shot: 'If you were in England, you would not be allowed to get drunk,' he said bluntly.[11]

There were few recruits that evening, but that was the least of the troubles.

> ### The Easter Rising
>
> Tensions boiled and by Easter civil unrest erupted. On Easter Monday, 24 April, insurgents seized important sites in and around the city centre of Dublin. British forces arrived to contain the uprising and a bloody battle ensued over six days. By the time of the surrender the following Saturday, there were 485 deaths and more than 2,600 wounded. Sentences of death were passed on 90 accused and sixteen were immediately executed.
>
> Coincidently Patrick Pearse, the Commander General and one of the sixteen, had been born at 27 Great Brunswick Street, just one door from the recruitment office Issy had visited. The North King Street Massacre, the scene of some of the most vicious fighting, occurred outside another office he had attended.

Chapter 17

Disaster and Splendour

Having been officially posted to the 3rd (Special Reserve) Manchester Regiment on 15 December of the previous year, Issy had left Dublin in January and was back in Cleethorpes providing training and coordinating reinforcements when the Easter Rising unfolded.

On 25 February he was on parade at Weelsby Camp as General Officer Commanding Humber Garrison inspected the coast defences and presented decorations. Issy's promotion to sergeant had come through on 7 March, and he was still at the base with the 3rd Battalion on the night of 31 March when a German Zeppelin was seen approaching.

Earlier in the day, a train bearing a fresh group of soldiers, many of whom had only been in the army a few weeks, had arrived at Cleethorpes station. They were billeted in houses along the sea front as well as at the local Baptist chapel. After dark an air-raid warning was given, just as it had been every other evening throughout the latter part of March. The Zeppelin, one of five, had been headed to London with its fleet when it developed engine trouble. The pilot decided to divert instead to Cleethorpes and attack the Grimsby docks. Spotted at 1.30 am on 1 April, it immediately began to drop bombs when the anti-aircraft gun at the nearby Waltham Wireless Station opened fire.

Three bombs fell – the first on the Baptist chapel, the second on the council office and the third on a street. The Zeppelin circled and more bombs were dropped in the surrounding fields of Humberstone.

The chapel took a direct hit. The night was very dark and no lights could be shone as the bombing had not stopped; rescue efforts were difficult and it took three hours for the killed and wounded to be removed. Volunteer nurses of the VAD who had practised first aid in their spare time acted valiantly – many had probably never had to apply a bandage for a serious injury before and now they had dreadful ones to deal with.

The total casualties were 31 dead and 51 wounded. On 4 April, five were taken by relatives to their home towns and 24 were carried on eight motor lorries covered with the Union Jack and floral wreaths to the Cleethorpes Cemetery. There, a service (in which Issy would have taken part) was held with all of the 3rd Battalion Manchesters along with other regiments, the Navy, the VAD and local townspeople. A soldier who died on the day of the service was interred two days later with his comrades, and another who died on 6 April was taken home.

Once again, Issy had escaped death.

✣

In between the terrible events in Ireland and Cleethorpes there was some good news. On 3 February King George V held an investiture at Buckingham Palace in which he decorated a number of officers for distinguished service during the war. Among the recipients were three VCs, one of whom was No. 168 Sergeant Issy Smith, 1st Battalion of the Manchester Regiment. The other two men were Corporal Bassett, the first New Zealand VC who succeeded in laying a telephone line under heavy fire, and Piper Laidlaw, who mounted the parapet at the Battle of Loos and played his pipes (until he was wounded) to draw his company, shaken from the effects of gas, out of the trench and on to battle.[1]

A great crowd gathered to see the VCs arrive. The day was wet and cold but it didn't dampen anyone's spirits. The proceedings went ahead and the newspapers reported that the King displayed a knowledge of the records of each man and shook them warmly by the hand as he thanked them for the particular deed of heroism. Issy's VC, which the King dutifully pinned to his chest, read:

ACT. CORPL. I. SMITH.
1ST BN. MANCHESTER REGT.
26.
APRIL.
1915.

Later, a photo titled 'Decorated by the King' showed a smiling Issy, dressed in a long trench jacket, standing alongside two women, one in a fur pelt and the other in a rain jacket, who the paper claimed to be his mother and sister. Although the picture is grainy, the woman on the far right is Elsie, who had arrived a few weeks previously. The woman in the centre of the photograph is unknown, but is clearly not his mother.[2]

After the big day, a celebration was held at the Carlton Hotel in Edinburgh, where Issy was given a royal toast and a gift of a silver casket on behalf of the Edinburgh Jewish community.[3]

For the next few months, life for Issy was relatively quiet and in August he found time to enter the welter-weight competition at Stamford Bridge. He was defeated by a Sergeant Barton. A few days later he played his old challenger Ted Broadribb at a charity event in Marsh's Yard in Esher, with the proceeds going to a fund to provide comforts for soldiers in France. New contests were excitedly scheduled, but before they could be held, Issy was once again deployed to war.

> Sergeant Issy Smith V.C. left England on Saturday for France, and consequently will not be able to fulfil his boxing engagements. It is not generally known that Lord Rothschild has invested a considerable sum of money in War Loan

Bonds for Smith, in recognition that the latter was the first Jew soldier to win the Victoria Cross in the present war.
– *Illustrated Police News*, 24 August 1916

The only detail the paper got right was that Issy had left for France. On 4 September 1916, Issy embarked at Marseilles for a different theatre of war.

Chapter 18

The Ill-fated Campaign

The Middle East had become a focus shortly after the war began. In August 1914, Britain sent an expeditionary force to protect its recently acquired oil interests in Abadan, in southwest Persia (now Iran). With all the major powers now anticipating oil to be a key asset of the future, the new discovery had to be safeguarded.

Abadan was not the only location in the Middle East worth protecting. Next door, an area of the Ottoman Empire shared the same topography. Known as Mesopotamia (literally meaning 'between the rivers'), it was situated between the Tigris and Euphrates river systems but also included south-eastern Turkey, eastern parts of Syria, Kuwait and regions of Persia.[1] It became the jewel in the crown for several interested parties, for a variety of reasons.

Mesopotamia was an ancient land, with Babylon once its proud capital. The current rulers, the Ottoman Turks, had lived in the region for 400 years and intended to keep it. The Arabs and Kurds, predecessors residing there, valued its holy cities; in addition, the United Kingdom had promised to support Arab independence if they revolted against the Ottomans.[2]

Britain, which already had various treaties in place, held hopes for untapped riches of oil in the East, and along with France and Russia were looking to finish off the diminishing Ottoman Empire and carve the region up for themselves.[3] Germany also saw the latent capacity for oil, and had nurtured an alliance enabling concessions for a railway from Berlin to Baghdad that would provide access for goods trade in the Persian Gulf. None of the parties wished to relinquish the opportunities that lay before them.

Britain also considered troops in Mesopotamia to be vital for other reasons. Firstly, if the railway was to be completed and an agreement not to extend it breached, German soldiers could be transferred to the Gulf in as little as a week, posing a serious threat to British-held India. Secondly, if the Ottomans – already in an alliance with the Germans – chose to enter the war, Mesopotamia was a main entry point. Thirdly, the German-Ottoman alliance had begun a propaganda campaign to incite followers of Islam to anti-colonial revolts in the hope that this would break the colonial power's grip.[4]

A presence was necessary to maintain British prestige in the eyes of the 70 million Muslims in British-India, especially those in the British Indian Army who were currently deployed at war. An Arab revolt would greatly assist, but it would not disguise the elephant in the room. By fighting the Ottoman Empire, Britain would now be at war with a Muslim power. There would be mutinies and desertions, and it would take strong leadership and a decisive victory to maintain sovereignty.

On 31 October 1914, the Ottomans followed Germany into the war.

At first, as the British troops arrived in Mesopotamia, there was relatively little resistance and things went smoothly. After capturing the fort of Fao and the town of Basra in November 1914, the 6th (Poona) British Indian Division led by Lieutenant General Sir Arthur Barrett moved up the River Tigris. The area, however, was inhospitable country. Most of the land was alluvial plain and desert – flat, seasonally hot and cold and with no protection from winds, dust, rain or enemy. Temperatures could be extreme, over 50 degrees Celsius in summer, and there was little water except from the rivers – which were themselves problematic. Shallow in parts and a haven for mosquitos, they rose when the snow in the northern mountains melted in the spring and flooded with the compounding rain in the wet season, causing the few roads along the banks to become bog. In the summer they turned large areas into salty wastelands. Transport by watercraft became the only suitable mode of carriage although even this was impacted by conditions, the wrong equipment and attack.[5]

Yet reliance on the river systems had further drawbacks. Basra was the strategic entry point from the Persian Gulf, but moving upriver by boat created significant risk as the access to support and supplies became more distant.

With no other options, the army proceeded. Instructed by Commander General Sir John Nixon and now led by Major General Charles Townshend, there were some successes (albeit with infantry losses) at Qurna and Kut-al-Amara ('Kut') before a harrowing fight at Ctesiphon, 32 km from Baghdad, brought a halt to progress. Townshend's army, now only two-thirds its former size after the loss of a total of 4,500 men, retreated to Kut on 25 November 1914. The town, which was surrounded on three sides by the river, appeared to be a good defensive position; Turkish reinforcements weren't expected as they were tied up with the Gallipoli campaign and a Russian threat to Armenia.

But it wasn't long before Kut was surrounded by the enemy and a long siege began. General Nixon was removed for this failure and General Sir Percy Lake took over.

Issy's old regiment arrived in January 1916 (while Issy was in Dublin) in an attempt to rescue the 15,000-plus soldiers and camp followers now trapped.[6] Consisting of the 3rd (Lahore) Division, 8th Indian Infantry Brigade and the 1st Battalion Manchester Regiment, they arrived at Basra on 9 January and were upstream at Ali Gharbi, not far from Kut, by the 17th. They joined the 7th (Meerut) Division, who'd been their fighting comrades at Neuve Chapelle.[7]

There were challenges immediately for the 1st Manchesters. Being winter and the flooding season, the rain was unrelenting. A Sergeant Hurst, last seen at 6.30 am on the side of a barge, disappeared without a trace – presumed drowned. On the 19th they were at Orah, near Hannah, and were given orders to attack the enemy in the village and across the river. Yet the rain did not stop and the banks were a quagmire; fighting was fierce and their medical officer was wounded. There was no cover of any kind and troops were forced to camp on a marsh in freezing temperatures and pouring rain, with No. 4 Company ordered to protect the waterlogged guns. The Battle of Hannah, as it came to be known, was unsuccessful and resulted in the overall loss of 2,700 men.

Hospital facilities, or the lack of them, became a major issue. Provision had been made to manage 250 casualties. There were now more than 4000 and with the cold, rain, mud and vermin, men began to die from sickness as well – anything from sandfly, typhus, yellow fever, scarlet fever or relapsing fevers; malaria, cholera, dysentery, measles, mumps, scurvy, plague, smallpox, cerebrospinal meningitis or heatstroke. At times, the wounded and sick had to wait ten days to be assessed in camp before walking, injured or debilitated and sometimes with wounded enemy, to the river – a distance that could be ten miles. The steamers that arrived – which luckily could move up the river while the water was high – were crowded, and the wounded were transported in among the sick, back to Basra.[8]

More reinforcements arrived in February, partially covering the losses. Meanwhile, fighting continued, including the dropping of bombs on campsites by enemy aircraft. In March Captain Shipster, whom Issy had saved at Ypres, arrived with a further draft of men for the 1st Manchesters. Another attempt to move closer to Kut was scheduled on the night of 7 March; the troops advanced to the muddy trenches at Es Sinn and the following day an attack was launched on the Dujailah Redoubt.[9] By evening, they were forced to abandon after being overwhelmed by thick clouds of dust from machine guns and very accurate enemy fire. The Battle of Dujaila was a failure, with a heavy cost of 3,500 men. It became apparent that the likelihood of relieving the men at Kut was slim.

On 5 April a further valiant effort was made. The 13th (Western) Division (who had just been evacuated from Gallipoli and sent urgently to Kut) rushed the Hannah trenches and found the Turks asleep. Later in the day they drove the Turks from the nearby Fallahiyeh trenches. No. 1 Company 1st Manchesters pushed forward to the Abu Roman mounds, but there were heavy losses and Captain Shipster was wounded in the process. Combats and casualties continued (despite excellent rescue news to the contrary being reported in London), and on 17 April another furious battle ensued at Sannaiyat, with more soldiers lost.[10]

By the end of the month, all relief efforts had failed and 23,000 casualties had been suffered, more than the number of men trapped. It had also become apparent that the enemy had been underestimated; while the power of the Ottoman Empire had lessened over the centuries, the resilience of the Turkish fighter had not. Accustomed or otherwise indifferent to heat, gales, rain and disease, the Turkish soldiers had dug themselves in and successfully repelled all attacks from the Kut garrison and the relieving forces. On 29 April, General Townshend and the remaining 13,000 starved and weakened British and Indian troops surrendered after 147 days, the longest siege and biggest surrender in British military history up to this point.[11] Coming so soon after Gallipoli, this was a humiliating defeat.[12]

On 1 May a London newspaper published a photo of the 'Sunny Street Scene in Surrendered Kut', noting 'it has certain aspects which yield romantic effect to the camera'. Right now, however, there was nothing peaceful or romantic. 'Mespot' as it had become known, was in a dire situation.[13]

Back in London, a flurry of criticism abounded regarding the disastrous state of affairs, and demands were made for both an inquiry into what went wrong and fresh troops to be resupplied with proper equipment and support.

On 23 August, a letter was received from Sir Victor Horsley, a volunteer field surgeon in Amara, south of Kut, highlighting the failures. Sir Victor wrote:

> ... [the failures] are due to the non-provision of transport.
> There never has been in this country adequate transport

for food, and there never (until March, when our solitary hospital steamer arrived) has been any medical transport whatever; nothing but the foulest store barges and steamers used on their return journey to the base to carry the sick and wounded.[14]

The letter was written in early July. It arrived in London after Horsley's sudden death from heatstroke and severe hyperpyrexia on the 16th of the same month.

✢

While the British and Indian governments debated the mess and how to recover, the 1st Manchesters remained in Mesopotamia and did their best to keep the enemy at bay. Now in the midst of summer, the extreme heat was debilitating and gales blew through, stirring up suffocating dust that was only disturbed by bombings from enemy aircraft. Sickness in camp was compounding; with the lack of hospital ships many perished before proper medical attention could be given, such as the battalion's Captain Vaudry who died from cholera on 2 May and was buried on the banks of the river. With the severe lack of good water and the difficulty in transporting it, a large number of men were struck down, succumbing to fever. On 15 July the enemy shelled the camp's water supply.

Aside from water, food was also a challenge. The supplies sent in the lead-up to the surrender had been barely adequate; now rations were at a minimum while the transport and logistics for the next offensive were planned. The right foods for each race and religion were stretched, and what arrived didn't always travel well. In the scorching sun, tins of corned beef could pour out like soup.

Then there was the problem of rest. Weary soldiers on the Western Front could be rotated out of the front line. For the troops positioned several hundred kilometres up the Tigris, there was no respite.[15]

During July Lieutenant General Sir Stanley Maude was made Commander of the relief forces. Although he had arrived at the end of the siege to head the III Indian Army Corps and had been instructed to simply hold the line, he immediately made changes. Taking a fresh focus on logistics, he reorganised and resupplied the British and Indian forces with 166,000 men, two-thirds of whom were Indians. The 1st Manchesters began receiving new drafts from the end of June.[16]

Issy arrived in September 1916, apparently surviving his ship being torpedoed on the way.[17] Attacks on shipping vessels by German U-boats had been steadily increasing since the war began, with the international rules regarding protection of passenger and certain merchant vessels (such as relief ships) soon abandoned. Although only 28 U-boats had initially been in service around the British Isles, the numbers had quickly grown after a novel scheme was devised of cutting off supply and starving Britain into withdrawing through constant ambush. In May 1915, after the sinking of the ocean liner RMS *Lusitania*, the attacks had lessened for a time over fears that this might induce the US to join the war – the loss of so many civilian lives (including 128 Americans) had caused disbelief and indignation.

By 1916, however, the sea warfare was back on the rise and 227 Allied ships had been wrecked; in the month Issy travelled, roughly 80 U-boats were circling and more than 40 Allied ships were lost. It is not known if he was rescued from a sinking ship or if the crew were able to make hasty repairs and limp on, with damage, to Basra.[18]

In any case, he made it in September 1916, only to be struck down within a fortnight with malaria. After being hospitalised for several days and taking a short recovery spell in the Royal Indian Marine workshop, he rejoined both his regiment and his close friends Sergeant James Rooke and Alf Burley, who were also posted there. Alf had now lost all three of his brothers – Frank in 1900 and the other two sadly during the previous year – George in Gallipoli and William in France.[19]

On 29 September the battalion moved to Sinn Aftar to take over the line of the Tigris as far as the mouth of the Nassafieh Canal.

Although not the heart of summer by then, it was still stiflingly hot with temperatures frequently over 40 degrees.

In addition to the reinforcements, better equipment arrived and work began in earnest to improve both the efficiency of the waterways and the surrounding land. While others worked on constructing new railways, Issy's battalion spent the next two months making roads to various points on the river for access and supply dumps. Much of this work had to be done at night – the enemy still occupied positions on both sides of the Tigris and regularly opened fire. On 10 December, the troops were relieved from Sinn Aftar and moved to Cholera Creek, and then a few miles further each night as work was completed. Almost every day several men were killed or wounded and others sent to hospital due to sickness. Christmas Day 1916 passed without mention, perhaps remembered quietly by the small numbers of Christian soldiers.

On 9 January, Issy's battalion launched an attack on Turkish trenches in a bend of the river north-east of Kut. The 1st Company 'left their trench and went over well together, but owing to excitement broke into a double too soon and arrived at the Turkish trench before the artillery fire had lifted. Some casualties were caused by this.'[20] A heavy fog also hampered efforts and several times the troops accidently fired on each other. The fog lifted and the fighting continued in the open and in the trenches all day. By evening they had captured the Turkish trench and gained 50 yards beyond – with heavy losses. Seven officers were killed and five wounded, 80 other ranks were killed and 136 wounded. Ten men were missing.

A Turkish document recovered from the trench managed to be translated. It read as follows:

> By telephone
> To
> IMAM MUHAMMAD SECTOR
> 8 Jan 1917
>
> The steadfastness of the troops on the Imam Muhammad Sector in face of the enemy's violent bombardment, and

especially of our infantry who held their ground in spite of bloody losses during today's bombardment in the mist, is above all praise.

The Corps Commander kisses the eyes of all ranks and thanks them. I too kiss all their eyes and thank them …

Sgt Acting O.C.
45th Division
Ismail Kakki

A week later, four replacement officers and 61 fresh troops arrived to fill the gaps. For the rest of the month, the battalion remained in small working parties and in reserve. At night, the enemy could be heard digging, but stopped 'when a Lewis gun paid attention to it'.[21]

By 28 January, Issy was working closely with the Inland Water Transport division, moving river craft. In February they moved closer to Kut along the Hai river, slowly and progressively pushing the enemy back bit by bit. Yet still the hold on the town remained.[22]

On 4 February a Turkish deserter swam across and surrendered. This was not unusual: several had previously approached the camps and volunteered information about military strategies or relief of shifts.

By the time they reached Kut, the troops were dodging enemy shells from biplanes and sniping from the enemy set up strategically in the town itself. In mid-February they were instructed to ready themselves and the infantry moved into positions at nearby Sannaiyat.

On 17 February they attacked. Turkish trenches were captured, only for them to be retaken in a counter-attack. For the next week, the troops held various positions to assist the rest of Maude's forces and on 24 February the enemy was successfully forced out. Kut was recaptured, and two days later a burial party was sent out to deal with the aftermath.[23]

For the remainder of February and early into March, enormous quantities of shells, ammunition and other war material was recovered from the hastily retreating Turks. But the troops could not relax. Parts of the battalion were involved in establishing picquets each day, sometimes a front of up to 2,400 yards (over 2 km), to protect against fresh enemy attack. Other picquets were required on the roads to stop Arabs raiding the convoys of supplies.[24]

Lieutenant General Maude began his advance on Baghdad on 5 March, reaching the Diala River, a tributary of the Tigris that began on the outskirts of the city. On 8 March a battle to cross it took place over several days.[25]

Meanwhile, Issy and the troops withdrew from the picquets at Kut and marched towards the city; en route at Aziziah on the same night (8 March) they took over the defences there. On the 10th they took a difficult trek via Ctesiphon in a blinding dust storm, stopping six miles further on at Bawi. Tents were not pitched and they had a very unpleasant night in the weather.[26]

At 8 o'clock that evening the Ottoman authorities ordered the evacuation of Baghdad. Lieutenant General Maude captured the city the next day, issuing a proclamation a week later with the famous line 'Our armies do not come into your cities and lands as conquerors or enemies, but as liberators'. A small number of Issy's battalion were permitted leave in Baghdad on 15 March.

Britain was relieved. Under the headline 'Captured by British, Remarkable Advance', a London paper printed the story of the river crossing, an excerpt of which stated:

> … our forces were engaged with the enemy on the line of the Diala on the night of 8 March. Our troops succeeded in spite of bright moonlight in effecting a surprise crossing of the Diala and in establishing a strong post on the right bank of that river…
>
> … During the night of 9 March the passage of the Diala was forced, and our troops advanced four miles towards Baghdad …
>
> This advantage in spite of blinding dust storms and a violent gale …[27]

The reality was somewhat different. In a cablegram sent by a Mr

The Ill-fated Campaign

Edmund Candler, a war correspondent who witnessed the crossing, the events read as follows:

> ... Immediately the first pontoon was lowered over the ramp the whole launching party was shot down in a few seconds. It was a bright moonlight, and the Turks had concentrated their machine guns and rifles in the houses on the opposite bank.
>
> The second pontoon had got into the middle of the stream when a terrific fusillade was opened on it. The crew of five rowers and ten riflemen were killed, and the boat floated down the stream.
>
> A third got nearly across, but was bombed and sank. All the crew were killed, but there was no holding back.
>
> Crew after crew pushed off to an obvious and certain death ... and the pontoons drifted out to the Tigris to float past our camp in the daylight with their freight of dead ...
>
> ... On the second night, the attempt was pursued with equal gallantry. This time the attack was preceded by a bombardment ... The barrage secured us the footing. Not the shells, but the dust raised. Later, in the clear moonlight, when the dust had lifted, or settled, the conditions of the night before were re-established. Succeeding crossing parties were exterminated and pontoons drifted away, but a footing was secured.
>
> The crew of one boat which lost its way during the barrage were untouched, but they did not make the bank in time. Directly the air cleared, a machine-gun was opened on them, and the rowers were shot down and the pontoon drifted back ashore.
>
> A sergeant called for volunteers to get the wounded out of the boat, and a party of twelve men went over the river bank. Every one of them, as well as the crew of the pontoon, was killed.
>
> Some 60 men got over ... The Lancashire men, surrounded on all sides but the river, held it through the night,

all the next day and the next night against repeated and determined attacks delivered in the dark or at dawn ... The whole affair was visible to our troops on the south side ...[28]

Part of the 38th Lancaster Brigade of the 13th (Western) Division were called upon to perform this dreadful task. It might just as easily have been the 1st Manchester Regiment, who at the time were holding the defences at nearby Aziziah.[29] Coincidentally, the very next Jewish VC recipient, Jack White, was awarded his medal for one of these crossings. The citation reads:

No. 18105 Pte Jack White, R. Lanc, R.

For most conspicuous bravery and resource.

This signaller during an attempt to cross a river saw the two Pontoons ahead of him come under heavy machine-gun fire, with disastrous results.

When his own Pontoon had reached midstream, with every man except himself either dead or wounded, finding that he was unable to control the Pontoon, Pte White promptly tied a telephone wire to the Pontoon, jumped overboard, and towed it to the shore, thereby saving an officer's life and bringing to land the rifles and equipment of the other men in the boat, who were either dead or dying.

For Jack, Issy and the rest of the troops deployed to war, it would appear that a soldier's survival rested largely in the hands of the government and the military authorities, whose decisions could be wise or diabolical. There was also sheer luck.

The Siege of Kut Al Amara

The Siege of Kut Al Amara, or Kut, lasted 147 days. The survivors became prisoners of war and, despite the press reporting otherwise, were badly treated. Most were malnourished and wracked with sickness. Although some prisoners were exchanged for Ottomans, the remainder were paraded through the streets of Baghdad, marched across the Syrian Desert (and shot if they faltered), incarcerated in jails with criminals, or forced to work on the mountainous section of the railway from Constantinople to Baghdad. The mortality rate for the British (accounting for those who could not be found) was 65 per cent. For the Indians, the number was close to 60 per cent.

During the siege, Major General Townshend never visited the hospital in Kut where his men were dying. He sent radio messages to London seeking a promotion and ensuring his dog Spot would not suffer. Reported by the press as being a friend of the Turkish General Enver Pasha, he was taken to Baghdad and given a guided tour of various sites before leaving for Constantinople where he was greeted with a formal guard of honour. There, he witnessed some of his starving and broken men on a death march but only enquired about them once.

He was transferred to an Island on the Sea of Marmara and treated as an honoured guest, which included living in a comfortable villa, having receptions held in his name at the Sultan's palace and use of a Turkish naval yacht until the end of the war. In 1917, during his time in captivity, he was granted Knight Commander of the Order of the Bath. On returning to London after the war, he asked for a major promotion but was refused. When the British proposed trials for crimes against humanity, he indicated he would defend Enver if the latter was called and denied that the death marches ever occurred.

Despite his indifference to the fate of his men, Townshend apparently could not fathom why he was not given another military post.

In 1917, an official inquiry and report into the disaster found that a twofold responsibility between the India Office (who determined policy) and the India Government (who managed the expedition) was unworkable; similarly controlling the expedition from India was a mistake. The advance to Baghdad was based on political and military miscalculations and conducted with inadequate resources, resulting in the loss of 13,000 in the siege and 23,000 in the failed attempts to rescue them.

The largest share of responsibility for the failure was placed on General Sir John Nixon. While General Sir Percy Lake was also removed due to his inability to achieve a successful result, he was not held to blame. The Commander-in-Chief in India, Sir Beauchamp Duff, was apportioned responsibility. Duff, Nixon and Townshend all received heavy criticism. A psychologist and historian later wrote: 'Through a mixture of self-interest, personal ambition, ignorance, obstinacy and sheer crass stupidity, this trio sealed the fate of some thousands of British and Indian soldiers.' Duff was rumoured to have committed suicide in January 1918 from shame, but an inquest ruled that he died by misadventure.

Edmund Candler wrote a book titled *The Long Road to Baghdad*, published in 1919. In it he described:

… a struggle in which blunder piled upon blunder made it evident to the troops that their sacrifice was in vain. And not merely in vain, but as it seemed at the time, thankless. For the forces which fought to relieve Townshend … were ill-fed, ill-equipped, and their sick, in many cases, untended.

Lord Montagu of Beaulieu, who spoke in the House of Lords where the report was debated, noted that he found the expedition to be short of equipment, clothes and food. When he wired Lord Kitchener, he received a reply asking him not to make any more demands as everything was required for France.

Chapter 19

End of the Fight

The fall of Baghdad might have brought welcome news to Britain, but it was quickly overshadowed by events unfolding in Russia. Riots broke out in Petrograd in late February 1917, and when the police and soldiers joined the revolt, Czar Nicholas II had no option but to abdicate on 15 March.[1]

Significant changes began immediately, but what wasn't clear was Russia's commitment to the war. Fears arose that the revolution would weaken the country's will to continue the fight against Germany, prompting the press to quickly dispel British anxiety with stories that 'the new Russia is a much more formidable enemy for Germany than the reactionary Russia … which has passed so swiftly and completely away …' and 'Russia will participate with abundant zeal and energy in the final stages of a conflict in which she has borne a full share of travail and sorrow.'[2]

How much, if any of this news reached Issy isn't known; nor can his views on it be assumed, even though the rebellion forced the removal of a regime that inflicted much grief upon his family.

Regardless of what he knew or thought, or what the future held, nothing appeared to change in Mesopotamia. The capture of Baghdad did not signal an end to the fighting; the 1st Manchesters continued north through Baquba and Shahrban towards the Jabel Hamrin mountains, where the enemy had a stronghold.

On 24 and 25 March a terrible battle ensued. Ten officers were killed, 76 of other ranks wounded and sixteen went missing. There are stories that Issy was wounded at Baghdad, although nothing in his records shows this. Sometime during the fighting, the end of his nose was broken by flying shell, but otherwise during his time to date in Mesopotamia he appeared to have been relatively unscathed. Others were not so lucky. Second Lieutenant Butterworth, a Manchester comrade of the same age (26 years) was wounded in March 1916, hospitalised for sickness in December of that year and one of the sixteen missing in action in March 1917.[3]

While the fighting and dreadful losses continued, a new military strategy was working quietly in the background that would bring momentous improvements.

It had become apparent from the Mesopotamia inquiry that the river transport service was grossly inadequate and largely responsible for the tragedy at Kut. Ongoing shortages of food, equipment and hospital facilities were compounding the issues for the troops still present and it was impossible to mount a new front that had any chance of success. A withdrawal now would signal further weaknesses in the once invincible British Empire and would put both prestige and the war at risk. A radical change was required.

When the 6th (Poona) Division had first arrived in November 1914, the limited number of vessels was sufficient for a small British force to protect the oil fields not far away. As soon as an advance onto Baghdad had commenced, problems had increased exponentially.

Basra was an ancient port and relatively unchanged from the sixth century when it was built. The city was situated on small areas of slightly higher dry ground surrounded by the muddy alluvial plains. In the rainy season even the higher ground flooded. Although the river systems were the principal mode of transport, the facilities for this purpose – docks, boats, handling equipment and storage warehouses – were basic and, in many locations further upstream, non-existent. Ocean ships had to anchor in the middle of the river and wait, sometimes for days, until lighters could unload them. Only certain types of smaller watercraft could navigate up the river systems (depending on the season) and these were often impeded by sandbars, narrow channels or shipping congestion – not to mention enemy sabotage. Supplies had to be sent in small quantities and transferred across the muddy marshes along the riverbanks by men and mules. Unloading heavy equipment over the boggy ground was impossible.

In 1914 the fleet, which was managed by the Royal Indian Marine from the India Office, consisted of three steamers and sixteen lighters. Nothing was modern or suitable. More craft were ordered, but the process was plagued with problems, and in January 1916, when the battle was being fought at Hannah, there had been 10,000 men and twelve guns available for reinforcements that couldn't be sent upriver in time. Later, it had taken nearly two months to send 12,000 men and 26 guns a few hundred miles. In the meantime, the lack of food and treatment of the growing number of sick and wounded had been – and was still – getting worse.

The process for delivering new boats was a shambles. Most were sent in sections to be reassembled at Basra, but they arrived without any numbering or instructions for assembly and were delivered wherever the ships landed; parts had to be searched for up and down the beach and could arrive months apart. Finding a particular piece for the completion of a vessel was almost hopeless. Some sections were too large to be handled and sank when efforts were made to assemble them in the river. Remaining parts that were sent back to Bombay (to be built there and towed back) added risk, cost and delay. The work required to send, assemble, erect and fit out steamers and barges was completely misunderstood, and without the right equipment and conditions to build and maintain them, the projects were a disaster.

Just as Issy arrived in September 1916, the War Office took control and the Royal Engineers (RE) Inland Water Transport (IWT) of Mesopotamia was established. An enormous expansion began; a range of departments were set up and a large staff of 7,171 staff employed.[4] The existing fleet was assessed and new equipment immediately organised. Some of the new boats were built in England with parts numbered, then dismantled and sent out to be re-erected. Others, such as hospital ships, were completely constructed in England and sailed out in a convoy, with just a few attacked and sunk by the enemy en route.[5]

With the operations in Mesopotamia growing, more vessels were needed, along with personnel with experience in the field. On 1 April 1917 Issy officially transferred to the Royal Engineers and the next day, joined IWT. Not having had any leave for some time, he was granted four weeks which he took in Egypt, likely visiting his family.

He departed on 4 May 1917 travelling on HT *Edavana* from Basra and returned on 8 June 1917 on the HT *Nile*. Both ships were used to transport sick to India, with HT *Nile* reported as having an outbreak of plague in February. Thankfully, this time he escaped infection and arrived back to settle into his new role.

Over 1917 and 1918, IWT set to work. Aside from the expansion of the fleet, the dockyards were developed, workshops erected, machinery installed, control stations opened, river access and irrigation improved, storage increased and supplies stocked. New slipways and bridges were also built.

Efforts by IWT on the Upper Tigris resulted in the capture of Tekrit on 6 November 1917.[6] Sergeant Rooke, who had remained with the 1st Manchesters, saw this battle. Although he was reportedly wounded in December 1917, it is more likely this was delayed reporting and he was actually injured on 5 or 6 November, when the main fighting occurred. A total of 106 soldiers were casualties, three being officers who were wounded. On 12 November, the brigade received a message from Lieutenant General Maude congratulating them on their gallantry.

Six days later, on 18 November, Maude was dead. A week earlier he had received as a guest a Mrs Eleanor Egan, an American war correspondent, and on the night of 14 November, in order to show her the sights of Baghdad, had taken her to a theatrical performance arranged in his honour by a local Jewish school. During the evening coffee was brought and he took milk with it but she didn't; two days later he was ill but trying to push on.

On 17 November, London papers printed a telegram received by Field Marshall Sir Douglas Haig, commander of the British Expeditionary Force in France, from General Maude, thanking him for his kind message regarding his success at Tekrit. More papers proudly detailed his well-managed campaign, claiming that enemy troops could not be matched against the formidable Lieutenant General Maude. Britain was therefore stunned to hear the very next day of his sudden death from cholera.[7] He was replaced by Major General William Marshall.

With Baghdad secured, priority was now given to the little-known Egyptian Expeditionary Force (EEF) and the Egypt and Palestine campaign – the latter country being under Turkish rule. By this time Issy's friend Alf Burley, who had been promoted to Colour Sergeant, had transferred to Egypt. Issy, still employed by IWT, joined him there, before Alf was sent on to Persia.[8]

Initially the main task of the EEF, which had been created in March 1916, was to protect the Suez Canal, a key communications link for the British Empire and a safe means of passage for the Indian and Anzac troops deployed to France.[9] The establishment of Egypt in 1915 as a military base and training area for Imperial Forces had put huge demands on facilities and resources. Inland water transport had been set up on the canal in order to supplement the limited railway and road networks which were now under strain. Tugs, steam barges and lighters as well as sailing, canal and river craft had all been acquired to deliver varying tonnages of supplies and cope with fluctuating water depths of both the canal and the associated lakes. The main material transported was road metal (broken stone to make or repair roads), but coal and stores, including food for the horses and mules, were also sent.

Royal Engineers staff coordinated supply and maintenance, just as they were doing in Mesopotamia.[10] Issy was employed in Alexandria, under the General Headquarters of the EEF in Cairo, superintending the loading and offloading of cargoes. With the equipment heavy and a good deal of the labour force unskilled, the work was often dangerous. On 5 August 1917 Issy landed in hospital after accidently receiving a large cut over his right knee while on duty.

By March the following year the EEF, which included Australian and New Zealand troops, had significantly expanded its operations, and advances were now being made by Lieutenant General Sir Archibald Murray on Gaza in an attempt to destroy the Ottoman forces in southern Palestine. At this time the British War Cabinet was not united over where to best allocate resources (Western Front or elsewhere); however, two failures at Gaza in April and May 1917 prompted the immediate replacement of Murray with General Sir Edmund Allenby in June and an expansion of the corps in Egypt. Wasting no time, Allenby set about restructuring, retraining and preparing the troops for a fresh assault on the Ottoman defences ensconced between Gaza and the inland town of Beersheba.

A third and subsequently successful Battle of Gaza took place in the first week of November 1917. Allenby and his troops then advanced on Jerusalem, occupying it on 9 December. As a mark of respect for the Holy City, Allenby dismounted his horse and made his entry on foot.

Some historical accounts suggest that Issy was at the fall of Jerusalem. In a letter written by Issy in 1940 to a Major Barrett, where he gave an overview of his service history, he mentioned taking part in the fall of Baghdad, joining IWT and being sent to Palestine.

'After the fall of Jerusalem, I was attached to G.S.I., General Allenby's Headquarters until demobilised in 1919 when I returned to Australia.'[11]

He made no reference to any involvement or presence on his part in Jerusalem. Without further substantiation, his participation in this battle is only speculative.[12]

With regard to headquarters, General Allenby had, in fact, two operations bases. On replacing Murray in June, Allenby had taken over the headquarters in Cairo before restructuring and establishing a new 'battles headquarters' in Palestine near the city of Khan Yunis on the Gaza Strip, close to the battlefront. The original base in Cairo became the administration and control centre for martial law in Egypt. The headquarters at Khan Yunis was a significant army operation, with a railway line established east of the canal and many depots and camps set up behind the lines.

A letter written in September 1917 from the British High Commissioner for Egypt to Sir William Robertson, Chief of the Imperial General Staff in the War Office, was full of praise for the set-up, noting the difficulties of a desert campaign and '… evidences of clear adaptation to local conditions and complete readiness and efficiency … at every turn …'.[13]

The IWT's, and hence Issy's, responsibilities at the headquarters were generally not in the thick of the infantry battles, but more in the securing and landing of supplies via the waterways to assist them. Issy continued to work in Alexandria where, in January 1918, he was held at Port Said with emphysema. He spent a further period in early September in hospital before being discharged 'overseas' on 19 September 1918. As he was reported to have been in Palestine, it was initially assumed that he was despatched to the other headquarters there to manage nearby inland water services for the battlefront. The closest inland waterway in the region where operations could have been managed was the Dead Sea, a salt lake with a main basin 31 miles long and 9 miles across at its widest point, just 26 miles from Jerusalem. However, this body of water was currently occupied by the enemy.

Earlier in the year, Allenby had been forced to send nearly two thirds of his troops to France and Flanders to support the push at the Western Front. In Palestine, the force was replaced with mostly new and untrained Indian units. Having spent six years in India and further time in Mesopotamia with the 3rd (Lahore) Division, Issy had considerable experience working with different cultures and dialects, and hence an appointment there would make sense. If this was his role, it did not last long, being interrupted shortly after his arrival with yet another hospitalisation on 28 September, this time for bronchitis.

During that month, Allenby had pushed on to northern Palestine, and fierce fighting in Megiddo from 19 to 21 September contributed to the collapse of the last formidable Turkish Army. Captain Shipster, who had rejoined the Manchester Regiment on 16 March 1918 and transferred with the brigade to Palestine, was killed in action at Megiddo on 20 September. He was aged 28. No doubt Issy learned of this terrible news.

Less than eight weeks later, on 11 November 1918, the war came to an end.

On 21 November, Issy was discharged from hospital with the medical notes stating he was suffering from 'bronchitis, gastritis and tachycardia'. He returned to Cairo to report to the Deputy Director of Inland Water Transport for light duties.[14]

World War I

Tragically, WWI, one of the largest wars in history, had now claimed more than 37 million casualties from the armed forces as well as many millions of civilians – not just from war, but also from starvation, disease and exposure.

Mesopotamia

To this day, little is known about what was endured in Mesopotamia. In June 1917, a Private George Tyson, soldier of the Lincolnshire Regiment, attempted suicide while held in a cell. He claimed he had been twice to France, once to Mesopotamia and also to the Dardenelles. He was willing to go to France again, but not to Mesopotamia. He was charged as an absentee and handed over to a military escort.[15]

In a meeting in the House of Commons on 22 November 1918, the British casualties in Mesopotamia up to the day before the war ended (which were agreed as incomplete) were 31,109 killed, 651,097 wounded and 15,355 missing. This may not have included the large numbers hospitalised for starvation, sickness and heat.

The signing of the Armistice at Mudros should have been the end of hostilities in the Middle Eastern theatre, but on 14 November 1918 Britain continued on to secure Mosul. This contributed to the controversy over the plan to combine the former Ottoman provinces of Basra, Baghdad and Mosul into one state under a nominated king. In addition, Britain was granted a mandate that the Arabs claimed was colonialism, as there was no clear promise of independence. In 1920, a major revolt broke out that was suppressed by British force – Alf returned with the 2nd Manchester Regiment, with whom he had transferred, to deal with this.[16] Instability and deep unrest continued in the region for decades.

The name Mesopotamia (a Greek word adopted largely by Westerners) was replaced with the Arabic name of Iraq, a name used for an Arab settlement in the area since the seventh century.

Inland Water Transport in Mesopotamia

From the time of its establishment in September 1916, Inland Water Transport lost 206 British officers. The number of casualties from other ranks and additional staff employed is not known, but not all of these casualties were due to the causes listed above. There were fatalities among the unskilled labourers as a result of the heavy and gruelling work.[17]

By the time of the signing of the Armistice, the IWT organisation in Mesopotamia was enormous, made up of 1634 vessels and 799 British officers (177 of them sergeants), 3,337 British other ranks and 38, 832 Eastern races, plus a number of followers for additional labour. At the peak, there were almost 50,000 men. IWT played a pivotal role in the campaign in Mesopotamia and in other theatres of war.

Palestine

Destruction, famine, epidemics and oppression took a terrible toll on Palestine. Not unlike Mesopotamia, promises had been offered and decisions made by the great powers with little consideration of the inhabitants. Many believed the land had been sold twice – to both the Arabs and the Jews – and the region has remained in dispute to this day.

Wound Stripes

In all, Issy was wounded four times, although it is not known which injuries were recognised. He was gassed twice near Ypres (possibly counted as one), lacerated at Alexandria and reportedly shot at Neuve Chapelle and Baghdad, although there is no evidence to support either of the latter two. The laceration in Egypt may or may not have been one of the four. The gassings and malaria attacks, which caused many subsequent hospitalisations, certainly plagued him for the rest of his life.

The British Army began awarding wound stripes in 1916 with authorisation from King George V. They were granted only to those who had appeared on a casualty list, and were worn vertically on the left sleeve of their uniform. 'Wounded' included gassing and shell shock but not accidental or self-inflicted injuries. Initially the stripes were made of gold Russia braid but the material grew shabby quickly, so brass versions were produced which could be removed and polished. These remain in the family's possession.

Dunsterforce

In 1927, an article noted that Issy had given brief particulars of his service, namely that in Mesopotamia he had served under 'Colonel Dunstable', and while in Baku he was awarded the Russian Cross of St George for locating a Cossack Patrol that had lost touch with Colonel Dunstable's force. Neither of these details was correct.

Firstly, the Allied command was actually a secret force under Major General Lionel *Dunsterville*, 'not Duns*table*', a force known colloquially as *Dunsterforce*. The mission was to protect the oil installations and railways at Baku in Azerbaijan and organise local groups to help guard the routes to India and Afghanistan. It was dangerous due to factional unrest among the many local ethnic groups; for this reason, men 'with dash and intelligence' were carefully selected for the task. Although a small number were chosen from Mesopotamia when Issy was in the region, there is no evidence to indicate that he joined them.

Secondly, receiving his Russian Cross for locating a Cossack Patrol during the expedition, a previously unheard-of story, could not be true. The Russian medal was awarded to him in 1915, well before *Dunsterforce* had been instigated.

Why this was incorrectly reported, like so many other events, could possibly be due to Issy's reluctance to give details of his war efforts. Over the years he was labelled 'modest', 'incurably shy' and, at one stage, 'mute' – it was therefore up to the journalists to fill the gaps and, to further enhance the story, they created more dare and adventure for greater readership.

Fifth and final Jewish recipient

There would be just one more Jewish recipient of the VC recognised during WWI. Captain Robert Gee, born in Leicester, England and the holder of the Military Cross from the opening day of the Battle of Somme, was awarded the VC on 30 November 1917 during the Battle of Cambrai in France. He was also Mentioned in Despatches three times.

Chapter 20

Joys and Challenges of Returning Home

Following the long-awaited news that the war had ended, Elsie immediately made plans to cross the globe again to marry her fiancé. It had been a long wait – since 1912 – and she prayed that this time the attempt would be 'third time lucky'.

Issy was granted three weeks furlough on compassionate grounds. To reach London at the same time as his bride-to-be, he was to embark at Port Said on 18 January 1919. But first he made an important stop.

A few members of his family still lived in Egypt – his mother Eva, sister Olga and sister Fanny with her husband Isaac and their five children. Due to his escapades in London and time at war, his visit in May 1917 was the first in more than fifteen years.[1] No doubt he planned to tell them of his upcoming nuptials, if they had not been told already. Given that his parents were Orthodox Jews and Elsie was a gentile, it was not clear how this would go down. According to the history books, they did not take it well and disowned him, but this can only be partly true at best. His father Moses had passed away more than ten years earlier – long before Elsie was even in the picture.

Whether Eva was happy about the news is unknown; however, there is another story of the visit, this time passed down by descendants. According to the tale, in addition to the honour of his Victoria Cross, family members believed that Issy received both a tidy sum of money (which he quickly drank and squandered) and a set of china crockery with a royal seal. He took the gift of the china home and gave it to his sister Fanny, who promptly threw it on the floor where it smashed! Life had been difficult during the war, with Fanny struggling under the weight of family responsibility as well as care for the local poor. She had battled on and yet here was a brother, the story went, who had been blessed with good fortune and was unwilling to share it, save for a few pieces of tableware.

Whatever the truth, Issy left Egypt bound for London and, according to his service records, was officially home (back at the barracks) on 12 February 1919. Yet apparently, four days earlier on 8 February 1919, he had married Elsie Porteous McKechnie at the Camberwell Registry Office, with Issy's good friend Alf Burley and Elsie's sister Flora as witnesses.

Issy recorded his details as Israel Shimlovitz, otherwise Smith, Sergeant of the Royal Engineers VC, bachelor and plumber, residing at 7 Vivian Road, Peckham. He listed his father, Moses Shimlovitz as also otherwise Smith, deceased, with the former occupation of tailor (even though from family accounts, Moses' job was simply to push the machine pedal for Eva with his one good leg!).

There has been much thought as to why Issy gave just his Hebrew name of Israel (and not Ishroulch) and more curiously, his surname as Shimlovitz. Perhaps this was an error on the part of the person completing the certificate that Issy, in his typical fashion, did not correct.

Despite Elsie disowning her father in 1911 and claiming she had no parents, she nonetheless recorded her father John on the certificate, listing his profession as coach painter. Although she also had an occupation as a seamstress, she did not note it. Strangely, she put her age as 25, yet she was four months short of turning 27. Issy recorded his age as older, 29, although he would not celebrate that milestone until September of that year. The reasons for the anomalies are mystifying.

On the paperwork, the words '…according to the rites and

ceremonies of the...' were crossed out, and replaced with '... by the certificate before me'. In the following month, on 23 March, the marriage of Israel Smith VC and Elsie Porteous McKechnie was solemnised by Jewish rites at the United Synagogue London.[2]

Being an Orthodox congregation, Elsie would have had to satisfy the requirements of Jewish Law, or *Halacha*, in order to marry there. To do this she had to convert to Judaism, though for an Orthodox conversion the steps were far more onerous than progressive or liberal Judaism, taking anywhere between eighteen months and five years to achieve. She had had many years to prepare, having met Issy in 1912; yet it is possible there was some flexibility extended by the rabbi, given the Great War and Issy's VC.

The couple lived at Peckham for a short time before moving into 30 Navarino Mansions, a group of tenement blocks opposite and just metres from Issy's old school in Sigdon Road, Hackney. The Mansion buildings, developed as an estate for Jewish artisans from the East End, were built by a company founded by Sir Nathan Rothschild.[3]

On 30 April Issy was discharged from the army, having served a total of fourteen years and 241 days. In addition to his earlier medals, he received several more – the 1914–15 Star, the British War Medal and the British Victory Medal.

The 1914–1915 Star was given to soldiers for various theatres of war between 5 August 1914 and 31 December 1915 – in Issy's case, most notably for his participation in the Western European theatre in France and Belgium, where he was awarded his VC. Although it included Mesopotamia in the Asiatic theatre, he would not have received the medal for that purpose as it was issued for a period prior to his arrival there. Interestingly, though, it also included German New Guinea from September to November 1914, although Issy's involvement is this campaign is still shrouded in mystery.[4]

The British War Medal 1914–1918 was given by King George V to mark the end of the war. The Allied countries decided to each award a victory medal to commemorate the Allied victory over the

Central Powers – Issy therefore received the British Victory Medal as well.⁵

While Issy elected to leave the army (again), Alf continued on, based at Aldershot. On 31 July, just a few months after Issy and Elsie's nuptials, Alf married Flora in Wandsworth London.

But despite the euphoria of the war's end and the celebrations (at long last) of the two marriages, the year took a downward turn. Elsie's sister Isabella died suddenly, a loss compounded by the death of their brother Norman two years earlier, and Issy became very ill.⁶

While records indicate that Issy suffered episodes of ague (chills and fever, which he believed to be due to malaria), the nature of Isabella's malady isn't documented. What is known is that at the time Europe was in the grip of the Spanish flu, with some autopsies on soldiers revealing malaria and influenza as dual infections.

The first wave of flu had reached London the previous year in June 1918, having travelled south from Glasgow. It appeared to be almost gone by August, but a second more deadly wave hit in mid-September.

Across the water in France, soldiers who caught a mild version of the 'three-day fever' in the cramped conditions of the trenches stayed where they were and recovered quickly.⁷ But those who contracted the more virulent version were escorted out on carts, through villages and to makeshift hospitals where the deadly disease spread. Female employees were warned not to wear 'pneumonia' blouses, while sick workers in munition factories were told to push on to keep up with the insatiable demand, but if continuing became impossible they were sent home on the tram.⁸ Returned soldiers, arriving back on cramped troop ships, were met by patriotic crowds who lined the streets to welcome and thank them for fighting so hard for their liberty. The flu travelled like an invisible enemy, from ports and railway stations to cities and suburbs and out into the countryside.

Hospitals were overwhelmed, resources stretched thin by the sheer numbers of cases as well as the lack of hospital staff; nearly half the doctors and nurses were still away on military service as war wounds did not simply disappear with the signing of an armistice. The difficulty in obtaining a doctor, for those who could afford one, coupled with the speed at which victims were infected, caused a significant increase in deaths. Many soldiers who had survived four years of horrific warfare died on their return within weeks, unable to beat the infection. The elderly, the young and the healthy fell ill, with no one exempted. Such was the number of fatalities that one London workhouse reported at its guardians' meeting that 'amongst the victims were the majority of the Board's workmen, including joiners, the result being that there was no one there to make coffins.'[9]

When Issy arrived in London at the end of January 1919, a third and only marginally less deadly wave began. Just as citizens should have been rejoicing with a fanfare of postwar activities, town halls and entertainment venues closed and public gatherings shut down. Whether this changed his wedding day in February from a significant event to a small gathering cannot be determined conclusively, but knowing Issy's private nature, it is unlikely to have affected it.

The pandemic most certainly inhibited the recognition and celebration of many other soldiers' days in the spotlight. From February to May, the influenza catatonia spread through Great Britain with no resistance and many public events were cancelled. Manufacturers were forced to curtail their production and some businesses shut up shop as staff took sick. Schools closed their doors after children succumbed.

A variety of treatments were proposed. Some were widely promoted: brisk walks, a good night's sleep, porridge, carbolic soap, Dr William's Pink Pills and Venos Lightning Cough Cure, to name a few.[10] Whisky or brandy were also highly recommended, but like doctors, were hard to come by. As a teetotaller, this did not help Issy.

There were also some strange and highly questionable remedies: electric shock treatment, eating raw onions and soaking beds with cold water. In some factories and public places, no smoking rules were relaxed in the belief that cigarettes could somehow prevent infection by being a germicide. Issy was a heavy smoker and may well have followed this advice. Yet his throat and lungs, damaged from the effects of chlorine gas, could not deal effectively with smoke nor flu, nor indeed any other disease with respiratory implications.

Not that a great deal could be done about it. Healthy or not, everyone – including Issy – had to weather the storm and wait until the dreadful flu had run its course.

Chapter 21

Postwar Slide

A flu pandemic and a serious health issue were not the only tumultuous events Issy encountered in 1919. The country he had returned to, after the turmoil of world war, was in revolt.

Since his arrival, Britain had been rocked by violent strikes and race riots from merchant seamen, dockers, engineering workers and the army – all seeking restitution for a host of grievances, including pay, working hours and living conditions.

Less than two weeks after the signing of the Armistice on 11 November 1918, Prime Minister Lloyd George announced that the task was 'to make Britain a fit country for heroes to live in.' The perception for many of those returning from war the following year, however, was that this was a project that hadn't even started.

For the soldiers, the discovery that migrant labour had filled jobs to make up for war service caused anger. Frustration grew with the delay in being demobilised, a task that was moving at snail's pace (Issy's took three months). But compounding their angst was the government's suggestion that conscripted troops be sent to Russia as military intervention against the Bolsheviks, to crush a tide of communism they feared might sweep across Europe. This wasn't a 'return to a fit country as heroes', this was more of the same – ongoing war. Tired and embittered, they reeled with horror. Desperate to be relieved of duty, they mutinied.

On 7 February 1919, the day before his wedding day, such an

example of mutiny occurred. Issy, currently a quartermaster sergeant while awaiting his demobilisation, was at Victoria Station in London coordinating a large party of soldiers who had been on leave and were returning overseas. The men had gathered at the station as required, but due to stormy weather in the Channel, the leave boat was cancelled. Unfortunately, this fact wasn't conveyed to the military authorities in time for them to make alternative arrangements. The 1,600 men were now stranded in town.

On learning of this news, the soldiers were furious. Having spent most of their money during their leave, it appeared that they would now need to spend the night in the overcrowded city using their own resources – an unpleasant prospect. A demonstration was staged at the Railway Transport Office before the men marched to the War Office and then on to Horse Guards Parade, where they held a meeting. Apparently, a similar problem had occurred the previous week, and those men had been given seven days' new leave. The same privilege was demanded.

Two major generals and a brigadier general explained to the soldiers that a block of hostels had been made available where they would get a meal, a bed and a hot shower. Issy made a speech urging them to take up the offer, but the men, seeing only his Inland Water Transport badges on his shoulder straps, howled him down, assuming him not to be an army soldier but entirely responsible for the boat cancellation. Already aggrieved at the delays in being demobilised, they eventually calmed down and boarded the waiting lorries after being given a guarantee that those with immediate demobilisation papers would be processed the next day.[1]

Problems, though, were not limited to soldiers – unhappiness spread like the flu. Waves of strikes, or the threat of strikes, began for more industries – steel, railways and transport workers as well as miners, cotton workers, bakers and renters. On 31 July, the day of Alf and Flora's wedding, even the police held a strike. By now Issy had been demobilised but this did not prevent him from being recalled and issued with a police truncheon to help keep the peace.

The boycott went for several days; whether he was called away during the wedding festivities we will never know.[2]

All of these revolts put the government on high alert – the overall disorder, they believed, was not just disorientation and dissatisfaction after four years of war, but the beginnings of an uprising not unlike the overthrow of Russia just two years earlier. As riots broke out, protesters clashed violently with police; by midyear, Britain was in the midst of its own 'Red Summer'.[3]

For Issy, finding peace and regular employment was going to be a struggle.

✢

In August, in the midst of the turmoil, a letter reached the Smith household. Addressed to I. Smith Esq., VC, it read as follows:

>The Gas Light and Coke Company
>Gas Sales Department
>129-131-133 Mare Street
>(Triangle) Hackney, N.E.
>August 6th, 1919
>Dear Sir
>　I beg to inform you that the company will send and exchange your Cooker free of charge, on the distinct understanding that we are not to be held in any way responsible for the explosion which happened on the 5th instant.
>　A fitter will call for the purpose of carrying out the work at the earliest opportunity.
>Yours faithfully,
>Inspector-in-charge[4]

The blast from the cooker must have given Elsie, the primary meal provider, a terrible fright. In addition to her own safety, she had another to worry about – she was now five months pregnant.

According to the baby, who wrote about her own childhood some 70 years later, the pregnancy wasn't good news. Expectant mothers were not to be seen in public and were to hide themselves at home until after the birth. Even then, infants were not to be brought out on show until they were healthy enough; their attendance at formal events was generally frowned upon, if not forbidden. Olive Hannah, a huge 14½ pounds, had bronchial and eczema problems from the start and the doctors recommended Elsie have no more children. The arrival of a sickly child in the midst of a dreadful pandemic meant the baby would be confined to the flat in Navarino Mansions where she'd been born. Elsie had been looking forward to a plethora of high society functions and gala events in recognition of Issy's prestigious award. For a while they had a nanny and her sister Flora to help; however, for the most part Elsie remained at home and Issy attended without her.

But before social festivities could be enjoyed, Issy's pressing requirement was to find a job. As the flu began to decline in the second half of 1919, existing businesses reopened and new ventures started up, mostly funded by private investors whose entrepreneurial initiatives had been stifled during the war. For those who had made good money manufacturing supplies for the war effort, life couldn't be better and they did their best to capitalise on it – jazz clubs and cocktail bars flourished. Issy became the manager of a London nightclub that entertained aristocracy and wealthier classes from a new generation keen to throw off all encumbrances and misfortunes of the war. The story has it that one of the club's most frequent regulars was Edward, Prince of Wales, who enjoyed the nightlife and the ladies. Apparently, his visits ended abruptly when his mother, Queen Mary, learned that he was using the upstairs rooms to consort with some of his female friends. The club was shut down and Issy found himself out of work.[5]

Not long after, Issy obtained employment as a representative for T. Davies & Co. Cycles, with the company proudly reporting in a local newspaper that he was likely the only member of the cycle trade who had earned the VC.[6] Originally the manufacturer of bicycles, accessories and rubber goods, the company, cognisant of the rapid growth in motor vehicles, had moved instead into the sale of British and Continental tyres. In December 1919, when Olive was born, Issy listed his occupation on the birth certificate as 'Motor mechanic, traveller, ex-Army'.

While the automotive industry was growing and car manufacturers had initially enjoyed a postwar upturn, progress was slow. The next year, as Britain's postwar debts began to bite, the purchase of motor cars, already beyond the reach of most, became a discretionary item for the wealthy few. As sales stagnated there was little need for tyres, and Issy found himself looking for work again.

Tough conditions, however, were not limited to this industry alone. A serious recession had hit the economy and public spending on a raft of new projects was cut. The percentage of those employed, which at the end of the war had been nearly three-quarters of the working population, dropped sharply as manufacturing seemingly vanished overnight.[7] To make matters worse, inflation had more than doubled since before the war and the value of the pound sterling had crashed.

Returned soldiers with disabilities found the going especially tough. Initially, for those with low level disabilities there was some hope of a job, but even that soon dried up. The severely disabled were out in the cold.

With so many disabled soldiers unable to work and needing ongoing medical care, the heavily burdened government managed its war pensions carefully, based on the level of impairment.[8] Aside from his decoration pension of 3s 6d per week, Issy received a 9s 4d per week disability war pension, levelled at 20 per cent impairment, as a result of the gassing and malaria acquired from service; Elsie was not eligible. The total, being 12s 10d, was the equivalent of just one day's wages for a skilled tradesman and hardly enough for a family of three to live on. An urgent reassessment of the family's future prospects was required.

But rather than join the long queues of desperate men and watch his savings whittle away, Issy had an idea. Australia had previously been fruitful for him, and he had acquaintances in Victoria who might have contacts. He decided to take a gamble and make a whirlwind trip there. If work could be secured, he would seek repatriation and return with Elsie and Olive. He would take a chance.

In early 1921 he departed from London on the RMS *Orsova*, bound for Melbourne. Having been commandeered during the war as a troopship, *Orsova* was now refitted as a magnificent ocean liner and was back operating a passenger service from London to Australia. Not surprisingly, Issy recorded his age on the manifest as 26 years (this time several years younger than on his marriage certificate) and his occupation as a mechanic.

RMS *Orsova*'s journey would take it firstly to Fremantle, Western Australia, then anti-clockwise around the country, stopping at Adelaide, Melbourne and Sydney before its last port in Brisbane, Queensland, on its return to England.[9] A celebrity on board always attracted great attention and it wasn't long before Issy was the hero of the children, who were delighted with his efforts to amuse them. He became a leader of all their sports and, accompanied by Tommy Noble, a champion English bantam-weight and the winner of a lightweight belt in New York, gave 'spirited exhibitions' before training a number of the boys in boxing.[10]

Word of his trip to Australia quickly spread, reaching *The Daily Telegraph* and *The Sun* newspapers in Sydney on the other side of the country the day after he docked in Fremantle.[11] In all, 32 papers in nearly every state from the cities to outback country towns heralded his arrival. Many reported him to be the first Jewish person to win the coveted Victoria Cross and nearly all sprouted the yarn – under big bold banners – that Baron Rothschild had given him £5000 in 1924 war bonds and that he had received other gifts totalling £11,000. He would settle in Melbourne, they announced.

Issy was forced to repudiate the claims, contradicting the rumours of the money from Baron Rothschild and the other significant sums. 'I'm far from being a millionaire,' he argued. With respect to his travel, he would probably settle in Victoria but had not definitely made up his mind, determining rather to settle in whichever state he could get the most suitable employment (although he had many friends in Melbourne).[12]

The Truth newspaper in Sydney, being a sensationalist paper that delighted in startling its readers, reported a few days later that 'Issy Smith V.C., who has returned to his old job of gas-fitting, informs all and sundry that the only reward he received was from the Metropolitan Gas Company, for whom he worked prior to 1914.'[13]

Issy arrived in Adelaide on 25 April 1921. A special court was held at the Outer Harbour Police Station that night to hear the case of four young men who, finding it difficult to obtain work in Fremantle, had stowed away on the *Orsova* for that leg of the trip. Issy, having being a stowaway himself more than once, offered to pay their passage, but the captain refused. The men needed to learn they could not travel for free and were each fined £2 10s costs plus the £5 fare, with seven days' imprisonment on default.

Issy disembarked in Melbourne a few days later. He visited his old employer, the Metropolitan Gas Company, and arranged for his prewar position to be kept open during his absence in England. He also attended the office of the Department of Repatriation and lodged an application for free passage to the Commonwealth for Elsie and Olive to join him and reside in Australia; he also applied for a War Service Home. For the very first time, he listed his date of birth on official papers as 18 September 1888.

Reaching Brisbane on 16 May, he was in time to rejoin the *Orsova* (being recorded as a gasfitter, aged 33). On his return to Plymouth, England, yet another newspaper proclaimed his arrival on 25 June.

Within a few weeks, the Department of Repatriation in Melbourne received a report from the Imperial Pensions Office outlining his health issues and percentage of disability. Issy, now reunited with his family in England, learned that his application for free passage had been denied. Once again, he was left pondering his family's future and how best to manage it with a health battle on his hands.[14]

The longer-term effects of his gassing, coupled with relapses of the malaria that had been giving him grief since the war, were getting worse. He now had a constant cough and shortness of breath, which was noted on his medical reports as emphysema, and from time to time bouts of fever forced him to bed. Any work was hard to find, but work for an ill soldier – even a highly decorated one – was harder still. The days of hero worship were gone, and in the struggle for existence it was every man for himself. With so many desperate yet able-bodied men also searching, the chances were little better than finding a black cat in a coal cellar.

On 29 December a new medical report by the Re-Survey Board downgraded his disability to temporary and from a previous 20 per cent incapacity to now less than 14 per cent. His pension, which had been adjusted accordingly and was already minimal, was reduced. Issy lodged an appeal.

Somehow his plight became known, with one paper expressing their bewilderment.

> It is surprising to read in the Jewish press that Mr Izzy Smith, the Jew who obtained the Victoria Cross during the war, finds himself in great distress and approaching destitution in consequence of being unable to obtain a livelihood. This, I understand, is in great part due to his state of health, consequent upon being gassed. When one considers the enthusiasm he evoked but a few short years ago, when the country's highest recognition for war bravery was conferred upon him, how he was declared to have brought un-dying glory upon the Jewish community, and how his name was always thrown with triumphant scorn at anyone who alleged that Jews were no good as soldiers or too cowardly to fight – it does not do the Jewish community credit that Smith is now compelled to seek charity.[15]

On 18 January 1922, two newspapers reported that a fund had been started to raise money for him, and to date it had accumulated £50. Others caught on, and on 10 March the *Hebrew Standard* reported that:

> Private Issy Smith, when he won the V.C. in the early days

of the Great War, was much feted at the time of his decoration, but has been much neglected since ... Word has come through that the one-time hero is now in very straitened circumstances, and that there is sickness in the family. His income from the government is about six shillings a week, and a fund has been started to raise enough money to start him in business that he might be able to keep his wife and family in a decent way ... It is hoped that the response to this appeal may be a fitting one, and that the promises made to our men that they would be well looked after be redeemed in the case of Private Issy Smith, V.C.[16]

Issy was able to keep his family afloat through the donations, however by March his health had deteriorated further. On top of the lung issues, he complained of constant headaches, fever and dizziness, trembling hands and pains down his left side. To compound matters, his nose and throat were inflamed and congested from septic tonsils, inducing bronchitis. A specialist recommended that his nose be operated on.

No surgery was performed, but at the next medical assessment in April his existing disabilities were returned to 20 per cent.

The infection gradually subsided and later that month, feeling a little better and with the charity money to assist him, he secured a job as assistant manager at one of the variety stage London halls, supporting a Mr Freeman, manager of The London, Shoreditch, at the front of house.[17]

In August 1922, he was able to make the pilgrimage to Ypres on the anniversary of the third battle there.

On his return, Issy became the secretary of The London Music Hall Christmas Fund, a committee formed 'To provide boots and clothing for the Poor Children of the District'. In December of that year, he arranged for the hall to be provided cost-free so that a series of concerts could be held. Boots and clothing were indeed purchased and given to the children from the money raised.[18]

By early the following year, his health had worsened again and he had to abandon his employment at the hall. A medical report noted that his fingernails were 'clubbed', that is, enlarged at the ends – a condition often associated with chronic disease of the heart and lungs. But there was far worse to come. He was now gravely ill with acute mastoiditis – an infection of the mastoid bone behind the inner ear, possibly brought on by the earlier untreated contagions.

In the 1920s this was a frightening matter. Patients with serious infections at that time found their health and lives imperilled; with antibiotics not yet developed, the risk of the spread of infection was high and could be difficult to stop, leading to catastrophic outcomes. To compound matters for Issy, the money for treatment had to be found. But there was no time. Immediate surgery was required to drain the ear and prevent further repercussions such as a brain abscess, meningitis or death.

On 23 January 1923, a Dr Francis Muecke operated. Dr Muecke, who was born in Adelaide, Australia, had trained at the Adelaide University and worked at the hospital there before moving to England. When war broke out he had joined the army before transferring to the RAF as a lieutenant-colonel. Now working as a surgeon in the Ear, Nose and Throat department of the Maudsley Hospital (which had been requisitioned by the War Department and was operating as a military hospital), he treated the critically ill Issy and saved him.

Much later, in 1935, Dr Muecke arrived in Adelaide on the passenger vessel *Aorangi* for an international medical conference of several hundred doctors from the British Medical Association. Issy, who had by then moved to Australia, heard of the trip and was one of the first to board the ship to see him. Overcome by emotion he welcomed him and shook his hand warmly.

'I am very glad to see you, laddie,' said Dr Muecke. 'I appreciate your action very much.'

The press was quick to note the event, with multiple papers reporting two separate incidents of Issy either being dangerously ill with merely hours to live and being operated on by Dr Muecke, or, alternatively, being badly injured during the course of winning his VC in 1915 and the surgeon saving his life by removing a piece of shrapnel from his skull.

They got at least one fact right. The two men shook hands.[19]

Chapter 22

The Royal Smack and Other Noble Events

Times may have been tough, but in among Issy's ill-health and the heartache of a deepening depression, there were periods of shining light.

On 20 June 1920, Issy joined more than 300 VCs, referred to affectionately as the Column of Courage, as they marched from Wellington Barracks in London to Buckingham Palace. Crowds lined the streets, dismissing the wretched shadow of the Spanish flu and shouting cheers at the heroes as they paraded by – Navy first, then Army and then Air Force. According to a local reporter, the men 'seemed to be divided between the necessity of march discipline and the desire to show the crowd which was honouring them in no uncertain manner that they appreciated the applause'. Many of the VCs, he went on, were recognised individually by the audience; but those who did not know 'were helped to knowledge by representatives of the Services who were present in large bodies'. Issy had worn four wound stripes, and as he marched a large Jewish gathering shouted for him.[1]

The heroes proceeded to Buckingham Palace, where a garden party had been arranged. King George V and Queen Mary, who had been waiting on the balcony, met the men on the terraced steps to the lawns. Each of the heroes was personally presented to the King, who apparently closely questioned those who had left the army about how they were now faring. Elsie and six-month-old Olive, surprisingly a guest, waited in the grounds for the party to start.

And so as the story goes, written a half dozen years later by a journalist with more than a hint of poetic licence, Issy and Elsie had been talking quite naturally with the King and Queen in the gardens when Olive, attracted by something sticking to the Queen's veil, leaned forward to pick it off. As Mary stepped back, George waved an admonishing finger at the baby while simultaneously announcing to her that she was a very naughty girl. He then took Olive, turned her over and administered a playful smack. Returning her to her mother, he told Olive, 'You won't remember this, so I will send you a note to remind you how naughty you were.'

In due course a messenger from Buckingham Palace arrived at Issy's home, with a certificate that read:

> This is to certify that Olive N. [sic] Smith was a naughty girl on the occasion of Their Majesties' garden party to the V.C. winners, held at Buckingham Palace.
>
> (Signed) George R.I.

The document was since held, the journalist concluded, at the home of Olive's grandparents in London.

If indeed there was such a letter residing with her grandparents, it could only have been with John, Elsie's father; but as the two were not on speaking terms, more than likely it was a conclusion concocted by the writer.[2]

Based on this news story, the incident might well have been considered pure fabrication if it wasn't for another account of it, discovered much later and buried in an unrelated article. This time it was told by Issy himself. Upon being welcomed to Adelaide in September 1927, Issy had been pressed by a reporter, as usual, for the intricacies on how he won his coveted VC. After shaking the question off with 'I could not leave the poor chap – he was one of ours', he then offered the following entirely unrelated event:

> My wife and I were invited to Buckingham Palace, and we took our six-months' old baby with us. At first we could not

pass the gate with her, but eventually, after much persuasion we succeeded in getting her past the palace watchdogs. The Royal Family made a tremendous fuss of her, especially the Queen.

Her Majesty was holding her in her arms when baby suddenly made a dart at the spotted veil the Queen was wearing. There was a rending sound, and a large portion of the veil came away in her fist. Her Majesty took it all in good part, and the King playfully smacked baby's face. He added that the incident should be preserved until the young woman reached the age of more discretion. So the story was written, and signed by His Majesty.

The reporter went on to note:

> As an outcome of that memorable meeting Princess Mary sent Baby Smith a doll for Christmas. She has taken an interest in the family ever since, and Mr Smith was invited to both her wedding and that of her brother, the Duke of York.[3]

Decades later baby Olive, by then a young mother herself, related the story of the gift of the doll to her own children.[4]

By the 1920s, association with royalty was no longer so extraordinary. Arising out of the ashes of war came a mixing of the different classes, from workers to high society, that changed the social landscape. Living and fighting shoulder to shoulder in the trenches had levelled the field – now a man from humble beginnings and an unequally, often poorly-acknowledged religion was proudly accepted into high society.

On 28 February 1922, Issy and Elsie did indeed attend the marriage of Princess Mary, the third child and only daughter of King George V and Queen Mary, to Viscount Henry Lascelles, the elder son of the 5th Earl of Harewood. It was a gala affair – the first major royal event after the war and only the second royal wedding at Westminster Abbey in over 400 years.

Then, on 26 April 1923, they were invited to another significant royal wedding. Huge cheering crowds lined the streets as the royal carriage passed on its way to Westminster Abbey. There, escorted by no fewer than eight bridesmaids, Lady Elizabeth Bowes-Lyon married Prince Albert Duke of York, the brother of Princess Mary and the second son of King George V and Queen Mary. Four years later, Issy and Elsie joined them again at a dinner hosted by the Government of Victoria in the Royal Exhibition Building in Melbourne, during the royal couple's visit to Australia.[5]

In 1936, the Duke and Duchess came to the throne as King George VI and Queen Elizabeth, the parents of the future Queen Elizabeth II.

Prior to these events, on 11 November 1920, Issy had stood at Westminster Abbey with 100 other VC recipients in a guard of honour for the body of the Unknown Warrior. This had been both a touching and sobering event, captured on film. The coffin of the unknown soldier, brought from France, was initially drawn by six black horses and led by 1,000 schoolchildren and a division of French troops amidst the calls of trumpets and bugles. Transferred via HMS *Verdun* to a 19-gun salute, the coffin had arrived in London and made its way through crowded streets to Whitehall, where it stopped in front of the newly built Cenotaph, which King George V then unveiled. The procession, which included the King, the Royal Family and Ministers of State, had proceeded solemnly to Westminster Abbey where the VC guard of honour had been waiting. Although the century-old film is blurry, it is possible to pick out Issy marching along with the other heroes.

When King George V died in 1936, Issy became a guest at the memorial service on the steps of Parliament House in Canberra.[6]

Issy also led two memorial services. On 9 August 1921, he and Sergeant Harry Kenny VC unveiled the St John at Hackney War Memorial, dedicated by the Suffragan Bishop of Stepney.[7] And in August 1922, Issy and Sir John French (known as the Viscount French and recently appointed Lord Ypres), laid a wreath at Cloth Hall, Ypres, on behalf of the Ypres League. The League, of which Sir

John was president, had been formed as a veteran's society for those who had served there. It had as its patrons King George V, Edward Prince of Wales and Princess Beatrice, the youngest daughter of Queen Victoria, who lost her own son Prince Maurice of Battenberg in the 1st battle of Ypres. Nearly 800 pilgrims travelled to the town for the commemoration. Issy had the honour of placing a wreath on the cenotaph on behalf of Princess Beatrice. The Princess had been rarely seen following her youngest son's death and was now mourning the loss of her second son Leopold who had died just a few months earlier.[8]

Yet along with all of these significant and formal ceremonies, there was one more amusing royal story. In 1929, Issy was invited to join Edward, Prince of Wales, at a dinner in London – an invitation that turned into a ludicrous debacle and made headline news. The dinner, to be held in the Royal Gallery of the House of Lords, was for recipients of the Victoria Cross. The card, embossed with the emblem of the British Legion in one corner and the bronzed VC medal in the other, read:

> His Royal Highness The Prince of Wales, Patron, Admiral of the Fleet Earl Jellicoe, President and the National Executive Council of the British Legion requests the pleasure of the company of Issy Smith, Esq V.C.

Issy, who was by this time living in Australia, also received the following accompanying letter:

> It is realised that this invitation may possibly arrive after the date of the dinner, but it is forwarded in the belief that you would like to keep it as a souvenir. A general invitation to all recipients of the Victoria Cross has, however, been circulated constantly through the press during the last three weeks.
>
> London, October 26.

Also included was a copy of the menu, program, toasts and the names of those to be present.

Extraordinary as this was, the wording of the letter, which could be interpreted as bordering on insulting, was not the main highlight. The parcel arrived seven weeks late, having roamed two countries in search of a non-existent address after the official responsible for addressing the Prince's invitations sent it to Melbourne, New Zealand. With the address written by hand, five date stamps slapped on haphazardly and red, blue and black ink as well as blue and illegible pencil scribbled all over, it read as follows:

> Not known to Post Dept Wellington
>
> Not New Zealand
>
> Try Base Records
>
> Try R.S.S.I.L.A.
>
> Not Wn. Try W4
>
> Back to Melbourne Victoria
>
> Not Wade Street Hintedartis Co (?)
>
> Try R.S.S.I.L.A. ANZAC House, Collins Street Melbourne![9]

Finally, someone suggested 'Latham House, Swanston Street, Melbourne' and that's where it turned up. It made the news in Melbourne, Adelaide and Tasmania. Later, Elsie added it to the scrapbook, where a newspaper clipping of the earlier general invitation in search of the VC holders was also placed. At the foot of that article, the text read:

'What has happened to all the V.C.s who have been lost sight of or submerged in the civilian struggle for livelihood? Where is Issy Smith, the Jewish V.C.?'[10]

Chapter 23

Desperation

For Issy, the next two years, from the start of 1923, were a battle on multiple levels.

Following the urgent surgery in January, he spent two weeks at the Central London Throat, Nose and Ear Hospital at Gray's Inn Road in London. Next, he was transferred to the London Hospital in Whitechapel to recuperate before moving to 'a mental home in Esher' for ten days, suffering 'nervous trouble'.

Whether this was a psychological wound from conflict (shell shock), the culmination of multiple traumas and stresses piled on top of one another (stacked trauma) or some other medical condition isn't clear. In any case, it wasn't short-lived. From June to November Issy became an inpatient at one of the convalescent facilities at the Queen's Hospital at Sidcup, Kent – the major centre providing plastic surgery for soldiers who had sustained facial injuries.

He then spent several months in a home for neurasthenic ex-servicemen. 'Neurasthenia', another outdated term, was used to describe a range of symptoms including physical and mental fatigue, loss of appetite, insomnia, depression and generalised aches and pains. Like shell shock, it was a common diagnosis; however, both terms were ill-defined. A review of case records suggests that shell shock was seen as a 'contagious psychological response of the weak', mostly affecting the lower ranks. Officers, on the other hand, were generally considered to have neurasthenia, requiring a transfer to specialist facilities for more gentle psychotherapeutic treatment.[1]

At the beginning of the war shell shock was not sympathetically regarded, causing much debate. Soldiers sometimes presented with hysteria, tremors, shaking or stuttering as well as loss of awareness, speech or hearing. The public struggled to understand this afflictive health issue: having been sheltered from the atrocities of war due to the strict media embargoes, it was difficult for them to fathom. 'Hearty' men with no family history of mental illness were expected to recover quickly from battle trauma and have no ongoing medical conditions. Similarly, this was an affliction that would not affect well trained and properly led men. A decorated soldier whose bravery and courage had been clearly demonstrated would certainly not suffer from it.

Within the military, there were mixed views. While some doctors felt it was due to nervous and mental exhaustion from a terrifying experience or prolonged strain or hardship, other ironhanded doctors believed that soldiers who broke down showed a lack of resolve or even cowardice, and if it was prevalent in a battalion, it was a disgrace, remediable by humiliation and punishment. In 1915, a British Army order stated that:

> Shell shock and shell concussion cases should have the letter 'W' prefixed to the report of the casualty, if it was due to the enemy; in that case the patient would be entitled to rank as 'wounded' and to wear on his arm a 'wounded stripe'. If, however, the man's breakdown did not follow a shell explosion, it was not thought to [be] 'due to the enemy', and he was to be labelled 'Shell shock' or 'S' (for sickness) and was not entitled to a wound stripe or a pension.[2]

Nevertheless, as the number of shell shock victims rose during the war and the strength of the front lines diminished, the problem could not be ignored. A new military priority grew out of necessity; more research was done and different treatments were trialled, although it remained contentious as soldiers and their doctors were often in disagreement as to the cause. Trauma therapy centres did emerge, including a mental welfare society created by Sir Frederick Milner in 1919 for neurasthenic ex-servicemen. Issy did his best to recover there before attending Queen Alexandra's Military Hospital, Millbank, situated by the River Thames.[3]

On 23 December 1923 a Special Board reassessed Issy's health with the view to a final position on the award of his pension entitlements. Earlier in the year, on 22 May, a Pensions Appeal Tribunal had been held to consider the nature of his surgery. The condition of Mastoid Septum Rhinitis was accepted and added to his disabilities of bronchitis and laryngitis from the effects of gassing, along with the malaria.

Issy described his nervous complaint and ongoing recurrences of coughing, vomiting, dizziness and attacks of malaria, while a specialist also noted nasal infection, left ear discharge and pain over the left temple. A few weeks later the Board summed up its findings, noting 'A case of slight Bronchitis and Emphysema with laryngitis and discharge from left ear. Malaria – no disability now. General condition good. Pension continued at 20 per cent rate.'

Issy returned home and the family moved to another apartment in Navarino Mansions. Life seemed promising for a while: he advised the Board that he had obtained employment as Reception Manager for the London Club, a social organisation for professional men of London. The newspapers also noted that he joined the London Lodge of the Wolves, where at their meeting of 18 January 1924, he was the only initiate for their new officers' election the following month.[4]

Unable to stand the inside work, it wasn't long before Issy became a traveller for the chocolate department of J. Lyons and Co. He was out of work for a period and then joined Eaton Chocolate in a similar capacity. In between travels, he visited the London hospital as an out-patient twice a week.[5]

Times, however, were becoming more difficult. With England's period of prosperity well and truly over, interest rates were high and British exports expensive. The impact of the significant cutbacks in investment and the lack of development in streamlining operations, particularly mass production processes, were crippling the economy. Chocolate and other gourmet goods were a luxury and sales fell. Issy, ill again, found himself once more out of work.

On 16 December 1924, at his next health reassessment, he was clearly irritable. Suffering from all of the same ailments, as well as severe headaches, sleeplessness and depression, he admitted that he had made three suicide attempts.

The medical board finalised their report. Making no mention of these serious health revelations, the documents stated that there was no evidence to connect the nervous condition with his current invaliding disabilities for which he received a 20 per cent pension. No treatment was required.

In a follow up report made a few weeks later, it was noted that his condition would become materially worse within two years. Nothing was done.[6]

Issy struggled on, but by the end of 1924 he was unemployed and out of money. With little alternative available to him, he pawned his medals – the sale netting him just £20.

News of this event hit the papers in the UK and Australia simultaneously, with headline banners such as 'VICTORIA CROSS WINNER REDUCED TO POVERTY' and 'JEWISH HERO'S PLIGHT'. In the land down under, the story reached most states, every major city and several outback towns.[7]

Back in the UK, rescue efforts were underway. A Mrs Hertz, wife of the Chief Rabbi who was President of the Jewish Historical Society of England, and a Mr Gustave Tuck stepped in to help. They set about obtaining twelve subscriptions of £10 and gave the total of £120 to Issy. Meanwhile, the medals, which had been purchased by the Society, were taken out of pawn and put on display at the Mocatta Library, University College, with the arrangement that Issy could obtain them at any time with repayment of the original amount he received for them.

Sometime later, he did just that.

The Mighty Ones

On 26 September 1924, *The Land* newspaper wrote an enlightening but unsubstantiated story, titled 'The Mighty Ones, Echoes of Ghosts':

> Ten years ago Britain drew the sword against advancing Germany and began the supreme struggle of her existence. Today the London Conference has reached agreement upon its vast problem; an invitation has gone out to Germany, and her delegates are asked to be in London tomorrow.
>
> And where to-day are the Titans of ten years ago? An English editor – Hannen Swaffer, supplies the answer. Battenberg, Fisher and Tug Wilson are dead. So are Kitchener and Roberts and Townshend. Jellicoe, in far New Zealand, engages in controversy about Jutland, while Beatty walks down Whitehall unrecognised. Few hear of the Earl of Ypres or Sir William Robertson, who writes of Prayer Book revision. [...] Izzy [*sic*] Smith, the first Jew to win the Victoria Cross, keeps order at a London dance club [while] Asquith leads a party without a policy and Lloyd George gropes for power. [...]
>
> The Kaiser is forgotten at Doorn – 'and, in the darkness where he sits, regret rebuilds its dream'.

Chapter 24

Lights! Camera! Action!

It might have been the 'Roaring Twenties' for Britain at the beginning of the decade, but by the mid-1920s the British Lion was morphing into a domestic cat, with its mighty roar diminishing to the pitiful meow of a kitten. The British economy, which had been steadily contracting, had lost its former economic predominance, and unemployment was at record levels. Thousands of families, just like Issy's, were suffering.

In April 1925 Winston Churchill, the newly appointed Chancellor of the Exchequer,[1] announced the return to the Gold Standard. This monetary system had been successful before the war in creating certainty for international trade and bringing stability with low interest rates. Although it had been abandoned to fund the war effort, there was an expectation that it would be returned to restore the economy. Setting it to its prewar rate, however, was considered by many to be a mistake. The pound was over-valued, making exports too expensive. Manufacturing demand fell further, along with wages, and the remainder of the decade continued with a long and painful slide into depression.

Given Issy's perilous position of ill-health and unemployment, this could have been disastrous for him, but in February of that year he was thrown a lifeline. Perhaps out of sympathy for his plight and his desperate need to pawn his illustrious medals, he was offered a part in the new upcoming comedy stage production of *Khaki*. A career in entertainment was born.

Although money was tight for many, theatre was still relatively popular and a much-needed form of relief. During the war it had been a way to escape reality, even if the production was about war itself. Many of the shows were in the form of light humour, which along with the laughter instilled a sense of pride and national unity. Even though it was now more than six years since the Armistice, a war storyline still drew the crowds, and *Khaki*, a wartime comedy, featured prominently.

Described as a 'revue without music', the show's storyline followed a man by the name of Harry Graham and his servant Josser, a gardener, who are sent by a Captain Partridge on a wartime mission so dangerous their chance of escape is remote – the purpose being so that the captain can marry Graham's wife and gain access to her forthcoming inheritance. Graham and Josser are captured by the enemy and several attempts are made by villains to kill them, but each time the comical Josser comes to the rescue to the great amusement of the audience. Exactly what part Issy played we don't know, but according to many press promotions, he and Josser, played by a Tom Heathfield, were the two leading artists. Issy 'soon became a favourite', with one paper noting that 'Sergeant Issy Smith VC, whose gallantry the public still remembers, figures in the play and was received with loud applause by the audience ...'

Khaki was performed twice nightly and generally for two weeks at a time at major theatre houses across the United Kingdom, beginning in Northern England. By May 1925 it was performing in Methyr, Wales, and by July the show had moved to Belfast, where Issy enjoyed some celebrity. He signed an autograph album with the following little rhyme:

> It's hard to lose the friends we love. We'll meet again I hope.
> It's harder still to find a towel when your eyes are full of soap.
> Sincerely Yours,

> Issy Smith VC
> Khaki Co
> Hippo, Belfast
> 23.7.25[2]

Midway through the season, in June, Issy exchanged greetings on stage with Captain James Leach, another soldier from the Manchester Regiment awarded the Victoria Cross, who was appearing in the amateur production of *A Messenger from Mars*.[3] By September the performance was in Ilford, close to Issy's home in Hackney, London. Elsie and Olive were able to rejoin him.

By the end of October *Khaki* had run its course, and Issy was now working with Eddie Fields, a popular music hall artist who was performing with his 'Rascals' band.[4] In February 1926, the two were working in Liverpool, with Issy accompanying the band in a background of 'artistic tableaux' – the theatrical technique of freezing on stage for dramatic effect. Featuring with Issy was the American actress Marion Davies, who was acclaimed for her roles in various Broadway musicals and films, particularly comedy.[5] Her notoriety had soared in 1917 when she became known as the mistress of the newspaper tycoon William Randolf Hearst. More recently, however, her name had hit headlines with the mysterious demise of film producer Thomas Ince, who had boarded Hearst's yacht on 16 November 1924 as guest of honour for his 42nd birthday – and died. Despite reports of death by acute indigestion or heart failure, rumours abounded that Hearst had accidently shot Thomas. Believing that Marion and Charlie Chaplin (also on the boat) were having an affair, he had intended to shoot Marion, Charlie or both, and in the havoc that followed, it was claimed, Ince was collateral damage.[6]

On the night of 11 February 1926, however, these rumours were forgotten and all eyes were on another celebrity couple. As the curtain dropped in preparation for the close of the second performance, the audience was taken aback by the sudden invasion of members of the cast in an impromptu act. From one side, dressed as a drum major, came one of the main actresses, leading another dressed as a blushing bride with an old curtain as a veil. From the other wing and to the music of 'Welcome the Bride' came Eddie Fields with his best man, Issy. A rushed, comic 'ceremony' was performed and the stage couple (with a stand-in for the real bride) blew kisses and waved, under a shower of confetti, to the roar of cheers from delighted patrons.

The pantomime caused a British media sensation. Rumours had been circulating of Eddie's courtship of Josephine Trix (real name Josephine Yeiser), one half of the famous Trix Sisters who were performing at the London Apollo, although to date anything more than courtship was pure speculation. The sisters were an American vaudevillian double act at the height of their careers in London. Having begun in New York, they had honed their skills in the USA and Canada before finding fame in Paris in cabaret, with recordings now selling all over Europe. Josephine, who had stunning looks, a beautiful soprano voice and a flawless dance routine, was often billed as 'The Sweetheart of London' and was in great demand.

'We met for the first time four weeks ago …' said Eddie to a local paper.

> It was a case of love at first sight, and on 5 February we were married at Holborn Registry Office, with only Sergeant Smith V.C. present as a witness. We determined to keep everything secret; not even Miss Trix's sister and partner, Helen, knew anything about it.[7]

A journalist, eager to get the full story, immediately contacted the sisters after the startling reveal. He reached Helen, but to both their surprise, she still knew nothing of the marriage, despite it being a week after the actual event.

'It is quite likely,' she said. 'We know Mr. Fields, but my sister has said nothing to me.'[8]

Helen was reported to be furious and the famous Trix Sisters broke up, not reconciling again until 1928.[9]

Eddie continued performing with the Rascals, but Issy's role with the band was short-lived. Soon after the wedding exposé, he was employed by Gaumont-British, one of the largest film producers and cinema chain in the country, to work on the film *Mademoiselle from Armentieres*.

Films were big business. Cinema venues and patron attendances, which had been building steadily before the war, were now rebounding and outstripping the demand for music halls and theatre. Sound film ('talkies') had not yet arrived but cinema entertainment was popular, with some film fans going as often as three to four times a week. It was not just for its affordability; Hollywood studio productions were capturing the fascination of British audiences.

This foreign novelty was, however, reaching an alarming level. According to the Board of Trade, British films had comprised about 25 per cent of all films prior to the war – now in 1926 they had fallen to 5 per cent.[10] More British productions were desperately needed for jobs and the economy. The war theme was still one of the best paths to a box office winner; having previously inspired patriotism, it now conveyed a heroic message of victory while also helping bereaved families feel comforted that their loved ones were not forgotten.

Filmmakers approached the British government seeking financial cooperation, and when this was granted, several companies went into production simultaneously. Issy soon found himself involved in two productions, joining the set of *Mons*, made by British Instructional Films, as well.

Government guidelines stipulated that the pictures not be unnecessarily exaggerated and that every person employed in them must have taken an active part in the war. Everyone connected with the production of *Mademoiselle from Armentieres* was an ex-serviceman – this was apparently achieved with all 10,000 men except one, a man who was blind in one eye and could not enlist. Issy played the part of a platoon sergeant.

According to press reports the whole film, with the exception of a scene at Buckingham Palace, was made in just six weeks. In one particular piece of filming, Issy's mixed platoon of soldiers/actors were sandwiched between two regular companies of soldiers. When a director's request to move to the left was given, the company officers barked the command in typical army style: 'A Company! Move to the left in fours – form fours – left! B Company! Move to the left in fours – form fours – left!' Issy's actors had no place in the battalion formation but Issy did not miss a beat. 'Gaumont Company! Move to the left in fours – form fours – left!' he shouted, and his group moved with matching precision.

By July word was out that *Mademoiselle from Armentieres* was in the making and newspapers reported that Issy was taking part. The film was released in September, and across the country it was widely promoted as 'the most thrilling British film of the war yet produced'. Issy and another veteran, Colonel English DSO, were listed in the advertisements along with Estelle Brody, an up-and-coming star. By November, the film had been sold to France, Belgium, Holland, Switzerland, Spain, Portugal, Burma, Ceylon, Egypt, Australia, New Zealand, South Africa and India. It was later picked up by Metro-Goldwyn-Mayer (MGM) in America. One newspaper reported that the figure paid for the Australian rights was the largest Australia had ever paid for a British film.[11]

The producers were keen to describe the film as a 'soldier's story' with 'a quality of reminiscence', however a little scuttlebutt gave it more spice. The film was loosely based on a wartime trench song of the same name, made popular with marching British soldiers. The song, however, had many versions, some with risqué lyrics deemed not fit for polite company! And then there was the scandal of the mademoiselle, a lady purported to be 'of uncertain age and doubtful virtue'. Rumours circulated that 'mademoiselle' – who in the film is a French woman who falls in love with a British soldier and feeds misinformation to a German spy – was actually a living person who kept an *estaminet* (a shabby café) and acted as a real spy. The public were eager to know who the real mystery woman was and interest in the film flourished.[12]

In the same month, *Mons* was also released. Labelled as a Great War epic, it too was a silent film, this time based on the August 1914 battle and retreat of Mons, one of the earliest confrontations of the war. Like *Mademoiselle from Armentieres*, the film aimed to be a convincing and accurate representation of war made using ex-servicemen. Every actor had had army service, as required, and the War Office had granted access to all official records to enable the scenes to closely mirror actual events. Others involved in the production but not acting in it directly were also ex-army and contributed their war experiences. It is not known what role Issy played.

Yet there was a slight difference between the making of the two productions. The director of *Mons*, a Captain Walter Summers DSO, MC, MM had actually fought in the battle. He enlisted as many of the survivors who had fought with him as he could find and, interwoven with the story, had them relive their actions with daring manoeuvres that included the blowing up of bridges.[13]

Of course, the making of war films with realistic looking action drama came with inherent dangers and didn't always go to plan. Leonard Keysor, the third Jewish VC beneficiary, was injured on the film set of *For Valour* while re-enacting his part at Gallipoli where he earned his decoration. In a trench scene he was picking up and throwing back bombs, just as he did in the war, when a flash-powder dummy bomb exploded in his face. He was knocked unconscious, one eye blinded temporarily, his jaw fractured, a tooth broken and his arms and legs peppered with cuts and burns causing more than 150 lacerations.

A year later, Leonard sued the producer. He argued that he'd been told the filming would be perfectly safe, and yet smoke bombs had been thrown carelessly into the trench and the electrical timing of explosions of gunpowder was faulty. It had taken him five and a half weeks to recover and, despite an operation on his jaw, his mouth was permanently disfigured. He was awarded £675 in damages.[14]

Chapter 25

The Lure Down Under

During 1926, Issy attended a number of functions, including a sports day for the Lancashire Fusiliers in commemoration of the landing at Gallipoli and an awards night run by the Berner Street Old Boy's Club.[1] But behind these community attempts to lift spirits and boost morale was an underlying fear. Prices were continuing to rise, work was getting harder to find and poverty for many was a very real possibility. After the success of the Bolsheviks in Russia in 1917, the threat of revolution and communist uprisings still prowled in the undergrowth.

In May 1926 the miners, whose pay had fallen dramatically from immediate postwar levels, went on strike. Faced with longer working hours and more wage cuts that brought them to the poverty line, they marched through the cities, joined by workers from buses, trains and docks, from steel, building and iron works and from printers, electricity and gas companies. Large processions advanced, waving red flags, chanting slogans and clashing with the police. The government called for thousands of special constables and two battalions of guards to help control the crowds and safeguard food supplies picketed by strikers at the London Docks. After nine days the strikes were called off and miners received even lower wages and longer hours than before. The fight for improvements to working conditions had amounted to nothing, and welfare queues grew.

Hardship was felt not just by the miners but across the nation.

Whether there was no more film work for Issy or he simply grew tired of the constant struggle to find regular employment is anyone's guess. In any case, after *Mademoiselle from Armentieres* and *Mons* were released in September 1926, he applied to Australia House in London to be repatriated to Australia. This was the lucky country, where business was booming and the standard of living was reaching lofty heights.

But if he thought repatriation was going to be easy, he was to be bitterly disappointed.

When war was declared in 1914, Issy had returned to England as an Imperial Reservist. From the beginning, pay and conditions had been better for Australian soldiers than for their British comrades, and in 1919 the Australian Federal Government had promised the same advantages for returning Imperial Reservists resident in Australia prior to the war. Unfortunately, this promise hadn't passed smoothly to the Repatriation Department and in 1919-20, reservists faced a common problem trying to access the offer. There was a great deal of confusion regarding entitlements, and if Issy had sought to resolve this directly with the department during his whirlwind visit in 1921, he had failed. In 1926, he was still trying to negotiate with the Australian authorities in London.

The Australian newspapers, which had been quick to claim him as one of theirs on the announcement of his VC, soon caught on and printed details of his predicament.

"REPATRIATION PROBLEM' and 'V.C. SHUTTLECOCK WANTS TO COME BACK' the headlines claimed; the stories going on to report (incorrectly) that he had been repatriated to Australia after the war, had returned to England in 1922 and was now wanting to return again. Perhaps it was assumed that his brief visit in 1921 had been a permanent stay followed by a change of mind and he had simply returned to the Mother Land; regardless, the false assumption of being repatriated twice was reported and the articles noted that: 'He is now ineligible for repatriation or an assisted passage because he is married.'

Marriage may well have been the issue. Following the war there had been a hurried flood of brides after the Australian Government made an offer of free passage to wives of Australian soldiers who married before 1 September 1919. So many jumped at the offer that the situation became a logistical headache, with 'bride ships' flowing into the country during 1919 and 1920. Where this left the Imperial Reservists wishing to return with their spouses was once again unclear – were they entitled to the same advantages as had been promised, or not?

Issy sought special consideration from the Prime Minister of Australia, Stanley Bruce, and it wasn't long before a decision was returned. 'V.C. WINNER NOT WANTED', the banners cried. 'TURNED DOWN AT AUSTRALIA HOUSE'.[2] Bizarrely, a Sydney newspaper also reported that: 'the English boxer, Issy Smith, is not to tour Australia. His recent defeat has caused his engagement to be cancelled.' Issy was not boxing at the time.[3]

One newspaper, however, highlighted the incongruity. 'It seems absurd that a man who has fought and won glory for Australia should be refused a grant that is open to any British subject who has not happened to reside here before […] Here is evidently an earnest man who wishes to return to the land for which he fought, and is refused assistance, not because he is not deserving or is not likely to make good, but because he accidently comes under a law designed for an entirely different class of person.'[4]

In January 1927, Issy returned to Australia with his family anyway, funding the passage himself with assistance from the Jewish Board of Guardians. Disembarking in Australia on 12 January 1927, he did his best to avoid the press, but there was to be no escaping them. Stepping down from the SS *Orsova*, he refused to discuss the challenges he had faced with Australia House. 'I am here now. It's all over, why talk about it?' he said. The papers, always keen for the smallest titbit of gossip for their readers, regurgitated once more the story of the illustrious Rothschild gifts promised to him. Issy was forced to debunk these claims and the papers duly printed an update.

'It had been reported previously that he was to receive the sum of £11,000 granted from various sources in recognition, but he has not had one penny of this amount.'[5]

✢

As a young child, Olive knew nothing of her father's migration troubles, but instead remembered vividly her own experience journeying out. As the ship was readying to leave England, she stood at the end of the long pier with Issy and Elsie, waiting to embark. In the distance she could make out two small figures at the water's edge, the silhouette of a man and a woman, silently watching.

Suddenly a small boy who was with them broke free and ran the length of the jetty, reaching her completely out of breath. Not much older than her, he wasted no time with greetings of any kind – instead, breathing heavily, he shoved a bunch of French comics in her hand and ran off without a word. Olive related later in life that she thought the two solitary figures were Issy's parents – her grandparents – and this was the closest they were willing to come to see their son and meet their granddaughter, now that he had married a gentile. The child, she believed, was a cousin.

One of the figures might have been Eva, Issy's mother, as it has never been proven that Eva disowned Issy – except that she never went to England. But the other certainly couldn't have been Moses – he had been dead for some twenty years. The most likely scenario was that the location was not England but in fact Port Said, a stopover on route, and Issy's sister Fanny and her husband Isaac were seeing them off. The boy was probably their son, Alfred – and indeed Olive's cousin.

Whoever it was, Olive never saw them again. The journey out was also the last time Issy would ever see his close friend and 'brother-in-law', Alf Burley.[6]

In 1925 Alf and Flora had gone to Rangoon, Burma, with A Company of the 2nd Manchester Regiment, where Alf was Company Quartermaster Sergeant. Later, A Company moved north to Mandalay.[7] The two couples kept in touch, with Elsie's sister Flora often sending gifts of brass animals, pots and beads. When Alf retired after 24 years' service, they returned to England in May 1928 and Alf took a job as caretaker at Dame Alice Owen's School for Girls in Finsbury. During the Great Depression, a visit by either was out of the question. Once Issy and Elsie departed, a ship's passage halfway across the globe for a social occasion was a luxury neither could afford.

✣

On arrival in Australia, conditions appeared to be rosy and a great opportunity for Issy and his family. Many countries had suffered as a result of the war, and although Australia had not been immune, it had fared better than most. Australian businesses had done their best to be resourceful, moving into new areas of production when international trade was disrupted and supplies had dried up. Manufacturing had been going well and, in some industries, had expanded rapidly. With more homes connected to electricity, demand for new electric appliances and other consumer goods had grown. So too, had the trade unions – the larger ones now had stronger national links.[8] The commencement of mining at Mount Isa in 1923 boosted hopes and BHP was on its way to a bumper year in steel output.

With these developments, the country was confident that growth in real estate and the rollout of public works in the form of new infrastructure would support immigration and build the economy. But by the end of 1926, the presumptions, many of which had been based on speculation, began to crumble. Commodity prices started to fall, imports flooded in and British banks warned that the high levels of borrowings for the raft of projects planned were unsustainable. By 1927, there were growing signs that the brief postwar boom was ending.

Issy arranged for the family to move into 46 Margaret Street, Moonee Ponds, a three-bedroom Edwardian terrace, and applied for a Commonwealth pension. In the meantime, a six-month advance of his existing pension was sent from the UK while the process was transferred to the Repatriation Department in Melbourne. The amount, which was still fixed at the 1921 rate of 9s 4d per week for war disabilities and 3s 6d for the VC, was now marked as final for life. With no entitlements for Elsie or Olive it was not enough to live on, and to support the family he took up work as a stove inspector with his old employer, the Metropolitan Gas Company. He also had small earnings to keep him going from *Mademoiselle from Armentieres*, which was still playing in cinemas around England. Issy joined the RSSILA and the Melbourne Hebrew Congregation in Toorak Road.[9]

Olive, now seven, was enrolled in the local school. Each day she was despatched with two lunches – one of which contained a liquorice stick. The lunch with its additional item was dutifully deposited with the headmaster, to be given to a child who would otherwise go without. As the children sat around to eat, Olive always knew which child got the meal on account of the sticky dark snack.

On 25 April 1927, commemorations were held for Anzac Day, with every state of Australia observing, collectively for the first time, a form of public holiday.[10] The Duke and Duchess of York attended, and Issy took part in a special march with the 28 other Australian VCs; a photo was taken of the line of men waiting to enter the Royal Exhibition Building for a service.[11] Another photo was taken of Issy chatting with Stanley Gibbs, a young man awarded the Albert Medal for gallantry during peacetime, who attended with them. Just a few months earlier, on 3 January, Stanley had been on a boat at Port Hacking in NSW when he heard a scream and saw that a large shark had hold of a boy in chest-high water. He immediately dived in and swam to help. Climbing onto the shark's back and grabbing its dorsal fin, he kicked and punched it until it released its grip. He managed to get the badly injured boy on board a nearby rowboat, but unfortunately, he could not be saved.[12]

By July, *Mademoiselle from Armentieres* was enjoying success in Australia, having been reported to be 'another illustration of the fact that Britain could make films equal to the world's best'. After a three-month stint at the Crystal Palace in Sydney, the film was now at the Majestic in Melbourne.[13]

The day before its private preview screening, Issy walked into the theatre's offices and said he would like to see it because he was one of the cast. As there were 10,000 soldiers in the production, no one got excited until it was discovered that this was the VC who had starred as the platoon sergeant! Suddenly there was a hunt for him in the theatre – that was different! The story, 'Leading "Armentieres" Player Found in Melbourne' became news.

He was invited the next day to join members of parliament, military and high government officials who were attending the film. A few days later, arrangements were made for him to meet with soldier inmates at the Caulfield Military Hospital and escort them to an afternoon screening. The group travelled in a fleet of all-British motor cars and Issy made an appearance on stage where he spoke about the film's production. A photo of 60 gentlemen and Issy holding their hats in front of a huge poster of *Mademoiselle* was later published in *Everyones* [sic], Australia's major film industry trade magazine.[14]

Mr Smith had appeared in twenty pictures, various papers claimed, and this was the first in which he had been given a part (or a leading role, as others suggested). He was a natural on film and caused many laughs. He had managed music halls in England and toured as a comedian in a musical comedy. Much of the humour in this film, it was said, had been provided by him.[15]

Where the story of the 'twenty pictures' came from will never be known. It would have been difficult for Issy to have been part of that many films, and there is no evidence that he was. A line in a newspaper story suggested that he appeared in *Ypres*, another production made in 1925 by Captain Walter Summers, the director of *Mons*. This would make sense, given it was the location of his heroic deed and he would have known a good deal about the battle there. Yet during that year he was mostly travelling with the stage production *Khaki*, which performed twice nightly, leaving little spare time to be on the location of another set. *Ypres* was released in October 1925, just as *Khaki* ended.[16]

Another article claimed he took part in the productions of *Every Mother's Son* and *The Flag Lieutenant*. There were two productions of *Every Mother's Son* made at the time, one in 1918 in the US (which can easily be discounted) and the other in the UK in 1926. The latter film, which is classified as a drama, has only a tenuous connection with wartime (a plot of an ex-soldier marrying his ex-sweetheart despite her having a child by a squire's dead son) and no details exist of precisely where it was filmed; it is therefore difficult to ascertain whether Issy had an involvement in it. The film *The Flag Lieutenant* (which does have a fighting plot) also had two productions, one in 1919 and the other, a longer one, in 1927. The latter film was directed by Maurice Elvey, who also made *Mademoiselle from Armentieres* that same year; both films being released in October 1927. Given it was the same producer, it is entirely possible that Issy had input in *The Flag Lieutenant* while acting on *Mademoiselle from Armentieres*; but without any further detail, this cannot be confirmed.[17]

Nevertheless, Issy was immediately engaged in Melbourne by Australasian Films, an Australian film distribution and production company, to tour with the picture and speak about aspects of the war and how the film was made. *Everyones* ran a feature article on 17 August announcing Issy's entry into the industry and his role within Australasian Films as exploitation manager for Victoria. 'By his war record and the attention his presence commands by his knowledge of production and his understanding of the human note that must be struck to win popular response, Sergeant Smith, V.C. is a notable addition to the industry's ranks,' it read.[18] The *Mirror* reported it slightly differently. 'Izzy [sic] Smith, who holds the V.C. and the medals of half a dozen European countries, has deserted his very ordinary job in the Sydney gasworks and taken on a year's contract with Union Theatres and Australasian Films boosting British pictures.'[19]

As the Majestic was not a long-run theatre like the Crystal

Palace, *Mademoiselle from Armentieres* moved progressively for short stints, and within weeks Issy found himself travelling in and out of Melbourne, giving introductions at various screenings.[20] In early August, after visiting Ballarat and Bendigo, he was in Geelong lecturing at the local theatre. While there, he was welcomed at a Diggers' reunion dinner of over 300 returned men, held by the RSSILA. General Sir John Monash, who had been one of the main organisers of the annual commemoration of Anzac Day and whom Issy knew through the Jewish community, sent his apologies for being unable to attend.[21]

By the end of September, *Mons* was screening in Australia; Issy arrived by train in Adelaide to speak about the film and the great retreat in 1914. He was greeted at the York Theatre by the Adelaide branch of the RSSILA and a representative from MGM, through whom the film had been released in Australia. Reporters trying to interview him came to the conclusion that he was 'incurably shy' after he wouldn't be pressed on his war escapades but offered them instead a funny and possibly fictitious story concerning an overdose of bully beef.[22]

Issy stayed in Adelaide for several weeks, giving an introduction to the film in afternoon and evening sessions. The Mayor and the Premier of South Australia, along with 60 members of the State Cabinet and their wives, attended one evening in the opening week. They did their best to hear, among the constant interruption of applause, the almost insurmountable difficulties Issy described occurring on set as they tried to make the film an accurate record of the event. Afterwards, the party met with him personally to express their gratitude at such 'a magnificent effort by British producers'.[23]

When the season concluded in Adelaide, Issy returned to Victoria, stopping in Portland on 22 October for a few nights while *Mademoiselle from Armentieres* was playing. He was given a civic reception by councillors and returned servicemen at the Mac's Hotel. Later, at the cinema, he gave one of his usual lectures and made an appeal for the encouragement of British productions, which he said were gradually coming into their own.[24]

On 26 October he travelled by train to Lilydale in time to meet Elsie and Olive, who had arrived to join him at a series of engagements at Healesville for the screening of *Mademoiselle from Armentieres*.[25] After speaking at the local school, a Mr Harvie, who introduced Issy, urged the children to always show preference for Empire-made pictures.

For the family, leaving Moonee Ponds on that day was perhaps a good idea. A storm had been brewing in the form of a gangland war centred around the racetracks, including nearby Flemington Racecourse. On 27 October 1927 it erupted. Joseph 'Squizzy' Taylor, a standover man with a fearsome reputation and a history of charges for assault, armed robbery and murder, was out and about in search of one of his rivals, John 'Snowy' Cutmore. At a house in Barkley Street a gunfight ensued between the men in which both were fatally injured.

A few years later, in 1930, Richard Buckley, an associate Squizzy was accused of aiding in the murder of a bank manager seven years earlier, was captured in a house in Bowen Street, Moonee Ponds, just half a mile from Issy's home.

Chapter 26

Things Don't Always Go to Plan

Travelling suited Issy. Having had a lifetime of being on the move, it took him no time at all to settle into the role of a Victorian film salesman. At the start of November 1927, he was in Wonthaggi; by the end of the first week he was in Horsham, then in Kooweerup he was on time for the Armistice memorial service on 11 November. There he was given a civic reception, where he mentioned that he was a little disappointed that he wasn't given an opportunity to speak to the children, but soon he had everyone laughing when he stated that he would be pleased to return again when he 'could buy potatoes cheap enough'.[1]

He was sent off to Echuca on 21 November with great fanfare and well wishes. A day later, at Moama, the schedule was adjusted. He was given time to speak to the children at a local primary school and his medal case was passed around for all to view. By early December he was back in Melbourne visiting the suburb of Sunshine and then it was Melton's turn, where many returned soldiers were invited to meet him in person.

Invitations didn't just extend to a meet and greet. There were welcoming fanfares on his arrival and civic receptions to follow. Generally, on the announcement of a forthcoming visit, the towns concerned got busy with preparations, publishing details in the local papers to ensure everyone got involved. On Issy's arrival in Sale on 19 December, the Gippsland Light Horse Regiment was ready, forming a guard of honour at the train station to receive him. At Traralgon, Issy's health was toasted at a dinner held by the local branch of the Returned Soldiers' League. Musical items and speeches were then rendered and partying continued into the wee hours with the final singing of 'Auld Lang Syne'. On route to his next stop at Warragul on 30 December, Issy sent a note of appreciation, one of many he did throughout his journeys, thanking the organisers for their gracious hospitality.[2]

There were also sideline events scheduled specifically for his visit. On 6 February 1928 at Wentworth, just north of Mildura and across the river into New South Wales, he was taken to see the weir and Lock 10 under construction for the Murray-Darling water system. Then, at Warracknabeal, the stakes were upped and he was met by the captain and crew of the local fire brigade in full regalia, before being loaded onto the fire engine and taken at full pelt up the street – with bells clanging and men shouting as they went! Issy was later described as being 'the acme of modesty' and quite embarrassed at the show of appreciation that continued into the evening at a public reception held for him.

A few days later at Jeparit, back in Victoria, he was a little more comfortable with proceedings. Asked to sit in the president's chair in the Memorial Hall and move a motion, he announced to the delight of the audience that the local rates, which were already very low, should be reduced to sixpence in the pound! The story was humorously reported under the heading 'Issy any good?'[3]

Of course, there were events that didn't go so smoothly. On 1 February 1928, a civic reception at Mildura organised by the RSSILA hosted Issy, along with Gustave Froelich of Germany, the world's amateur champion backstroke swimmer and H Kofler of Austria, the champion amateur diver of his country. This might have been a little awkward – but not overly problematic – until Froelich and Kofler were invited to attend a smoke social arranged specifically for Issy that evening. They accepted the offer and all hell broke loose.[4]

'TACTLESS INVITATIONS', the papers cried, prompting *The*

Age in Melbourne to print a summary of the League's meeting held immediately afterwards, in which the following motion was carried without dissent:

> That this general annual meeting of the Mildura branch R.S.S.I.L.A. deplores the extraordinary action of a member of the committee in inviting a German and an Austrian, who happened to be visiting the town, to the branch's complimentary reception to Sergeant Issy Smith, V.C. The branch, while not wishing to perpetuate war-time enmities, considers that the presence of these two visitors singularly inappropriate at such a returned soldier's gathering. That this particular instance be not permitted to be cited as a precedent, and that in future should an invitation be desired for any foreign visitors or for others who are not members, the committee shall deal with all such requests.
>
> A further motion that the vice-president who issued the invitation be asked to resign office was defeated, only three voting for it.[5]

What Issy thought of the whole affair was never recorded.

Not all was going so smoothly for Issy's daughter either. Elsie, frequently at home without Issy, had busied herself with Olive's education. Arranging for her to have additional classes out of school, Olive was taught piano, elocution, tap dancing, ballet, French, German and Latin. Elsie, being a tailoress, made costumes for her to wear at the many performances. Learning so many disciplines at once stressed the young girl, causing her bronchitis to flare and her body to break out all over in eczema, until finally she had a breakdown. On the doctor's advice she was sent to live in the country, in nearby Olinda, for twelve months.

Chapter 27

Britain vs. Hollywood

In April 1928 Issy attended the Anzac Day service in Melbourne, joining a procession of 25,000 returned soldiers who marched from Princes Bridge to a service held for them in the Exhibition Building. Once again, he made the papers on the day, this time in a photo with two men whose military ranks were not described but were simply listed as 'two old imperial men'.

For the next few months, he continued touring for Australasian Films. With Olive boarding in Olinda, Elsie was now more often by his side.

Up until the mid-1920s, the film company had been largely focused on the distribution of imported American and European films, rather than the riskier business of making their own.[1] Given the growing enthusiasm for American films, the company decided to invest in the creation of several Australian/Hollywood productions with the help of an American director and several Hollywood stars, whom they brought to Australia. *For the Term of His Natural Life* had been released in June 1927 and *The Adorable Outcast* was a current release in June 1928, but the films were not doing well.

The cost of production was too expensive and films with sound were coming which would quickly date them; so far, the company had lost £30,000. It may have been concerns over the company's financial future or the fact that *Mademoiselle from Armentieres* had wrapped up in Melbourne that encouraged Issy to jump ship – in any case, he left and joined Cinema Art Films Ltd and was duly employed as their Victorian country representative.[2]

Cinema Art was a young company, having only begun operating in late 1926 as a distributor of foreign films. The company was established as the Australian branch of British International Pictures, which had at its headquarters in Elstree, Hertfordshire, a significant film studio. However, the directors soon announced that on the whole, British films were too costly to compete successfully and they had begun securing films from UFA (Universum Film Aktiengesellschaft), a German motion-picture company based in Berlin that made exceptional silent films with artistic flair and clever camera work. 'Art films', as they became known, were more experimental and creative, and not designed for mass market appeal; UFA had been enjoying acclaim for their productions and had already distributed several films through Australasian Films, where Issy had previously worked. But by early 1927 the worldwide and increasing popularity of Hollywood films had almost driven UFA to bankruptcy; in March they were only just afloat, having been rescued by a powerful investor by the name of Alfred Hugenberg.

The German association didn't appear to be of concern to Issy, but it was not lost on one eagle-eyed newspaper. 'Thus we have the spectacle of a V.C. winner exploiting the goods hailing from the country in opposition to which he won his V.C., it read.[3]

In July 1927 Cinema Art Films announced that it had merged with UFA, along with Exhibitors' Alliance Films in New Zealand. Issy was promoted to manager. The press release stated that film producers of America and the United Kingdom were prepared to negotiate for film rights by treating Australia and New Zealand as one market. This provided more favourable terms than if the countries negotiated separately, and enabled a saving in overhead costs.[4]

That same month, the manager of Cinema Art Films, Leslie Keast, appeared before the 1926–28 Royal Commission into the Moving Picture Industry in Australia, where he was asked whether his company's promotion of German films was creating a 'German atmosphere' in Australia. He explained that the company carefully chose films focused on 'subjects we believe will elevate the industry and encourage the desire of films of an artistic nature, while of course, due regard will be given to popular pictures'.[5]

Ensuring the recognition of quality British films became Issy's number one priority. He wrote to *The Herald* about this, attaching a letter sent from America which had lauded the British film *Picadilly*, and on 13 June 1929 his communication was published:

> **BRITISH FILM PRAISED BY U.S. REVIEW BOARD**
> Put on 'Exceptional' List
> To the Editor
>
> With reference to comments in the *London Star* on British Films, of which cabled extracts appeared in *The Herald* on June 8, the following letter, sent to Mr J. D. Williams by the National Board of Review, proves that the British pictures being released in America at present are as fine as any that have ever been shown in that country.
>
> Referring to the statement by Charles Lamb, that 'British pictures are all silent and damned', I asked a wise showman the other day what he thought of the present peculiar situation in our business. He gave me this answer: 'Bricks, mortar and showmanship'. What he meant was that the show business requires fine theatres, and that, sound or silent, stage or screen, British or foreign, it takes a good showman to put the shows over.
>
> This year's British International productions are as good if not better than any silent film produced in America today.
>
> – Yours, etc.
> Issy Smith, V.C.[6]

Shortly afterwards, Issy was dealing with a challenge that had developed into a dispute dubbed the 'War of the Talkies' – the need for new technology and the fight over who could supply it.

Films were in the process of transitioning to sound. Although these were generally referred to as *talkies*, the addition of sound could relate to productions that were fully speaking *(all-talkie)*, partly speaking *(part-talkie)*, with sound effects or just with music. Regardless of the format, film projectors with sound attachments, amplifiers and speakers were required to run them. The problem was that in late 1928, the Western Electric Company (WEC), a major supplier of the equipment and one of the few commercially viable sound systems available in Australia, was too expensive for most cinemas to install and run. In addition, WEC had set up restrictive clauses in their contracts with film distributors, preventing the distributors from supplying films that did not utilise their equipment – their argument being that the films would be inadequately portrayed if shown on something else. This tactic, believed to be an attempt at a monopoly, prompted many companies around the world to urgently develop their own systems and argue for interchangeability. On 27 June 1929, Issy launched a protest, again through *The Herald*:

> Refusing to enter into any coercive agreement with the W.E.C., Mr Smith said, 'our company recently began the making of talkie films at Elstree under the R.C.A. process. By this almost miraculous method, sound vibrations on a tiny mirror, held on sensitive taut filaments, are recorded on separate celluloid strips. The most important of the completed pictures are *Kitty* and *Picadilly*, both of which, reproduced by the R.C.A. equipment, have been declared by experts as being absolutely as good as any talkie picture shown through the medium of the W.E.C. apparatus.'[7]

A day later, he followed with another article.

> We have passed years in research work, and are continuing that work. We consider we have a duty towards our shareholders who are British, and we do not admit that they should be deprived of their investments for the benefit of any body of American shareholders.
>
> By the end of this year we expect to see our machines installed in 500 theatres. They are being installed in Italy, France, Belgium and Holland. Our system was adopted by

the State-controlled Ente of Italy, after a searching examination of all other devices available.[8]

Eventually, perhaps due to industry pressure, RCA and WEC agreed to make their systems compatible, and during 1929 the RCA system arrived in Australia.

Within weeks, Issy was dealing with another problem, this time to do with film censorship offences. Electric Theatres Pty Ltd, a company owned by Hoyts and to whom Cinema Art had distributed film, was charged under the Victorian Film Censorship Act for several violations, the primary one being the screening of five films, *Red Heels*, *Body Punch*, *Moulin Rouge*, *Synthetic Sin* and *Seven Footprints to Satan*, without advertising that they were not suitable for children. Issy, whose title was described as Film Exchange Manager, explained that the stamps on some of the posters had been covered up by the frames in which the posters were displayed. This possibly negated fines for two of the films, but Electric Theatres was fined £3 for each of the other three, plus 10s 6d in costs.[9]

Yet it wasn't long before all of these challenges – 'British', 'sound' and 'censorship' would roll themselves into one and give Issy a new dilemma. *Blackmail*, the highly anticipated British thriller directed by Alfred Hitchcock for distribution in Australia by Cinema Art, was banned.

Blackmail was proclaimed to be Britain's first sound feature film and had been voted as the best British film of 1929. The banning of it in Australia in October caused a sensation and initially no one understood why, after the chief censor, Creswell O'Reilly, declined to state the reason.

It had been expected that the film would achieve record runs in Sydney and Melbourne. Britain, it was claimed, had invested enormous sums with the coming of sound technology to produce films with 'the expressed intention of beating the popularity of American pictures by taking advantage of clearer diction of British actors and actresses.'

As the Melbourne manager for Cinema Art, Issy was asked to comment:

> The information I received on completion of *Blackmail* was that it was the finest film ever seen and heard in England. Then when it was exhibited all newspaper critics regarded its success as so important, affecting the British industry, that they treated it as a drama first night, and devoted great space to their reviews.
>
> In fact, some of the papers sent their ordinary dramatic critics, and all of them wrote highly of the talkie. They pointed out, in effect, that American exhibitors would have to take second place in the Empire if the standard of *Blackmail* with its English diction were maintained in future talkies.
>
> Many of the scenes were filmed in Scotland Yard, with the approval of authorities, showing interiors and men, and I cannot think that their subsequent release would have been officially permitted in conjunction with other sections that were regarded as objectionable.
>
> I am further surprised because in the last few months I have seen films in Melbourne in which the details and the theme of the plot might be deemed to offend the moral sense to an infinitely greater degree than anything in *Blackmail*.[10]

Even the actor who played the part of the victim expressed his bewilderment.

'It came as a shock to me to hear that the picture had been banned,' Cyril Ritchard, the leading Australian actor, told *The Sun*:

> The censor must surely take a rather narrow view. I do not think that the Australian public would object to it. The picture broke all records during the six weeks in London, and is now showing in New York.

The action of the film censors was indeed surprising, considering that the film had had such a remarkable reception in Britain and America. But Australian censorship was particularly sensitive, going further than the British system it was modelled on. It came down to the personal beliefs of the Censor Board as to what would be considered too violent or offensive for the ordinary, self-respecting Australian citizen. Additionally, films that attempted to make a hero of a criminal were frowned upon. While making films about real criminals or gangsters was not yet popular internationally, a trend for bushranging films had begun in Australia until the police succeeded in banning them in Victoria and New South Wales in 1912. Although a film titled *The Story of the Kelly Gang* had been made in Melbourne in 1906, a new film made in 1923 titled *When the Kellys Were Out* was not approved. Films of this type were not to be encouraged.[11]

Blackmail was not based on real events, but it did have violence. In the story, a girl kills a man who attempts to rape her and ends up being blackmailed by a witness to the killing. The plot was considered too daring and sordid. Cyril Ritchard concluded with his view:

> I am eventually stabbed with a bread-knife – a most undignified ending – after which an ex-detective and a doctor mutter over the body that was me. As in the other world, virtue triumphs, and vice eventually is punished. So that's all right, surely.
>
> Possibly the censor considers the suggestion to housewives thus to use the bread-knife is dangerous.[12]

Issy also weighed in. He said:

> The banning of this picture was never dreamed of. This will be regarded as a slur on British films, and to come at a time when the first lot of British talkies are on their way to Australia is most serious.
>
> If this can be regarded as a 'bad' film from the moral point of view, all I can say is that several 'worse' ones from Hollywood have already been presented in Melbourne without protest.
>
> A strong appeal against the decision will be made, and it is earnestly hoped that the ban will be lifted.[13]

An appeal was lodged and eventually the film was passed – after two minutes of footage from the apartment scene was cut, which included the murder. Ironically, the struggle in the apartment behind the bed curtain was the forerunner to the infamous shower curtain scene in *Psycho* (1960); reaching for the bread-knife was also similar to the scissors scene played by Grace Kelly in *Dial M for Murder* (1954). Both are now well-known scenes and are uniquely Hitchcock.[14]

Chapter 28

Chaos and Despair

From 1929 to the end of 1930, Issy was involved in a number of key events and featured regularly in the press.

In November 1929, while the debacle in the form of the Prince's invitation addressed to 'Melbourne, New Zealand' was circulating over the Tasman Sea, Issy attended the Governor's dinner for VC recipients given at Federal Government House by the Governor-General Lord Stonehaven and the Governor of Victoria, Lord Somers. A photo showing a smartly dressed Issy seated in the front row now lies in the archives of the Australian War Memorial. Issy also attended the Reveille Ball at the St Kilda Town Hall, a huge effort by returned soldiers to raise funds for those less fortunate.[1] On Anzac Day at the 1930 memorial service, his photo was again taken by the press, this time with another VC awardee, Lieutenant James Rogers.

Two weeks later, on 7 May 1930, he was a speaker at the City of Essendon's public meeting to obtain recruits for military service, a peacetime version of the rallies he had addressed in England and Ireland during the war. The compulsory military training system that had been in place for two decades was being replaced with voluntary enlistment, and Councillor James Fenton told the gathering that while he regretted the Federal Government's decision, he intended to make it work. Issy received a round of applause when he rose to make his appeal to the young men to join.[2]

In between these engagements, Issy completed his usual British Ministry of Pensions declaration form, required to be done twice yearly to collect his pension, and was surprised not long after to receive a letter regarding it. On the 15 May, the Repatriation Commission wrote advising that his date of birth did not agree with records. He was requested to furnish an explanation, along with his disabilities and any wounds from action. This was the first and only time his age was ever queried.

Dutifully replying the same day on Cinema Art letterhead, he advised that his date of birth was 18th September 1888 and that he was gassed at Ypres on 26 April 1915. 'These particulars,' he noted, 'are to the best of my knowledge and belief correct, but should you require further evidence, it will be necessary for me to sort out a considerable amount of correspondence, etc.'

Nothing further was heard on the matter. Given the army's awareness of the 'flexible' ages of millions of its recruits and the difficulties in some cases of providing proof, the explanation was likely accepted and the records simply updated.[3]

Sometime over the next few weeks Issy moved the family a short distance west to 54 Derby Street, Moonee Ponds, a more spacious three-bedroom Californian bungalow. This was the second move in a year – firstly from 46 Margaret Street to 10 Grace Street, another Victorian terrace just around the corner, and then to this new residence.[4]

For Olive, who had returned home from her convalescence in Olinda, it was a convenient half mile to St Columba's Convent school, which she was now attending, without the need to cross the railway line to get there. The convent, which was run by the Sisters of Charity, was Roman Catholic and not Jewish. Curiously, Olive noted in her memoirs that it was the only school that would take her.

In early July Issy was listed in the paper as the new Victorian agent for Australia and New Zealand Pictures Ltd, whose head office was in Wellington. Not much is known about this company, other than a mention of an American affiliation which would enable the import of Hollywood films in addition to the British films he was already managing with Cinema Art. This would have been of immense benefit to the Australian public, as almost overnight American movies had become a mammoth industry and Hollywood productions a sought-after recreational pastime.

On 10 July 1930 he featured again in the newspaper, this time to comment on a primage (uniform customs) duty that was to be imposed on all imports, including films. The new duty was part of what was reported to be 'the most crushing budget in the history of Australia' – created to reduce Australia's significant deficit of £14,000,000. Fortunately, the duty did not apply to British films, but Issy noted that the industry had nearly reached its limit (in taxes), and that many of the smaller film exchanges would go out of business. He also commented that the government appeared to have overlooked the fact that film distributors were among the biggest customers of the postal department. The significant hike in postage costs (which was also part of the budget) was likely to result in a heavy curtailment in the postage of film.[5]

Then on 16 September, Issy wrote once again, this time to *The Argus*, clarifying a misperception about European films. The letter was published two days later, on his 40th birthday.

> Sir, – 'Keystone' says today that good European films never reach Australia, except by chance, and that *Metropolis* and *Variety* were screened here because an American exchange happened to distribute them. This is not correct. The three U.F.A. productions – *Metropolis*, *Variety*, and *Faust* – were distributed by Australian and New Zealand Pictures Ltd., and we are the agents for all U.F.A. films distributed in this country. In the near future the first U.F.A. talking picture is expected, namely *The Blue Angel*, introducing Emil Jannings. Will Fritsch in *The Girl in the Moon* and in *The Love Waltz* will also be coming shortly.[6]
>
> Yours, etc.
> AUSTRALIA AND NEW ZEALAND PICTURES LTD.,

(Per Issy Smith, Manager for Victoria).
234 Swanston Street, Sept 16 [7]

In August 1930, in between the newspaper stories, Issy met with his fellow Jewish returned comrades who had formed a gathering in the previous year under the stewardship of one Colonel Isadore Isaacson. The members, who included Sir John Monash, decided to inaugurate an association to be known as the Jewish Returned Soldiers' Circle. Lieutenant Colonel Isaacson, who had taken over as chief censor from Monash during the war, was elected president and Issy became a member of the committee.[8]

But in April 1930, a single contemptible event which affected Issy eclipsed all others, making headlines. The public learned, from information leaked to the press, that the government had decided to dispense with the principle of giving preference to returned soldiers in Federal Public Works, favouring unionists instead. This public bombshell caused widespread anger. Men had volunteered for war service, the community cried, interrupting their careers, leaving their families and risking their lives. For those who had not been killed, a huge number had lost their health – either suffering mentally from the dreadful experience or being physically impaired in some way. Nearly all had been handicapped by the years they had lost while away. They were courageous men who had proven their loyalty to their country and the community needed to do whatever was required to help them on their return. All promises that were made to them before they left had to be kept.

Yet beneath the surface, there was even more to it. In an open labour market, everyone could compete for employment. When the economy was strained, a disability became a serious handicap that threw all but the fully robust out of work. For an injured veteran with a basic pension, the only rescue from destitution and charity was a preference to returned soldiers.[9]

On 5 May 1930 a protest in Melbourne was announced, to be held at the Essendon Town Hall, with James Fenton and Issy as speakers. Other protests were planned across the country. The unionists, on the other hand, stood firm. Despite the worsening employment situation, they clung to the government selection and their wages and conditions with a tenacity not seen before, ignoring concerns raised over the Wall Street Crash and its emerging impact on Australia's ability to fund public works.

In Parliament, the topic was vigorously debated. When the recently appointed Prime Minister, James Scullin, argued that no returned soldier would be denied preference to employment if they joined a union, there was an uproar. On 7 May, under the threat of censure motions by the opposition, the government announced an unconditional retraction of the decision. The press noted that it was unfortunate there were so few ex-servicemen in the Federal Parliament and none in the Federal Ministry.

At the soldiers' conference in July, following opening remarks made by Sir John Monash, debate on the topic continued, in particular as to how it had managed to reach this point. The president of the League's Victorian branch, Mr Holland, explained his discussions with the Federal president once he had learned of the plan. 'I have done what I thought was right, and I give you my assurance that I was absolutely sincere,' he said.

'Are you aware that the Federal president has refused to employ returned soldiers at the Richmond racecourse?' Issy retorted.

'That is not correct,' a voice replied. Unfortunately, the follow-on was not recorded, though a new discussion and motion about the perceived exploitation of memorials was. A frustrated Mr WB Brown expressed his unhappiness at publicity hunters. 'We must protest emphatically against Prime Ministers, Amy Johnsons and others using our memorials for publicity and personal gain,' he exclaimed.

Two journalists captured Issy's comments: 'The way every Tom, Dick and Harry visiting country towns places sixpenny wreaths on war memorials is a disgrace,' he apparently said. 'Not even the Prime Minister should be allowed to do it except on Anzac Day.' This motion was defeated.[10]

Chaos and Despair

But the debates didn't end there. On 4 October 1930, another meeting was held at the Essendon Town Hall, again presided over by James Fenton. This time the protest was against the dismissal of a significant number of returned soldiers from the public service. A crowd of 300 attended and Captain Albert Jacka, the first official Australian VC recipient and now mayor of St Kilda, passed a motion against the dismissals, arguing that a system of rationing could have allowed many of the men to be retained. He called on the government to issue instructions for all possible work to be rationed and for the men to be re-engaged. Issy seconded the motion.[11]

No actions from the motion were forthcoming. In May the next year, the Postmaster General's Office announced that there was not the slightest hope of re-employment for the dismissed returned soldiers while present conditions prevailed. By July that year, it became a fight to avoid reductions in returned soldiers' pensions.

Belts tightened everywhere. The hopes and prayers for Australian prosperity were now cantering off into the distance, and in their place, the chaos and despair of the Great Depression was galloping in.

Not even Cinema Art was spared. Sometime in late 1930, Cinema Art ceased operating, and Issy's employment with them came to a sudden end. Having struggled financially after the Great Depression set in, it appeared that continuing the company had become uneconomic and it was voluntarily wound up.[12]

It may have simply been financial woes or perhaps, behind the scenes, there was more to the story.

When Alfred Hugenberg had acquired UFA in 1927, just prior to its merger with Cinema Art, nothing changed initially. However, Hugenberg, who was the chairman of the German National People's Party (*Deutschnationale Volkspartei*, or DNVP) in the Reichstag and owner of Scheri-Gruppe, a powerful media corporation, had not only acquired UFA but also controlling interests in various other film and newspaper companies. Soon, he had a near monopoly on the German media. He began insisting that UFA mainly focus on films promoting German nationalism, and while the company still produced internationally acclaimed films such as *The Blue Angel*, the producers were pushed to move away from this and make National Socialist films.

But Hugenberg's views went beyond being a mere patriot for country kinship. It was reported he was an annexationist, striving for the German Reich to become the world's greatest power, and was violently opposed to the settling of Germany's war reparations. He hoped to use nationalism via his media platform to end the current government and restore the country's fortunes. Through Adolf Hitler he saw an opportunity.

Hitler, whose power was on the rise, was able to utilise Hugenberg's media empire to promote himself into the public eye. Although the relationship between the two men was rocky, in February 1931 Hugenberg abandoned the DNVP and joined the Nazi Party in kicking his former party out of the Reichstag. Later, Hugenberg and Hitler released a joint statement agreeing to work together towards the overthrow of the 'Weimar system'. In October they appeared together at a right-wing rally in Bad Harzburg to lay the foundations to this end.[13]

Faced with the signs of a political outcry, it is possible that Cinema Art decided that an ongoing relationship with UFA was untenable, and the time had come for the merger with the German company to cease.

Chapter 29

Racecourses and Picture Houses

Insolvency for a business was one thing. Destitution for an individual was another matter entirely: it was humbling. Having lived most of his life as a battler, Issy understood hardship. Although he had had regular employment in an industry that could generally weather the storm and, until the departure from Cinema Art he was, for once, relatively well off, he did not revel in this prosperity. He reached out to support others.

On 28 April 1930 Issy had become a justice of the peace (JP), sworn in before Sir William Irvine, the Chief Justice. With the population facing ever increasing financial hardship, the importance of a JP who could understand the plight of others was invaluable. Issy was also able to act as an interpreter, given that he spoke at least five languages (Yiddish, Russian, Turkish, English and some Indian dialects).[1]

And months later, on 8 December, in one of many examples of his nature, he attended the mayor of Essendon's Relief Committee meeting where a local reverend was endeavouring to provide a Christmas 'spread' for children of the unemployed. Issy advised that he could arrange for the supply of fruit and ice-cream from various sources. It was also proposed that toys be distributed among the children and, although it was not reported, he probably did this also. In 1922 *The Sun* newspaper had established a toy fund in Australia to provide gifts to sick children at Christmas. Over the decades, it was believed that Issy started this fund, although to achieve this he would have had to establish it during his fleeting visit in 1921 or otherwise arrange it from the UK, where he was residing at the time. This would seem unlikely, the more plausible scenario being that he became involved once he reached Australia. Through the years, his son Maurice recalled that Issy made many toys and distributed them to various charities.[2]

There had been economic slumps before, most recently the investment collapse of the 1890s, but nothing like this and not on such a worldwide scale. Unemployment had grown rapidly, along with the number of mass demonstrations held by those out of work.

'The banks are full of money, and all the big shops filled with goods; money is being spent at racecourses and picture shows,' a Labor minister told a crowd in Melbourne, 'while hundreds of people in Victoria are starving and sleeping in parks at night – hunger, want, misery and destitution stalk the land.'[3]

There was a lot of truth in this statement. Firstly, money *was* being spent at racecourses and picture shows – by the city's wealthiest; but also by many who could least afford it. Secondly, people were resorting to extreme measures in search of a bed and a meal, and charities were severely stretched.

A good friend of Issy's, Henry Lubransky, was in the former category. A tailor by trade, he ran a successful outfit in Flinders Lane in Melbourne, where the majority of the tailors, dressmakers and furriers jostled for business. Issy often visited Henry to catch up for a chat or occasionally be measured for a smart suit.[4] Henry was also an excellent punter and was renowned in racing circles as one of the few who would bet £1000 on a horse at an ordinary meeting (as opposed to a big event like the Melbourne or Caulfield Cup). In 1925 he had cleaned up almost £15,000, paid at odds of 20:1, on a winner at Werribee when the track had only just been classed as a metropolitan racecourse. Then, in January 1929, he had placed £2000 on Aga Khan in the Standish Handicap at Flemington Racecourse and, on this occasion with a betting partner, scored the best part of £10,000 in winnings.[5] By the end of that year, after the most famous punter of the time, Eric Connolly, retired following a heart attack, Henry was considered his successor, receiving the unofficial title of 'King of the Victorian Punters'.[6]

When in between jobs, Issy worked for a bookmaker on the track as a 'penciller', writing the tickets for the punters and handling the cash. At times he also 'tic-tacked' – going down to the end to see what the other bookmakers were doing and signalling the results ('Joe has a horse at 8:1, we will pick it up.').

Issy wasn't blessed with wealth for splurging on the races, nor was he a punter himself, but on 4 November 1930, perhaps encouraged by Henry, he gave the local newspaper a tip for the Melbourne Cup. Phar Lap would win, he said, with Temptation as the place bet (he got the most famous bit right!).[7] It was lucky Phar Lap was still around to be a starter – three days earlier, two men had tried to gun the horse down in a drive-by shooting. Thankfully they missed, and Phar Lap went on to win, becoming the shortest priced favourite (at odds of 8:11) in Cup history.[8]

While racecourses were regarded by some as a stain on society, particularly during a depression, picture houses did not escape disapproval either. It was inappropriate, it was said, for people to be enjoying entertainment in tough times – even if it was claimed to be for relief – when others could barely manage to live.

But the real sticking point with picture houses came with the discovery of a small anomaly in the law. *The Theatres Act* allowed certain cinemas to open on Good Friday, Christmas Day and Anzac Day. This was intolerable as far as many were concerned, with the last one being a particularly sensitive matter.

Anzac Day had grown to be a sacred day; however, the community was divided on the extent of observance. There was a mass of conflicting opinions about the motives behind the controversy, ranging from spiritual and deeply respectful to entirely about private profits. Issy still had his agency with Australia and New Zealand Pictures and on 4 April 1931, he wrote a long letter to the newspapers. The editor titled it 'V.C. URGES BRIGHTER ANZAC NIGHT SPIRIT'.

Sir, – As a returned soldier and holder of the Victoria Cross, which I gained on April 25 [sic], 1915,[9] I am in the deepest sympathy with those who lost their dear ones during the Great War, and I have always endeavoured to help, on every occasion possible, those of my brother Diggers who are unemployed because of the financial depression in Victoria. I do not believe, however, that the closing of the amusements would improve the position of the returned men in any way.

Surely we can hold our march and services during the morning and afternoon, then relax in the evening in the spirit of rejoicing at the great deeds of our army, which resulted in such a wonderful victory, without having to sit at home on Saturday night 'all dressed up and nowhere to go'.

Let us bear in mind the most solemn ceremony in connection with the armies of the Empire during the Great War is the service at the Cenotaph in London on Armistice Day, at which thousands are present. This ceremony is held in the morning, when all business is suspended. The impressive and solemn ceremonies of remembrance finish at 1 p.m. and the community goes back to work, and business goes on as usual. Surely we can adopt a similar method in regard to Anzac Day, even if we suspend the time until later in the evening.

I am sure that our State president and secretary must feel that there is no better day to hold the march and services than on a Sunday, as the original Anzac Day occurred on the fourth Sunday of April. The opening of places of amusement in the evening would not in any way interfere with the commemoration of Anzac Day this year, which falls on a Saturday.

Let us, in these depressed times, be practical, and while not forgetting our illustrious dead, think of the living, and march on with a 'cheerio' as they would wish us to do, and rejoice at our entertainment in the evening in the spirit of the Anzac. We would thus have kept the day as a Day of National Pride in the deeds of our boys and rejoice at the victory in which they took such a great part.

I hope that the authorities will fall into line with the general opinion of the majority of the Diggers, and withdraw from their attitude toward entertainments being held in the evening of Anzac Day.

Yours, etc.

AUSTRALIA AND NEW ZEALAND PICTURES LTD.
Issy Smith, Manager for Victoria.
Melbourne 4 April.[10]

How much Issy's letter, or the timing of its appearance, had to do with what happened next is hard to know, but a furore erupted in the press. On 10 April, a motion passed at the Soldier Settlers' council meeting at Anzac House was printed in *The Herald*. It read:

> This conference, representative of returned soldiers in all parts of the State, views with profound disgust and loathing the threat of the picture theatre interests to desecrate Anzac Day by opening their theatres, and pledges itself to do everything possible to defeat the anti-Australian sentiment evident among picture interests, of which this latest decision forms the most odious and detestable example, violating as it does all decency and showing a callous and cynical disregard of the feelings of those whose fathers, sons, brothers, and relatives gave their lives in the service of their country, and in whose honor and memory the day has been set aside by State legislation.[11]

The Victorian branch of the Returned Soldiers' League also issued a circular to every branch in the State, expressing their opposition. 'A determined effort is to be made by the picture interests to defeat the intention of the Anzac Day Act,' the papers printed. 'The Returned Soldiers' League has got to organise to prevent this desecration of Australia's National Day.'[12]

Another article, published on 15 April, was directed personally at Issy. Although the original clipping is not available, a subsequent apology printed by *The Argus* and several other papers in May 1931 gave the general gist:

> APOLOGY. – With reference to the leading article on the matter of the observance of Anzac Day appearing in the *Sunraysia Daily* of the 15th April ultimo, some reference was made therein to a letter written to the public press upon the subject by a V.C. winner.
>
> Although Sergeant Izzy [sic] Smith, VC was not named, it is obvious that the reference was to a letter under his signature appearing in the Melbourne *Herald*. Our article also referred to Sergeant Smith in the following terms:
>
> One is a V.C. winner whose letter suggested that he was in the A.I.F., whereas in fact he is an Australian of four or five years standing with no touch of A.I.F. or Australian sentiment in the matter. Doubtless he wrote as he was told by the employers on whom he depends at present for a living, knowing that he would be sacked if he refused to sign the dictated letter.'
>
> We have since learned that these statements are incorrect. We find that Sergeant Smith was one of the first twelve men to enter the Broadmeadows Camp on the 10th August, 1914, and that he has been eighteen years in Australia, instead of the four or five years as stated in our paragraph. We have been assured by Sergeant Smith that the letter was written quite apart from his employers, and was not in any way dictated by them.
>
> Under the circumstances we regret that we should have reflected upon Sergeant Smith and we now apologise to him for the incorrect statements appearing in our article. The last thing we would wish to do would be to cast any reflection upon a man holding the highest award in the British Empire for heroism.[13]

The appropriate morals for the frequenting of racecourses and picture houses during a financial crisis may have caused dissent and debate, but these arguments became peripheral as the world economy deflated and Australia's businesses crumbled. A VC life-pass given to Issy for admission to local theatres and London's entertainment halls was likely defunct before it could ever be used – the giver, an entrepreneur by the name of Hugh D McIntosh who was part owner of the Harry Rickards Tivoli Theatre chain and the *Sunday Times* newspaper, was himself sliding into bankruptcy.[14]

But while much of the country sank, Issy refused to go down with the ship. On 30 December 1930, he wrote:

DISTRESS AT ESSENDON

TO THE EDITOR OF *THE ARGUS*

Sir. – Various organisations are doing wonderful work for the relief of the poor. The mayor of Essendon (Councillor A. Fenton) and his unemployed relief committee have been for the last 18 months trying to alleviate the distress in their districts and they have gone to no end of the earth. There are in the Essendon district about 1,200 out of work. The committee was able to supply all the children of these people with toys and each home with a 2lb Christmas cake. A picture matinee will be held tomorrow, when sweets and biscuits will be issued to all the children present. They also receive the help of the president and members of Tattersall's club. This club supplied 70 people with dinners and the freedom of the club for the day on Sunday last. All the children were given toys on leaving. If we could get other sporting clubs to do similar things for the poor, there would not be half the distress and poverty that we have at the present time. – Yours, &c., ISSY SMITH [15]

If it was possible to make a difference, Issy did whatever he could.

Chapter 30

The Politics of Elections

The Wall Street Crash of October 1929 had initially attracted little attention in Australia. At the time, economic ties to America were not strong and the flow-on effects of a stock market collapse were not fully understood; with so many things to worry about at home, not much consideration was given to what was going on abroad.

Yet it wasn't long before the ripple effects of the global economic crisis were felt. During 1930 the government was met with plummeting export incomes, mounting unemployment and a worsening budgetary deficit. The Communist Party of Australia – considered to be Australia's greatest menace – had also been making big gains through the trade unions and the struggles of the working class.

As the problems grew, Prime Minister Scullin went to attend an Imperial conference in London. James Fenton, now the Minister for Trade and Customs, acted in his place and, together with Joseph Lyons, the acting treasurer, called urgent parliamentary sittings to deal with the crisis. Both men held very conservative views that Australia was living beyond its means, and to trade out of the Depression significant cuts to government spending, wages and pensions were needed, along with an increase in taxation. These views contrasted sharply with inflationary policies proposed by others to encourage more spending and promote jobs. Amidst conflicting advice and opposing agendas, fierce debates arose in caucus that spilled into the public arena, causing unrest. The banks were blamed, called out as greedy financiers whose sole intention was to line their own pockets by impoverishing the working class. Other huge sums had been borrowed, it was claimed, from money-lending Jews. This led to renewed antisemitism, prompting Issy to write a letter to the paper.

> Sir. – I shall be glad if you will grant me a little space in answer to the repudiation talk by Mr Hogan, The Premier of Victoria, at the Hotel Windsor. My strong objection being the remarks made by the Premier that it was believed by some that the Government had borrowed huge sums of money from money-lending Jews. As a peaceful citizen of Victoria and a Jew, I take strong objection to these remarks as, I am sure there is no need for me to inform him, that there are just as large a money-lending people of other religious bodies – Yours etc.,
>
> Izzy [sic] Smith
>
> Melbourne, March 19[1]

When Scullin returned in early 1931 and replaced Lyons with a politician in favour of the more radical direction proposed to deal with the crisis, Lyons and Fenton promptly resigned. Fenton joined the newly formed United Australia Party led by Lyons and on 28 November of that year helped bring down the government through a no confidence motion. In one of the fastest campaigns in Commonwealth history, nominations closed on 5 December and a general election was called for 19 December.

The election was always going to be stormy. It wasn't just the political climate that was strained; many of the working class understood the implications and were disillusioned and angry. Employment opportunities, investments and savings had been drying up since the crash, and long dole queues were the norm. For the destitute there was little relief other than a government issue of surplus army clothing and tired old boots which made the wearers highly conspicuous. The cuts to pensions seemed particularly heartless and further burdened families battling to stay afloat. The mood was dark.

On the opening night of his local election campaign, Fenton knew there would be tension – his electorate in Maribyrnong covered the main industrial districts where many had been laid off. Perhaps in the hope of obtaining a fresh perspective, he asked Enid Lyons, wife of Joseph Lyons, if she would accompany him and speak. Also joining them was Issy, who had decided to try his hand at politics and was contesting the Melbourne seat against the longstanding Dr William Maloney. Issy's decision, said *The Herald*, was made because he believed that 'the present is the time when people who have principles should be prepared to stand by them'. The papers had previously highlighted the lack of ex-servicemen in politics and perhaps Issy had taken heed, although he listed himself modestly just as 'I. Smith, Manager, Moonee Ponds', without his military credentials.[2]

'I have not been associated with any political party,' Issy told the paper.

> I believe that Australia's greatest need is to return to Parliament men who can be trusted and whose very presence will restore confidence both in Australia and overseas. I am irrevocably opposed to Communists and I would have their organisation declared illegal, with penalties providing either deportation or gaol. What Australia now wants is a policy of sound finance, a sound protectionist policy, a sound defence policy, and a properly conceived scheme of Empire trade.[3]

It was going to take a good deal of work to get these principles heard. Enid recalled the emotion-charged evening in her memoirs:

> An angry crowd is always a disturbing sight, but under some circumstance and in some surroundings it can be a terrifying one. No one can tell the moment when the last barrier of civilised restraint will break. Only once have I seen such a sight, and if I were asked to name the most dramatic incident of my life I think I should choose the one

that occurred that night, when Sergeant Issy Smith stood and faced the crowd.[4]

That evening, a dreadful noise could be heard coming from the Moonee Ponds Town Hall as the Fenton party pulled up. Supporters, pacing and anxious, quickly warned that it had been building since 6 pm. The hall was now full, mostly of men who had come straight from the factories to vent their grievances. Tired, hungry and dirty, nearly 2000 had forced the doors open and stood for two hours waiting for Fenton, the 'object of their wrath' to appear. Another 500 who could not gain admittance gathered outside.

As the party walked on stage there was an uproar. Insults, jeers, catcalls, heckles and boos filled the room for the entire time, except for just three remarkable minutes at the very end.

At first the chairman stood and attempted to make his opening speech, but after five minutes he abandoned and sat down. Enid, sitting next to him, hadn't heard a word amid the din. Fenton tried next, shouting against the wave of anger; but the commotion only worsened, broken at times by the cries of 'Traitor!', 'Rat!' and 'Mongrel!' He persisted for nearly half an hour without losing his patience, possibly encouraged by the occasional cheers heard in amid the roar, but his unruffled demeanour annoyed the hecklers more, and eventually another committee member took his place. It wasn't long before he too gave in.

Fenton, strained and pale, leaned across to Enid. 'You don't know how I hate to expose you to this,' he said, 'but they might listen to a lady. Would you try?'

Enid nodded. Rising nervously to her feet, she surveyed a sea of fury. 'Be sports,' she attempted. For a moment the racket appeared to lessen and then it rebounded with umpire's whistles, bells and voices that shouted in unison.

'Get back to your kids!'

The shouting did not let up. 'Get back to your kids! Go back to Tasmania!' they cried. After five minutes Enid, too, sat down defeated. The chairman took over and tried again. The only two police constables on duty stepped in and removed a few of the most persistent interjectors, but they were immediately replaced by women who stood on chairs to hurl their abuse.

While the crowd howled at their speaker, Issy sat down beside Enid. 'Lord this is awful,' he said. 'This fellow doesn't know how to handle them. I know the idiom here. I live in these parts. I'll have a go. They'll listen to me!'

Enid was relieved. Issy was not only a respected VC winner but also a well-known member of the community. Perhaps they would hear him out.

Signalling to the chairman, he indicated that he was prepared to speak. The chairman made room and Issy stepped forward.

For the briefest of moments, the racket seemed to lessen. The audience knew him – he was one of them, a popular figure, and both a local and national hero since the war. He managed perhaps a dozen words against the clamour before the hoots and jeers returned and the mob shouted him down. 'You will count for very little on December 19,' he exclaimed at last. 'Mr Theodore will ruin the Labor party.'

Then, in the centre of the hall, a lone man raised his hand. For five minutes he stood, his arm outstretched, until it occurred to the crowd that he had a question. The noise fell to a dull rumble, then to a murmur, then to silence. At last, when everyone including the party on the stage was listening, he spoke.

With his face mottled with anger, his voice impassioned with hatred and each and every word crystal clear, he asked, 'Who killed Christ?'

A gasp rippled through the hall and the room fell deathly quiet. Issy stood on the platform, motionless for perhaps half a minute. Then, in the stony silence, in a voice fervent with feeling that could be heard in the farthest corners of the room, he said, 'Well, if you're a fair specimen of a Christian, thank God I am a Jew.'

Not another word was spoken and the audience dispersed. Years later, in an article to the press, Enid noted that Issy, the most dignified person in the hall at that moment, spoke with 'eloquence and vigour' – to no avail. The hall was full of hostile voters. Ultimately hatred and prejudice – which she considered passed for current public opinion – beat reason.[5]

✢

The meeting might have ended, but the hostilities did not. As Issy stood on the steps of the Soldiers Memorial in North Melbourne a few days later, an unruly crowd interrupted his first official address. Roughly 1000 people were gathered and initially they accepted the opening speaker Mr Dillon, the candidate for Essendon, until he began to talk about a sugar embargo. Suddenly the mood shifted.

'Where's Issy?' they shouted. As Issy stepped forward, smiling and waving, the hooting gathered momentum. 'You've as much chance of shifting Dr. Maloney as I have of shifting the Shrine of Remembrance,' someone yelled, to which there were cheers and laughter.

Issy maintained his smile. 'Come on, boys, be sports and –' he started. The crowd surged forward and an inner circle of approximately 200 young men refused to let him speak. Each time he tried, an uproar began. Issy patiently persisted, but when an insulting remark about his war honour was shouted his smile disappeared – right then, an egg meant for him flew past and smashed against the pillar of the memorial. The crowd became more antagonistic, with some shouting to 'knock him down and put the boot in'. As his supporters gathered around him to hold off the advance, a young man in a cap yelled cynically, 'Don't be afraid, Issy: we'll see you're not hurt.'

Issy calmly brushed aside his stalwarts and said to the young man in the cap, 'I haven't lost my courage yet.' This inspired a brawny interjector to lob an offensive remark about returned soldiers to which some of the crowd applauded. But one man defended Issy. 'I was at the same place with him. Give him a go,' he called. A group surrounded the man and warned him to keep quiet.

The wall of insults continued in the face of Issy's attempts to speak. When he said that he favoured the cancellation of all war debts, some of the crowd pushed clenched fists in his face and told him 'to cut out the fucking war'. Issy appealed for moderation, proclaiming that surely they did not wish to drag in the war at the 1931 election.

A protester shouted, 'Are you in favour of absolute preference to all unionists?'

'No,' Issy replied, and a tremendous calamity followed.

Issy descended the steps and the crowd lurched, hooting, calling names and reviling his religion. When the noise began to lull, Issy ascended again and a handful of people cheered. But this was quickly drowned by more hooting and howling as the mob rushed the memorial steps. Issy was crushed against the base and had to fight his way out. As he pushed towards his car, he was derided for not having enough money to hire a hall. Some people came forward and offered to subscribe money but Issy, tired and hoarse, shook his head.

At the car, a woman called out, 'Think yourself lucky you ain't goin' 'ome in an ambulance', to which there was much laughter.

When the car moved off, a momentous roar rose up behind him. 'IZZY WAS HOOTED AS HE FLED' a newspaper splashed in headlines, only to acknowledge in the story that 'they howled him down, hooted and counted him out, and finally threatened to remove him from the steps of the memorial by force. Smith then left.'[6]

Dr Maloney, at his own meeting at the Kensington Town Hall later that evening, heard of the incident. A seasoned campaigner at 74 years of age, and not one to hold back or allow party politics to surpass his chivalry, he addressed the large audience, prefacing his speech with the need for respect for such an honour as the Victoria Cross and calling for fairness.[7]

Many wrote to the papers the next day, denouncing the crowd's disgraceful behaviour. *The Herald* reported that Dr Maloney also telephoned the paper personally to say how much he regretted the tactics being followed to prevent his opponent from speaking.

'At North Melbourne last night, Sergeant Smith was interrupted so much he was not able to get a fair hearing. I believe in absolute freedom of speech,' Dr Maloney said. 'After all, my opponent has won the greatest honour that can be won and Australians should see that he gets fair play.'[8]

Others agreed, and many sent letters of complaint.

'This is the type of man that Melbourne has the opportunity to elect to Parliament,' a Mr Clarke wrote to the papers. 'A man who risks his life for his fellows, not once, but many times, would not lack courage when it came to a fight on behalf of the people. The unemployed have a gallant friend in Sergeant Issy Smith VC.'[9]

One paper attempted to defend the behaviour. 'It was more from sentimental support for Dr W. Maloney M.H.R., than from political reasons that Sergeant Izzy Smith, V.C. was howled down …' the article claimed.[10] 'A section of "the little doctor's" followers always gives his opponents for Melbourne seat a very bad time. Dr Maloney has held this seat for over 25 years, often uncontested, and many of his followers consider it audacious for a candidate to oppose him.'[11]

But despite the press, the campaign animosity persisted.

Speaking at Royal Park Grammar School, Issy was continually interrupted, especially by a Mr William Gullett, whose shouts and abuse meant it was impossible for Issy to be heard. Gullett marched to the platform, threatening to knock him off it. The police removed him from the hall but he scaled a wall and attempted to climb back in through a window. 'Lie down, you mongrel! If I get up on the platform, I will go you,' he hollered, before being removed from the window and escorted outside again.

A few days later he appeared in Carlton Court and was charged with behaving in an offensive manner. He was fined £5 with one month's imprisonment in default imposed.[12]

At the next meeting in Kensington Town Hall on 14 December

more police attended. When the UAP senator James Guthrie referred to Issy's war record, a man yelled, 'Cut with the sob stuff. Give us some politics.'

Issy then rose to address the crowd. 'I notice in the audience some of my friends from North Melbourne,' he said.

'Where do you come from, Jerusalem?' a voice called out.

'I am not ashamed to say that I am from the ancient Jewish race,' he replied, to which there was some applause. 'I think some of you are being paid to follow me around – I hope you are receiving union rates.'[13]

On 17 December, just two days before election day, an advertisement appeared in *The Herald* from CW Joyce, State Secretary of RSSILA, who made an open admission that it was he who wrote the accusing article on Issy regarding the Anzac Day observance some eight months earlier. 'I therefore regret the statement that he had been in Australia for four or five years only. I have not and never have had any desire to reflect upon Mr Smith personally. His long and distinguished career with the Manchester Regiment is well known to me, as is the act of gallantry whereby, on 26th April 1915, he won the Victoria Cross [...] I have not desired to suggest in any way that in this controversy he has expressed views which are contrary to his genuine convictions, nor do I suggest that he would, under any circumstances, express views contrary to his convictions.'[14]

If this was an effort to help Issy's political bid, it came too late. In less than three weeks, the whirlwind campaign was over, with Dr Maloney retaining his seat. The heavy vote for the non-Labor forces were startling and Issy's was a case in point, with the papers reporting that it was amazing the fight he put up and how many votes he had received (over 13,000, resulting in a 38 per cent swing). Maloney had represented Melbourne for 27 years, and his hold on the seat was such that 'many thought Sergeant Smith was wasting his time in contesting it.' Issy accepted defeat gracefully. In a brief speech, he said that he was satisfied the best man had won. A photo was printed in *The Herald* of the two men shaking hands.[15]

But not surprisingly, there was more to come.

The Argus reported that the posters for Issy Smith had been deliberately altered. The posters advised electors to vote '1' for Issy but under cover of night, the number had been carefully altered to '2' for Maloney. Care had been taken to see that the new number fitted exactly into the square – the printing was identical. The voting was rigged.[16]

Nothing was done about this scandal. Interestingly, when Maloney had stood for the seat of Melbourne in 1903 (after being soundly beaten in his first attempt in 1901), he had protested the narrow defeat. Appearing before the Court of Disputed Elections he argued that hundreds of ballot papers had been signed by ineligible persons and that postal submissions had been recorded on phoney ballot papers. The Chief Justice ruled in his favour and in 1904 a by-election was held, which he subsequently won.[17]

Issy did not challenge the 1931 result. Despite managing a huge swing in his favour, even with all the hurdles thrown in his path, he took no further part and withdrew from federal politics. Perhaps he thought the remaining margin to win the seat was too great. Or maybe he decided that the political arena, and everything that went with it, was a mug's game.[18]

Boxing Magazine Feature, December 1915

Issy (seated left) with unknown others, 1915

WAR'S WEDDING PRESENT

V.C. HERO FOR HUSBAND

FACTORY GIRL TO BE BRIDE

£500 TO START WITH

In a Melbourne clothing factory there is a bright-eyed, happy girl who is making arrangements to leave for England, where she is to marry the man to whom she is engaged, and from whom she has been separated by the war.

The girl is Miss Elsie Porteous, of Lennox street, Moonee Ponds, who is employed by Messrs Davies, Doery and Company, 96 Flinders lane, and the lover who waits for her impatiently at the other end of the world is Corporal Issy Smith, the first Jew to be awarded the Victoria Cross.

£500 FROM WAR OFFICE

Fate, which first brought the young couple together, has also kept them apart; but the war which separated them a year ago is now to be the means of bringing them together again, for the War Office has allotted Corporal Smith £500—£250 has been paid over to him, and £250 banked for his benefit—so that, financially, the way to matrimony has been made easy for them.

BROTHER INTRODUCES FRIEND

Three years ago a British regiment was returning to England from India, and the mothers, brothers, sisters, sweethearts and maiden aunts of the men flocked to Charing Cross station to welcome them home. To the station journeyed a young man named Smith, whose brother was a member of the regiment, and with him went a girl friend. The soldiers tumbled cheering from the train, glad again to look upon the grey skies of the homeland. Young Mr Smith espied his brother, Issy, and after a fraternal handshake, presented him to "My friend, Miss Porteous." The girl beheld a sturdy, well set-up young man, whose frank, good-humoured face had been bronzed by the sun in India, while he saw a pretty, typically English maid.

WORK IN MELBOURNE

Corporal Issy Smith had then served his ten years in the army, and secured his discharge. He worked as a plumber in London, and the friendship which had been established at once between him and Miss Porteous quickly ripened into a more tender emotion, and the two became engaged. Eighteen months ago Mr Smith, anxious to improve his position with a view to matrimony, he was sent to England, joined the First Manchester Regiment, and with it went to France. He was in the fighting at Neuve Chapelle and at Ypres. Here it was that Corporal Smith on April 26 did the gallant deed that won for him the Victoria Cross. On his own initiative he left his company and dashed toward the German lines to assist Sergant Rooke, who was lying wounded close to the enemy's trenches. Smith raised the sergeant to his back and amid a hail of bullets and exposed to the fire of machine guns, carried him 250 yards to the safety of the British trenches.

CIGARETTES FORGOTTEN

"We had halted in a field for rest," said Corporal Smith, in describing the incident, "and shells were rained on us from a German aeroplane. We got orders to run for cover at once and leave everything behind us. When we went to look for cover I suddenly remembered that I had left my cigarettes behind. I went back to get them, and had only gone a short distance when a Jack Johnson dropped among my platoon and killed or wounded

MISS ELSIE PORTEOUS

News of Issy and Elsie's engagement, October 1915

Issy and Elsie's wedding day at Hallam Street Synagogue, 1919

Elsie McKechnie, year unknown

WWI VC Cigarette card

Postcard, distributed at newsstands in 1915

Issy (left) in a welter-weight competition, 1916

Chapter 31

Life in the Public Eye

In among the political turmoil and in less than a year, the Australian public was rocked by the deaths of three renowned and highly respected men.

On 25 March 1931, Issy attended the military funeral of Major General HE Elliott, a senior officer of the Australian Army who gained a reputation as a courageous leader during the Great War. He had been suffering from the strain of his war service and after receiving treatment for high blood pressure, had taken his own life. Thousands lined the streets en route to the Burwood Cemetery.[1]

Then, on 8 October that year in a meeting of the House there was a hush as the death of Sir John Monash was announced. The Australian flag was lowered to half-mast.

A lawyer and a civil engineer, Monash had been recognised for many important works in Melbourne before embarking on an army career that led him ultimately to become the commander of the Australian Army Corps and one of the most outstanding leaders of the war. Over 300,000 people gathered along the route to the Brighton cemetery to witness the procession in his honour. Eight years later, at the annual pilgrimage, nearly three thousand attended, including military leaders, returned soldiers and the Jewish community. A photo was taken of Issy paying his respects at his grave.[2]

As the people mourned his passing, more bad news was to come. On 6 January 1932, Captain Albert Jacka VC was reported to be gravely ill.

Like Issy, Jacka had suffered a number of injuries during the war, including gassing, and never fully recovered from them. His health began to deteriorate in his thirties and on 14 December 1931 he collapsed suddenly following a council meeting. On 17 January, one week after his 39th birthday, he passed away.[3]

Thousands lined the streets as Jacka was given a funeral with full military honours. Eight of the nine pallbearers were VC winners from Victoria. The ninth was Issy.[4]

A fund was immediately set up to help his wife and child. Jacka had had a hard few years – in 1930 his business collapsed due to the Great Depression and he lost his home; in May 1931 his car was stolen and in August of that same year his father had a narrow escape when his house was destroyed by fire.

Issy wrote to the papers, with a contribution enclosed.

> I regret that our late comrade, Capt. Jacka V.C. who did not wish to burden other people with his troubles, came to the end of his life early, needing the assistance which unfortunately he did not receive. During his life I have known him to neglect his business to help distressed diggers. The public, I am sure, will appreciate the move to help his widow and child, and I sincerely hope all will do their utmost for them.

Following meetings in the St Kilda Town Hall hosted by the mayor and mayoress, various events, including cinema nights and a cabaret show, were organised to raise more. Issy's friend Henry Lubransky booked a party table at one of these charity events and in a little over two weeks nearly £620 had been pledged towards the purchase of a cottage. By May the fund had doubled and Mrs Jacka and her daughter moved into a modest house in Glen Iris. Sufficient funds were also available for a special memorial stone, and on 15 May Issy attended the 5000-strong ceremony at St Kilda cemetery, marching there with 500 members of the Army and Navy for the unveiling of it.[5]

✣

In the face of these tough times, Issy continued to be an active member of his community. As a newly appointed justice of the peace, he soon found himself engaged in a number of cases. In the early 1930s, the functions of JPs, the services of whom were voluntary, were wide and varied and could involve a range of activities from court duties assisting a Police Magistrate in a Court of Petty Sessions through to hearing bail applications and child protection matters. Indeed, a JP's power out of sessions could include issuing a warrant or a summons, ordering an inspection of property, remanding someone who had been arrested, committing an accused person to trial or even holding an inquest.

In the previous year, on 19 June 1931, Issy had sat at the City Court with the Police Magistrate, a Mr Freeman, and six other honorary judges to hear two minor cases. In the first, a man by the name of John Sinclair had been charged with having insufficient lawful means of support. He had been remanded the previous week and was given time to produce a witness who, he claimed, would give evidence of his means of livelihood. He had been unable to produce the witness, but his counsel said that if given further remand he would try to obtain evidence that Sinclair had been hawking rugs.

The Police Magistrate was in favour of this request but the majority of the bench thought that Sinclair should be convicted on the previous police evidence. Following deliberations, the Justices returned with the penalty of one month's imprisonment.

In the second case, a Mary Evans had been charged with stealing two pairs of stockings from Myer Emporium, valued at 6s 5d. In this instance the bench had been unanimous regarding a conviction, but not on the penalty. Four believed a fine was appropriate, and the other four felt a suspended prison sentence should be imposed. After the bench retired to consider the matter, the majority decision was a fine of £10 and in default, imprisonment for one month.[6]

By 1932 Issy found himself embroiled in far more significant proceedings. One of the cases in question, held at the Melbourne City Court on 27 January 1932, was more than petty sessions and was in fact a hold-up for GJ Coles takings that became an attempted murder. Issy sat alongside the Police Magistrate, Mr Freeman, on the bench to assist.

The court heard that on the night of 20 November, Constable Derham escorted two employees as they left the Coles store in Swanston Street with money in a bullion bag. As they entered Flinders Lane, two men quietly moved up behind them and pointed guns at the constable's head. Two more men appeared into view, also with pistols, by the company car towards which the Coles party had been heading. Within moments a shot was fired and the constable dropped.

The manager of the Coles store, a Mr Fitzpatrick, had left the shop basement moments earlier and was ahead of them and almost at the car when he heard the shot. As he turned to go back the other two employees, a Mr Kilpatrick, the assistant manager, who was carrying the money bag and a Colt pistol, and a Mr Bartley, a storeman, rushed past him. A second shot sounded, and when he turned again, Kilpatrick and Bartley had been bailed up against a wall, with pistols pointing in their sides. Kilpatrick gave up the bag and the man accosting him searched his pockets, snatching the pistol. More shots were fired, one in Constable Derham's direction, and then the men quickly sprinted to a waiting car with the takings – £980, the bullion bag and the Colt. A fifth shot was heard by witnesses as the bandits fled. Constable Derham, who was found lying in the gutter with a bullet wound to his head, was bundled up and put into the car, but the distributor cable had been stolen and it would not start. Eventually he was successfully transported to hospital and incredibly, he recovered after many months.

Seven men in total all pleaded not guilty. The Police Magistrate believed that the evidence against one of the accused, a Robert Brewster, was weak, but Issy and another JP on the bench thought that he had a case to answer. Bail was refused and all seven were committed to trial in the Criminal Court. In June, three of the men were convicted and each received 20 years imprisonment at

Pentridge prison along with fifteen strokes of the cat-o'-nine tails.

At the time of their arrest, a newspaper reported that one of the accused sensationally said 'A man never had a chance. It was a good clean catch; I would like to know who gave me away.'[7]

Issy sat on the City Court bench for many more hearings, but on 15 July he was an informant.

In a previously heard case, a man by the name of Robert Taylor, a motion picture exhibitor, was in the Bankruptcy Court being examined by the Registrar, with Issy as JP. When Taylor refused to answer questions, the inquiry was adjourned so that action could be taken to have him committed for contempt.

Outside the court Issy inadvertently ran into him, whereby the man called out in a loud voice, 'You think you are so fucking clever.' When Issy asked him to repeat what he said, Taylor grew angrier. 'You ought to go back to Whitechapel, where the other fucking Jews are,' he shouted.

Later in the Melbourne Court, Issy recalled the incident. 'Taylor was very agitated,' he said, 'and I was under the impression that he was about to commit a serious offence.'

The man was fined 20 shillings, and in default seven days imprisonment.[8] 'MAN INSULTS V.C.,' was the headline banner in *The Herald* that day.[9]

In between court bench appearances, Issy continued his other duties. He attended the Anzac Day service as usual, as well as a special luncheon held on 26 April in which seven VCs were guests. In a brief speech to the gathering, Issy explained that this was the 17th anniversary for him, as it was on this day, at Ypres, that he won his medal.[10]

He also continued to feature regularly in the press. Less than a year since running for office and still passionate about the welfare of those struggling financially, Issy was unhappy about the new Lyons Government's plan for recovery. Although this was always expected to be extremely conservative and focused on cuts to government spending, Issy was appalled at the budget and how tightly the reins would be brought in. He wrote to *The Herald* on 6 September 1932 to express his concerns:

> Sir, – During the last Federal elections when I opposed Dr. Maloney for the Melbourne constituency, I was informed by the executive of the U.A.P. that it was not the policy of the U.A.P. to reduce old age pensions, and it is my candid opinion that the U.A.P. has done a terrible thing to these poor old people. Why not increase taxation on those people who would be drawing £5000 or more each year? They could afford to lose 2/6d per week much more than these poor old people.
>
> Issy Smith
> Melbourne, 5 Sept[11]

Not long after, *Everyones* published the news that Hoyts Cinemas had taken over the Williamstown Theatre and Issy, formerly of Cinema Art Films, had been appointed house manager. Issy had also parted ways with Australia and New Zealand Pictures, the company having gone out of business in June.

On 10 October, a photograph of Issy appeared in the papers as he entered the Jewish synagogue in Toorak Road for the Day of Atonement.[12] A few weeks later, there was another important event, but this time it wasn't publicised. Issy's second child and only son, Maurice, was born.

Earlier in the year Elsie, feeling unwell, had gone to the doctors with some trepidation. She feared she had a tumour: a pregnancy was not what she expected. After the difficulties of Olive's birth, more children had not been recommended. Another baby was not on the cards.

Maurice was born at Trinafour Private Hospital in Moonee Ponds on 8 November 1932. A healthy infant, his weight and dimensions were not recorded on the certificate and he was simply noted as 'Male'. Issy's age, however, was recorded as 44, his birth being 18 September 1888 in London, England. His occupation was listed as Manager.

Elsie's details were not entirely correct either. Her age was reported to be 36, her birth date being 5 June 1896, and not 40 as it should have been (she was born on 5 June 1892).

The marriage date shown was also erroneous. The date of 1 February 1919 was a week earlier than on their general registry marriage certificate, and eleven days earlier than on Issy's service record. The Jewish wedding date was not mentioned. Olive, the older sibling, was listed as being of thirteen years of age, although she was two months shy of having that birthday.

During 1932, daughter Olive had spent her final year at St Columba's Convent. Shortly before the arrival of her baby brother, she sat an entrance exam at Zercho's Business College and won a scholarship worth £27 for a year's tuition in shorthand, typing and bookkeeping – to be taken up in 1933.

On 8 November 1932 Frederick Zercho, the founder of the College, was in the Melbourne Supreme Court listening to a matter regarding a woman being charged with perjury. That case had heard that the woman's brother, a Mr William Kinchington, formerly a policeman, had been charged with larceny and receiving, having been accused of stealing a toaster, a fan and a bottle of perfume worth a total of £7 from Zercho's home, which he had attended on a burglary callout. He was later acquitted of these charges, but was immediately re-arrested on a charge of housebreaking and absconded from bail.[13]

Even more interestingly, Issy was also in court that day, residing on the bench again with Mr Freeman, hearing charges against a bookmaker.

The City Court first heard evidence against two men, a Lou Lyons and Thomas Thirsk, who were charged with having run premises not authorised to operate as a gaming house. As part of a sting, a constable had written to a registered bookmaker, a Mannie Lyons, asking for betting prices, which he was given. He placed a bet enclosed with a £1 postal note and sent it to the address given, the Public Benefit Bootery in Bourke Street, after which he received confirmation.[14] He then went to the seventh floor of the building and overpowered

Thirsk, who, upon opening the door had attempted to strike him and slam the door shut. Inside, he and his police partner found Lou Lyons, piles of cash and betting sheets. Both men denied that any bet had been laid on the premises. Thirsk said he worked there and initially claimed that he was an employee of another man named Abrahams, but then later admitted he was employed by Mannie Lyons. The other man, Lou Lyons, refused to speak. Both pleaded not guilty, arguing that the office was merely a repository of records for legitimate betting transactions.

After all of the evidence was heard, Mr Freeman said there was a difference of opinion on the bench. One thought the case should be dismissed and the other that the police case just succeeded – it is not known which was Issy's view. The case was adjourned to 13 December while another case against Mannie Lyons was presented.

Mannie was charged with assisting in the conduct of a common gaming house at the same premises. But while the letters found there bore his name, which in itself was not illegal, there was nothing to link him with operating a betting syndicate in the building. When a constable had interviewed him at his home a few weeks earlier, Mannie had said that all bets were made at the racecourse and had refused to answer any more questions. The charge was dismissed but immediately afterwards the defence lawyer for the earlier case advised that in order to avoid coming back to court again, his clients would plead guilty. They were fined £3 each, with £2 costs.[15]

Sometime that day, amidst the court cases, Maurice arrived into the world. His birth might not have been expected then or more likely Issy was not permitted to attend, which was a common practice of the time. Either way, the newborn was oblivious to the means of business, the judicial system and the felonious acts which it oversaw.

Not long after, in January 1933, there was another case, this time of larceny affecting Issy's friend Henry Lubransky. Under the banner '£250 JEWEL THEFT, SNEAK THIEF RAIDS BEDROOM', the papers reported that while Henry was challenging friends upstairs to a game of billiards and Mrs Lubransky was playing cards with her sister in the breakfast room, a thief climbed through the downstairs bedroom window in stockinged feet and stole £250 of jewellery including rings, a watch and sleeve links. Mrs Lubransky had heard their dog bark at the time but paid the animal no heed.[16]

Thankfully there were no robberies occurring at Issy's family home. Instead, a few photos were snapped of Issy proudly playing with his new son in the garden.

Chapter 32

The Punishing Depression

Issy's role as house manager at Williamstown Theatre did not last long. By the end of 1932 he had been out of paid employment for some months, except for a week here and there. It was not surprising. The Great Depression was at its peak, with Australia among the worst hit in the western world and unemployment at over 30 per cent – surpassing even Great Britain and the US. The country was facing a crisis of unprecedented proportions.

Credit and export prices, the two factors upon which it had been banking for its future, had collapsed, and hardship like never before was being felt across the nation. Australians became distrustful and xenophobic – now, even British immigrants were treated with animosity, with unions accusing Europeans of taking Australian jobs and some workplaces pressured to use only 'Australian' labour. Desperate men roamed the streets, traipsing door to door with anything they could sell, or offering to do odd jobs for the price of a meal. Unemployed and homeless returned servicemen, who had become affectionately termed 'diggers', slept under newspapers and old army greatcoats.

When Issy was earning good money, he helped any returned soldiers who were down on their luck, sharing part of his earnings as needed – just as he had done before the war for the men who queued at the gates of his old employer, the Metropolitan Gas Company. In January 1933, his own situation was dire. Although still working as a JP and actively involved in many community engagements, there was no money forthcoming. This work was entirely voluntary, and without his most recent role at the Williamstown Theatre, he had no means to support his own family. He wrote a letter to the Repatriation Commission on 10 January 1933, highlighting his predicament.

> I am a commercial traveller by occupation, but I am unable to secure employment in any line although I try hard enough. I get relapses of malaria and a very bad cough, but this would not prevent me doing work should it be offering.

He went on to explain his financial woes.

> I have two children, my wife does not earn. She has just been discharged from hospital. My eldest child has had to go away on account of a nervous breakdown. My wife has no assets or income, we own no property. We pay 23/- per week rent. I have no money in any bank or invested. Our combined income is our war pension. I am in arrears of rent. Should I secure employment I will advise the Department immediately. I am getting £5 today from the A.I.F. Educational fund as a gift to assist me during the period of depression and on account of having no employment. I desire that my present circumstances be placed before the authorities so that I may be afforded any assistance that is under their power to give me, and I undertake to refund any amount that may be made available to me, should the authorities so desire me to do it, in the event of securing employment. Failing this, I make application for a lump sum from my pension to enable me to start in some business. I owe money to doctors – Dr J.H. Kelly £15/15/-, Dr Cresswell £8/16/-, Dr Park £5 and Trinafour Hospital £8/15/-.[1]

This total of £38 6s was a considerable amount of arrears: over three months' pay on a basic weekly wage of £3 3s 4d per week. With ongoing health issues and few job prospects, the debt would quickly escalate.

Within a week, Issy was notified by the Deputy Commissioner

that the Repatriation Commission had discontinued payment of lump sums of pensions under the *Australian Soldiers' Repatriation Act* but his application for a lump sum payment of his British war pension had been referred to the Ministry of Pensions in London for consideration. While waiting for the outcome, he signed the regular British Ministry of Pensions declaration in March to collect his pension: still at the old 1921 rate.

Almost six months later, on 3 July, Issy received a reply. Approval had been given from the Royal Hospital, Chelsea, England, for a grant of an additional allowance of 18d per day (the equivalent of the cost of a pound of butter) payable from 20 February 1923 from the Commonwealth Treasury, in conjunction with his 3s 6d for the VC. But there was a catch.

The Pension Issue Office in London had identified an overpayment of £16 14s 11d in rank allowance for the war disabilities from 1923 to 1927. As this had not been corrected, a further overpayment in the Commonwealth had occurred from 1927 to 1933 amounting to £21 0s 2d, bringing the total to £37 15s 1d. A reduction in the war disabilities pension to 8 shillings per week, or 16 shillings per fortnight, would be made.

The letter went on to say that the reduction enabled him to become eligible for a grant of Commonwealth pension at the rate of 9d per fortnight, making the total 16s 9d per fortnight. However, for three years he had also been overpaid the exchange and this amounted to £2 5s 5d. Further, the Commonwealth pension was not payable over the same period as the exchange and it was necessary to deduct 9d per fortnight which came to £3 3s 4d – making the total exchange overpayment £5 8s 9d. In summary, after all the adjustments, a total deduction of £43 3s 10d would be made to his pension calculated from 1923, and he would be paid the balance of £6 2s 9d. From here on, his weekly pension would be 8s 4½d.

For Issy, the upshot from a call for help was payment of the equivalent of two weeks of the minimum wage and a reduction in pension to two-thirds of a twelve-year-old rate. It was enough to cover just one-sixth of his January debt and one-third of his weekly rent.

In October 1933, possibly through a new awareness of the exchange impact as a result of Issy's claim, an agreement was reached with the British Ministry of Pensions that all imperial pensioners would now receive the benefit of the exchange on their war pensions. He began receiving an additional £2 2s 3d annually – not that this would make a great deal of difference.

Thankfully, Issy had not relied on government assistance and in the meantime had rescued himself. He now worked for Dunlop Rubber as a commercial traveller.

The company, an Australian branch of the renowned British parent, was primarily in the business of manufacturing automobile tyres, although they also made shoes and other rubber goods. Issy had experience in the industry, having previously sold tyres for T. Davies & Co.[2] Over the summer holidays of 1933 he was able to secure a job for his daughter there for a month. Olive, who was just turning fourteen, had completed her tuition at the business college during the year and was keen to enter the workforce. Casual work proved fruitful and she transitioned nicely into a permanent job, which kept her employed there for the next seven years – a great outcome during tough times.

Yet conditions within Dunlop Rubber were far from smooth sailing. Prices on tyres and shoes were moving steadily downward due to heavy duties and the spiralling cost of raw materials. Profits were being strangled, and not just from tariffs and import costs. A strike during 1934 by 230 engineers for better pay conditions caused a shutdown and pickets, and the dispute compounded when 35 ironmakers, blacksmiths and welders joined to also air their grievances. A flood from the Yarra River washed a portion of the Abbotsford factory away, along with dozens of motor tyres; two fires broke out in the shoe factories and several workplace accidents occurred, resulting in various injuries and a few deaths. By early 1935 shareholders were up in arms and there was outspoken criticism of the Dunlop board's management. In response, the directors launched a company overhaul: processes were reorganised, production rationalised and many senior staff dismissed – including a number of the engineers involved in the strike. Issy was not a member of the union and not in favour of pickets, but nevertheless became one of the many casualties. Olive noted in her memoirs that the 'kids' (herself and other junior staff) kept the company going for the next nine months and the family lived off her £1 per week wage until Issy found a new job.

It didn't take long. Soon he was a commercial salesman for Stokoe Motors, a company formed six years earlier by a Mr V Stokoe to sell Chevrolet and Oldsmobile cars. The company had been doing well despite the Depression, and in late 1932 expanded to become the Victorian distributor for the American automobile manufacturer Willys-Overland Motor Company.

The US company, best known for their military jeeps and the Willys-Knight, had been the second-largest producer of automobiles after the Ford Motor Company from 1912 to 1918. On the back of this success a period of acquisitions and factory expansions were undertaken before the Depression of 1920–21 nearly crippled them. Since then, they had been restructured by Walter Chrysler and had begun to show signs of recovery until the Great Depression of the 1930s hit. Various assets and their Canadian subsidiary were sold off and many models shelved, including the Willys-Knight. Just a 4-cylinder Willys 77 model went into production, and Issy moved into the smart new showrooms in Elizabeth Street, Melbourne, to manage the sales of it.

At the same time, not far away at Anzac House in Collins Street, Issy attended the first meeting of the Imperial Reservists who had been camped at Broadmeadows in 1914 as the war broke out. He was elected president of the new body, which became known as the '1914 Imperial Reservists of Australia', after which the group went on to meet on the first Thursday of every month.[3] He also joined the Commercial Travellers' Association and became actively involved in their activities. Being a commercial traveller, away from family, was often a lonely occupation. The association cared for its members by protecting them wherever possible from unscrupulous accommodation or business practices, and arranging fundraiser evenings, smoke socials and balls to enable travellers to connect with one another whenever they were in town. Issy regularly visited the club's premises in Flinders Street and provided support.[4]

On 20 June 1935 Issy's own travels came to an abrupt halt when he was involved in a car smash on the edge of the city. While travelling north along Exhibition Street, he was entering Rathdowne Street when a violent collision occurred with another car travelling east along Victoria Street. The other driver was uninjured and his machine only slightly damaged; however Issy's car overturned, pinning him. With cars still a limited commodity and the injured man a celebrity, this was big news and was broadcast all over the east coast.

'Wounded again,' one paper reported, printing a photo of the overturned car surrounded by onlookers, with a snap of a bandaged Issy. 'Sergeant Issy Smith, V.C (inset), was injured in the head and hand to-day when his car, which was turned over, was involved in a city traffic smash,' the photograph's caption read. Another paper printed a photo of a spectator peering closely at the front of the other driver's car amidst a crowd gathered around the two vehicles. 'Mr. Izzy [sic] Smith, a Victoria Cross winner … was extricated from the driving seat through a shattered window.'

'I did not see the other motorist, and the first thing I knew there was a terrible jolt, and I was over,' Issy apparently told a reporter at the Royal Melbourne Hospital. 'I didn't know whether I had lost an ear or what had hit me, but I decided to get out of the wreck in a hurry. I was trying to get through the shattered window when someone helped me out.'

Another journalist recorded a slightly different account, claiming both drivers applied their brakes to no avail and Issy suffered a lacerated scalp. 'I can remember the collision, but I had a knock on the head and things became very vague after that,' Issy reportedy said.[5]

Aside from a trip to the Royal Melbourne Hospital for treatment, there were no apparent repercussions from the accident. Issy recovered from his injuries and the company car was repaired; on weekends, the young Maurice enjoyed driving lessons, steering from his father's lap. This was indeed a novelty – few families had a motor vehicle.

Issy remained with Stokoe Motors where, according to the company, business was going very well. The sales of Willys cars had more than doubled over the six months to the end of the year, it was claimed. Exactly how many car sales this was and how many salesmen were employed to sell them isn't known. From 1929 to 1932, sales of new cars in the US had fallen dramatically by 75 per cent. Australia, still in the midst of a damaged economy, was on the road to a slow recovery, but the cost of a Willys 77, at £376 7s 6d, was out of reach for most Melbournians.[6] Issy wrote to *The Herald* on 20 July promoting the number of miles per gallon and the low service requirements. Whether this influenced sales or not can only be speculated.[7]

Paid on commission only, Issy's income was sporadic and money was tight. Even if he had cleared all of his outstanding medical debts from the previous years, his assets would have been paper-thin. Nevertheless, in May 1936 he donated to the German Jewish Relief Fund, set up to assist refugees mostly arriving from Britain and Germany. A few months later he donated to the Essendon Football Club, where he was a member, so that the prize for the best and fairest player could be given out.[8]

Later that month, as a result of his poor health and mounting bills, he applied for a Repatriation Treatment Allowance (TA). A year later, when he became a hospital outpatient due to another recurrence of bronchitis, the application was accepted. Next to the rank of 'Sergeant', written and underlined in red, it stated 'Private for TA purposes'. At the foot of the memo under the heading 'Remarks' it said 'Full Sustenance is being paid, to be adjusted with TA by journal entry'.

In May 1937 Issy had indeed been reduced to applying for the Sustenance allowance, his fortnightly pension of 16s 9d being woefully inadequate and his commission insufficient to support the family. Such a scheme had been introduced for the relief of individuals able and willing to find employment but unable to do so. It comprised some cash and mostly food rations, but a payment was also available on medical grounds if individuals 'were unable to follow an occupation on account of undergoing medical treatment'. Issy was paid £5 2s 11d from 17 to 31 May 1937 while he was treated, after deduction of his British and Commonwealth pensions.[9]

This might have eased the financial burden but it wasn't enough. Maurice, now a young boy nearly five years old, recalled dinners at times consisting of little more than bread and dripping. Meals were also regularly made comprising largely of matzos, the unleavened bread made from flour and water traditionally eaten on the Jewish observance of Passover. 'Matzos' became Maurice's nickname.[10]

The expenses continued to grow. Soon it was the young Maurice who found himself needing medical care, with the additional bills stretching the family to its limits. When he was in hospital with tonsilitis, Issy brought him in a model car that he had made himself, built to scale from scraps of tin, wood and resin. It was a copy of the Blue Bird, in which British racing motorist Sir Malcolm Campbell had broken the land speed record in 1933.[11]

Despite these tough times, Issy did not begrudge his position. On 27 November 1937, he wrote a letter to the *Smith's Weekly* in response to a story about bogus VCs.

> DEAR SIR, – I was very much interested in your article in reference to the bogus V.C.'s, and I certainly think that they should be shown up, and I admire your paper for the stand they are taking on behalf of the Returned Soldiers.
>
> In Column 3 on Page 2 there seems to be an error that actually the V.C. pension is £5 a year. I am the holder of the V.C., and the lowest V.C. pension is £10 per annum, paid quarterly. Of course, one can get more than £10 a year

according to his circumstances, but never less than £10 a year.

Thanking you very much for your article.

I remain,

Yours faithfully,

(signed) Issy Smith, V.C.[12]

But while details of his decoration were an open book, his war disabilities were not: Issy did his best to conceal his ill health. It was true there had been significant changes to attitudes and care since the war – the disabled were no longer sent away to institutions or viewed as the 'deserving poor'; returned servicemen with impairments were war heroes. On the whole the community was sympathetic and employers were encouraged to hire them to show their support.

Yet there was a problem. While visible injuries were unmistakable and understandable, internal issues and nervous complaints were inexact and incomprehensible. Revealing publicly his deteriorating condition was not an option: he would merely become a charity case worthy of pity. Worse still, the reality was employment opportunities would dry up, money would get tighter and relief from his financial troubles would turn into nothing more than a pipe dream.

The solution was a gallant veneer.

Chapter 33

Dark Clouds Loom

On 8 May 1937 Issy received a letter from a Captain Bracegirdle, military and official secretary to the Governor-General, declaring that His Majesty the King was pleased to institute a medal to commemorate the coronation of Their Majesties, and that one of the medals had been awarded to him.[1]

Two thousand medals were given out at that time to the citizens of Victoria who took a leading part in State or Federal affairs. The letter shed no light as to the specific reason why Issy was receiving it.

There is a possibility that it was for his contributions to the British and Australian film industry, or even for his time in politics. It could also have been for his services to the general community: he had been a justice of the peace for the past six years and involved for much longer in countless fundraising events for disadvantaged children and less fortunate adults. He was also well known and highly respected within both British and Australian circles, as well as in the Jewish community.

Yet the most likely reason for his medal was for his ongoing support of fellow returned soldiers and representation at many commemorative events. During the previous year, Issy had, as usual, been actively involved in the Anzac Day services and, as president of the 1914 Imperial Reservists, chaired their reunion when matters of military importance were discussed. Later that year, as a founding member of the Jewish Returned Soldiers' Circle, he had recited a prayer for the dead (*Kaddish*) at an Armistice Day observance conducted by the Jewish Burial Society. The president, Lieutenant Colonel Isaacson, had placed a wreath.[2]

Just six months later, Issy stood at the Lieutenant Colonel's graveside, mourning his passing.[3] Not long after, Jock Cameron, an active member of the Imperial Reservists Association, was also gone. The ruinous war was still taking its toll.[4]

But as family and colleagues paid their respects in the Melbourne winter of 1937, a new and terrifying realisation was looming. It wasn't just the old soldiers whose early deaths were feared. Globally, war clouds were amassing again and those who had been part of the first war knew of its futility. With such a heavy cost expected to lives and livelihoods, every side would come out a loser.

The situation had everyone on edge. The troubles in Europe weren't just coming from a single despotic state; they stemmed from multiple fronts and had been brewing for over a decade. Attempts had been made to keep the peace – with Japan, following the invasion of Manchuria in 1931; with Italy before and after the attack on Abyssinia in 1935, and with Germany after Hitler sent his forces into the Rhineland in 1936. To make matters worse, Italy and Germany had joined forces and intervened in the civil war in Spain. Aggression and brutality were taking hold and it was becoming increasingly apparent that a new world war was not only possible but probable.

As British Prime Minister Stanley Baldwin stepped down and Neville Chamberlain stepped up, appeasement negotiations continued and the Commonwealth clung to hopes for a peaceful resolution. In February 1938, as fears grew over the negotiations with Germany, Lord Halifax, Britain's foreign secretary, weighed in with his views. 'I do not believe, and never have believed, in the imminence of war. I believe that time is on the side of peace,' he said. 'In my judgement, greater progress would be made if we could rid our minds of the catastrophic conception of Europe always on the brink of an abyss, which I think is largely responsible for maintaining the background which makes the whole picture look so dark. Europe as I see it is not so much dangerous as confused.'[5]

In Australia Joseph Lyons, still Prime Minister since his landslide election in 1931, also favoured the appeasement approach and had been endeavouring to maintain friendly relations with Japan. But as concerns mounted, he began to allocate an increasing proportion of the budget towards defence.

Lyons was popular, yet the country was divided. Many felt Lyons' actions came too late and that Australia's military should have been strengthened long before. When Colonel George Wall (husband to Issy's sister Rachel) had visited Melbourne back in 1933 he had made his view of the state of affairs clear. Having moved to Sydney to take charge of military activities at Randwick, he was frustrated with the sluggish recruitment since his arrival. 'The youth of Australia have forgotten about military training and sport has completely overshadowed everything,' he remarked.

> Diggers do not want war, but Australia has to be prepared. It is no good Australians thinking that they are safe because they are far from the seat of wars. If Britain gets into trouble, Australia might have to look after herself and she could not do it without being prepared. It is obvious that six up-to-date cruisers have not been loaned to Australia for nothing.[6]

Yet little changed over the following years and the worries continued. Now, in the later part of the decade it was not just a war that was looming: a resurgence in antisemitism was also afoot, rising dramatically in Germany and making its way stealthily across the world. In Australia an undercurrent was building, and as the tensions in Europe worsened, it was becoming increasingly overt.

The young Maurice felt it from the outset. One day, after constant torment, he used Issy's boxing skills in the school ground to defend himself. To everyone's surprise, including his own, he left his aggressor sprawled on the pavement.

But for the young boy, another example of it was even more vivid. When Issy could afford it, he liked to take his family out to dinner. One evening, the venue was Café Florentino, the famous and rather exclusive Italian restaurant at the top of Bourke Street. The décor was formal and the dress code strict: Maurice, now six or seven years old, recalled sitting bolt upright at the table, wearing a Harris Tweed jacket just like his father. Elsie and Olive, also neatly attired, sat beside him, enjoying the ambience. The room was full and the clamour made it challenging to talk. After ordering their meals, the family abandoned their chatter and watched the activity as the waiters scurried about.

At a nearby table, a party of men who had drained several bottles and were sinking a few more suddenly spotted Issy; it appeared they knew who he was. The most rambunctious of the group began to make rude, racist jokes about him. The others snorted with laughter and, further encouraged, the man continued, raising the jests with more obscene language until a loud guffaw broke out. The room fell to a hush just as a waiter arrived at Issy's table with an enormous bowl of spaghetti. Surrounding diners squirmed in their seats, unsure what to do. Issy sat quietly with his back to the men – he did not turn or look.

Now with a captive audience, the man launched into a raucous tirade to the delight of the party who clutched their sides between howls of merriment. Just as the jokes reached their pinnacle Issy collected his dish, walked calmly over and without further ado, inverted the bowl on the ringleader's head.

For a moment there was stunned silence as the man sat motionless, a wig of aromatic beef bolognaise and white noodle about his crown. Then the room erupted and the other diners stood and applauded. Without another word, the group got up and left.

A fresh bowl of spaghetti was delivered to Issy shortly thereafter – on the house.

Chapter 34

The Appeals

I suppose I shall be a crock for the rest of my life, but it's all in the game.

— Issy, 30 September 1927[1]

Shortly after the award of the Coronation Medal in May 1937, Issy returned to see his doctor. His cough was constant and he had regular spells of dizziness, blurred vision, chills, sweating and pains in his back. He'd been forced to take a few days off work from Stokoe Motors.

At the Repatriation Commission's outpatient clinic, his blood pressure was recorded as 160/120 mm Hg – an above-normal reading. He was given some medicine for bronchitis, told to go to bed and report back in seven days. A medical sustenance allowance of just over £5 was granted for the next two weeks.[2]

Issy returned a week later, on 24 May, still very unwell. He had had more giddy attacks and had to sit or lie down quickly each time. Everything seemed to go around and his vision became hazy; in addition, he now had a constant throbbing pain in his left temple.

His blood pressure was taken again, this time giving a reading of 170/100 mm Hg. A series of question marks were noted on the case files. Vertigo? Labyrinthitis?[3] Hyperpiesis?[4] He was sent for further assessment.

On 3 June 1937, a Dr Pryde examined him, noting a new reading at 176/114 mm Hg, a level nearing the danger zone.[5] He made his diagnosis: arteriosclerosis.

Although this was entirely possible, if correct this pronouncement would have been remarkable. Arteriosclerosis, a condition of the thickening of the artery walls resulting in rigidness, was difficult to be seen except in an autopsy. In 1937 there was no specific method or means of proving the condition: the conclusion that seemed to have been drawn was that if the pressure was high, the pipes (arteries) were blocked.[6] Although some research had begun in America with the insertion of catheters into the arteries to examine them, little was known about heart disease, and the procedure was not common practice.[7] The long-term effects of recurring infections or chlorine gas on the lungs were also unchartered territory. It was guesswork.

Perhaps to back himself, the doctor requested an eye test: if the tiny arteries in the eyes were thickened, this might be an indication his diagnosis was correct. He also ordered Blood Wasserman and Kahn tests: although primarily used for the detection of syphilis, these investigations sometimes identified other diseases such as malaria and tuberculosis. Syphilis, in particular neurosyphilis, would explain his previous hospitalisation for a nervous condition. The latter diseases would explain the fevers.

Issy accepted the diagnosis of arteriosclerosis and later that day lodged an application for a disability claim for it along with an eye condition, assuming that the latter was causing the headaches.

A few days later the test results came back – all were negative. The diagnosis was final. For the remainder of Issy's life, the primary cause of his health issues was attributed to arteriosclerosis without any investigation of other possible factors.

If further consideration was given to the high blood pressure warnings and the danger lurking from their sustained levels, nothing appeared to be done about it. Issy was handed a pair of glasses and on 28 June, a Dr Tyrer and a Mr Usher recommended to the State Board that the claim be rejected. Within a week, the State Board accepted the recommendation.[8]

On 21 July 1937 Issy, unaware of his precarious predicament, requested an appeal, arguing that his present disability was due to the stresses and strains of war service. A long and very detailed process began, with pages upon pages submitted detailing his service and health records. Issy provided several affidavits outlining his postwar employment and the symptoms and suffering he had experienced.[9]

Diagnosing illness as being due to war service was difficult, especially when medical records during service were limited and any prior to the war were almost non-existent. Only a one-line summary could be offered for each of the injuries incurred during his service and nothing was available before he enlisted – although having run away at age eleven and joining at thirteen meant it is likely Issy never saw a doctor until then.

Conditions for which little was known were arguable. By 1932 arteriosclerosis and hyperpiesia (hypertension, or high blood pressure) had been recognised as occurring together and frequently among ex-servicemen. They were considered part of cardio-vascular disease, but their causes and association with each other were unknown. Without a clear link to war service, they tended to be ignored. Issy's case was no exception.

There were also challenges with the committees who reviewed applications and appeals. The panel members making the assessments often comprised doctors with army experience, many of whom held draconian views about health. Symptoms that appeared to be ill defined, vague, or a neurosis were frequently easily dismissed. Issy had spent some time in care for nerves and his complaints were at risk of being considered largely psychological.

After hearing the evidence, the decision for Issy's appeal was left to the same Dr Tyrer and Mr Usher, who again recommended it be disallowed. On 13 August, the State Board agreed with the recommendation and on 30 August the Repatriation Commission also brought down their decision. The appeal was disallowed.

But the case didn't end there. Even though a decision had been made, the following month the Commission forwarded the evidence on to the Ministry of Pensions in London for their view. As many of the Repatriation staff were ex-servicemen themselves, the case may have struck a chord with those sympathetic to his condition and perhaps it was hoped this would offer a lifeline. Alternatively, given Issy was not a member of the AIF but instead an Imperial Reservist whose pension was funded by the Ministry, their final decision may have been necessary.

Three months later, on 3 December 1937, a reply was delivered to the Commission on traditional royal letterhead. All of the evidence had 'been considered under special arrangements for dealing with late applications made more than seven years after discharge', it read. Unfortunately, the Ministry was unable to admit this application for a grant of compensation. The arteriosclerosis and eye condition were disallowed.

The decision was pivotal. As this condition was deemed *not* to be the result of war service, the cash-strapped British government was off the hook. All examinations for eligibility had, to date, been exacting – and for good reason. Significant debts were still outstanding from the Great War and another serious war was looming – any available money had to be readied for future hostilities. With such a delicate balance in the making, the focus had to be on the future of the Commonwealth … not the past.[10]

After being notified of the outcome, and with no medical or financial relief appearing to be anywhere in sight, Issy made a last-ditch effort. On 6 December 1937 he lodged an appeal to the War Pensions Entitlement Appeal Tribunal, a body set up in Australia eight years earlier to decide appeals against decisions made by the Repatriation Commission. He cited pains in his chest, dizziness and problems with his eyesight – being, as he believed, to be the result of high blood pressure caused and or aggravated by war service. This was his final court of appeal, with a date to be set. Later that day he was admitted to Repatriation General Hospital in Caulfield with bronchitis, a bad cough and pains in his chest and legs.

Once again, Issy was examined by Dr Pryde, the doctor who had diagnosed his arteriosclerosis. After recording his blood pressure at 175/110 mm Hg and listening to his heart and lungs, which he deemed to be satisfactory, he noted, 'Man's main complaint is related to the rejected arteriosclerosis – incidentally, he has every symptom one likes to mention: very introspective.' Issy was given some expectorant mixture for his bronchitis and discharged. Nothing was recorded about treatment. There were probably few recommendations available given the arteriosclerosis (the supposed cause of the high blood pressure) was not well understood. Diet and exercise were not mentioned, nor was smoking. The latter was likely not even considered.[11]

Like many of his colleagues, Issy continued to smoke after his war service. During the 1930s cigarettes were fashionable and men's 'smoking socials' became a cultural norm with an air of middle-class respectability. Cigarette advertising was widespread, lauding healthy virtues: even doctors were used in the marketing campaigns, promoting cigarettes not only for stress relief but also as a mental stimulant and an appetite suppressant. Issy smoked a tin of 50 Craven 'A's a day. The brand had two famous slogans: 'Will not affect your throat' and 'For your throat's sake'. Given his cough and larynx complaints, it might have been this campaign that encouraged him to choose the brand. In any case, despite issues with shortness of breath and frequent bouts of bronchitis, he smoked heavily and did not stop.

✢

The War Pensions Entitlement Appeal Tribunal, which had been set down for 18 February 1938, was heard in Melbourne by two lieutenant colonels (Mason and Dibdin) and a Mr Farrow. Issy represented himself. Surprisingly, and to his great relief, the Repatriation Commission allowed the arteriosclerosis and would now pay these costs. The British Ministry of Pensions still accepted no responsibility.

In Britain, arteriosclerosis was less of a concern as a different controversy with respect to pension payments was being fiercely debated. A condition found in men in wartime and referred to as

Disordered Action of the Heart (DAH) had been studied for more than 100 years and was now a hot topic due to its prevalence – yet it was contentious, as there was no simple medical explanation nor clear cut link that could be attributed to the war. A range of names such as cardiac neuroses, effort syndrome, irritable heart, Da Costa's syndrome and soldier's heart were bandied about along with various and varying symptoms – breathlessness, dizziness, chest pain, palpitations, anxiety and fatigue. These symptoms bore uncanny similarities to Issy's sufferings and often appeared after infections and psychological stresses, just as Issy's had done. Yet anything that presented so long after the war and could not be readily explained was subject to dispute.

Back in Australia a determined campaign had been pursued to have the arteriosclerosis, along with hyperpiesia, recognised: perhaps this was the reason for the turnabout and the sudden acceptance.[12] Then again, it could have been the influence of the man known as the Little Digger, Billy Hughes – the then Minister for Repatriation. Back in 1935 he had proposed that the policy for eligibility for the war pension be expanded to include soldiers suffering from tuberculosis. The government had since requested the Commission review *all* cases in which a negative decision had been recorded for soldiers suffering from tuberculosis. The newspapers, which were frequently the forum for political promotion, were quick to extend this more broadly, suggesting that the Government had now advised the Commission that 'all cases of unaccepted men were to receive renewed consideration tempered with the utmost sympathy'.[13]

Whichever was the reason, it was accepted at last and Issy now had one less thing to worry about.

Chapter 35

Into the Airways

Midway through the previous year of 1937, Issy had parted ways with Stokoe Motors and returned the Willys company car. In August, when his British pensions declaration form came around again for signing, he had listed his occupation as 'Traveller' – it is possible he was doing some work then for the Commercial Travellers' Association, although with doctor's visits and a detailed appeal process underway it is likely this was occasional at best. Later that month he had secured more regular employment, but it wasn't until December of that year that he was spotted there, seated behind a desk at the Civil Aviation branch of the Department of Defence located at Essendon Aerodrome, where he had become a member of the clerical staff. Quizzed jokingly by a journalist about the 'Smith Society of Civil Aviation Pioneers' which included Sir Ross Smith and his brother Sir Keith and also Sir Charles Kingsford Smith, Issy replied emphatically that he would not be attempting to apply for membership. This seemed to satisfy the writer, who noted for his own amusement that 'there were still enough Smiths to go around the Navy and the Air Force without depleting the Infantry.'[1]

Essendon aerodrome was the place to be. Indeed, the location made headlines on 21 November when a young seventeen-year-old from the Aero club made a parachute jump into a nearby paddock, becoming the first woman in Australia to do so. No doubt Issy saw the bodacious event, along with a few thousand spectators who swarmed the grassy fields to watch it.[2]

Issy settled into his new role, with the management team supportive of his need to attend regular Repatriation Clinic appointments. They were delighted to have him: in fact, the Melbourne Civil Aviation branch now had the privilege of boasting that 'it was the only Civil Service with two VC winners on its staff'. The other gentleman, a Major William Anderson Bloomfield, was a South African who was decorated for conspicuous bravery in 1916. He had been with the clerical department for nearly two years and had performed his duties admirably. Working alongside Issy, he was described as 'dapper and engaging' and was well liked by his fellow colleagues. In April of 1938 he gracefully retired and was given a heart-warming farewell.

Within days of his departure a scandal broke out, with the startling revelations splashed all over the papers. Apparently it was when he told the story of his investiture in Issy's presence that Issy knew he had never been in front of King George V. The facts became immediately clear – the man was not a VC winner at all. Instead, he had been masquerading as one, taking the name of the real VC hero who was still alive and well and working as the highly respected mayor of a small town in Transvaal, South Africa, where he had lived for the past 40 years. The bogus Major Bloomfield VC, the newspapers declared, had even been invited to Government House and included on the list of names for the Jubilee and Coronation medals![3]

The matter was quickly swept under the carpet by the embarrassed department with no charges laid, although a few of the public could not help but assert that the man deserved some recognition for his audacity, given he could impose himself so convincingly upon the Department of Defence for so long without detection.[4] Issy gave no such support.

Instead, a few weeks later Issy paid homage to his fallen comrades on Anzac Day. It was a particularly important occasion. Just six weeks earlier, Hitler had invaded Austria, to which Britain had raised little more than a diplomatic protest. Shortly, Hitler would be visiting Mussolini in Rome and it was feared the alliance would be strengthened. A show of defiance was required and huge numbers of Anzacs and supporters amassed across the country, with 40,000 gathering so tightly in Sydney that some 200 people were crushed around the Cenotaph.

In Melbourne Issy, a well-known figure, led the Imperial Reservists alongside the other military units in the afternoon march to the Melbourne Shrine. Twenty-two thousand men faced a cold, squally gale that whipped up dust in stinging eddies and challenged even the sturdiest to keep his balance. These men, the media said, had fought in a war to end all wars. Now, the tragic failure of this objective was being evidenced in a growing world storm of hostilities.[5]

As arguments over a likely war swirled about, Issy continued to battle his ill health, although now with more of his medical expenses covered. On 29 April 1938 he was sent for an x-ray, which indicated some enlargement of his heart. A Dr Maxwell recorded that his patient had a mottled complexion and that his eyes were not clear. His lungs also sounded harsh. When he saw Issy eight weeks later on 15 June, he noted that he looked much thinner. Issy complained again of shivers, sweating and pains in his back and legs.

On 29 June 1938, Issy was well enough to attend an evening out at a Soldiers Ball held in the Box Hill Town Hall, hosted by the local branch of the Returned Soldiers League. He and Elsie attended with three other VCs and their wives and four hundred guests. It was a joyous event.[6]

But a month later Issy took a turn, having a coughing fit at work and ricking his back. He was sent to the Repatriation Clinic where the resident doctor noted he could not bend, his calves were tender and his feet were cold. Issy was told no more medicine could be given than that which he had already and he was sent home. Compassion was even less forthcoming. In the files, the doctor wrote: 'the organic and functional disabilities of this man are so interwoven that a true perspective and prognosis is obscured and treatment consists largely of tactful encouragement calculated to keep him firm in his economic groove. For this reason, medical certificate discouraged and man advised to try to keep at work.'[7]

Issy called for his lodge doctor, Dr Park, and covered the bill himself.[8] Six days later, after a spell in bed, he was able to return to work. However dizzy attacks, coupled with shortness of breath, sweating and chills, were more frequent and the pains in his head and legs were unremitting. He now attended the clinic monthly, where the physicians noted that his pulse was increasing and he had regular headaches and pains in his chest.

On 1 October 1938, Issy attended the Commercial Travellers' Club House Dinner, a formal affair with guests His Excellency, The Governor of Victoria, the Right Honourable Lord Huntingfield KCMG and the Lord Mayor, Counsellor Edward Campbell. It was a ceremonial evening with speeches from the various presidents of the Chamber of Commerce and Manufacture and the Chairmen of the Wool Board and Railways. Before the night's end, Issy signed the back of a program and obtained the signatures of eight other patrons, including Huntingfield himself.[9]

Within a few weeks Issy was promoted to the ground staff at the Essendon aerodrome as an Aerodrome Control Officer. News of his appointment and a photo of him featured in *The Argus*.[10]

Yet before he could settle into the role, disaster struck the airline industry. The Australian National Airways Douglas DC2 monoplane *Kyeema*, flying enroute from Adelaide to Essendon, veered 25 miles off course and crashed into the Dandenongs. On board were eighteen passengers, including a Mr Charles Hawker, MP for Wakefield and a member of the UAP. There were no survivors.

This was not the first disaster: since the establishment of the airlines on a big scale in 1930 there had been six fatal accidents. This, however, was Australia's worst aviation tragedy. An enquiry began immediately and it was soon learned that the crew appeared to have mistaken either the towns of Gisborne or Sunbury for Daylesford and thought they were descending from the cloud to approach Essendon airport.

Aerodrome Control Officers, who had only been introduced fifteen months earlier, were responsible for the taking off and landing of aeroplanes in aerodromes – pointing a big torch with a green light to go – and providing advice on the weather. With the growing traffic it quickly became apparent that they could not control aerodrome traffic and check airline flights at the same time. The accident could have been averted, the Air Accidents Investigations Committee was told, if a Flight Control officer had been employed. A competent person on the ground could check the movements of aircraft, advise pilots of their positions in relation to other aircraft, monitor weather conditions and alter flight directions, preventing accidents and collisions near airports. In this instance, the officer would have noticed the path error immediately and could have advised the pilot to remain at a safe altitude until he had definitely established his position.

This was an important consideration as the amount of traffic and the associated risks were rapidly increasing. Initially it had been planned that in busy times commercial aeroplanes and aero club training flights would be under the Aerodrome Control Officer's control, and at quiet times the control tower would fly a flag and planes could take off or land without permission provided they obeyed ordinary aerodrome rules. But within months it had been realised that the airport was now the busiest in Australia, with a greater load than Mascot in Sydney, and specific hours for flying had to be set. Now, more than ever, an officer's focus and attention to detail was imperative while the report into the crash was completed and the necessary improvements were determined.

On 31 October 1938, Issy's blood pressure and pulse were at an all-time high. Attacks occurred when he returned home, and he commented to the clinic that he was in an embarrassing position regarding this as his private doctor, the young Dr Park, resented being called to him at night while he was the attending Repatriation doctor during the day.

Issy pushed on, attending the Armistice Day service in November and participating in the march of British ex-servicemen, walking with the 1914 Imperial Reservists from the Treasury Gardens. In the evening, a smoke social was arranged by the British Ex-Service Legion of Australia with a visiting London Official as guest of honour.

By the end of the year, following years of drought, the State faced a severe summer, extremely hot and dry. For Issy, working conditions on the tarmac of Essendon airport would at times have been unbearable; but he had little choice. The city was an oven and the countryside had undergrowth like kindle. By January several fires were burning on Melbourne's urban fringe and as the temperatures soared and the northerly winds blew, flames skipped large distances until on Friday, 13 January 1939 they combined into one massive fire front.

On that day, the young Maurice found himself at the hospital once again. A few weeks earlier, possibly in another confrontation about his heritage, he had been pushed over onto the gravel and had injured his knee. The accident might also have been his own doing. Just like his father, Maurice was renowned for his pranks, such as escaping out of the classroom window when the teacher wasn't looking or dipping the pigtails of the schoolgirl who sat in front of him in the inkwell on his desk. When it came to tricks on his fellow classmates, sometimes there was a little retribution. An affray and a subsequent laceration may have resulted.[11]

Regardless of the reason, an infection had set in and as no antibiotics existed, doctors were debating whether he should be admitted. He spent time in care as fire trucks raced to the scene of Melbourne's blazes and black soot and ash littered the sky.[12]

The fires were eventually contained and Maurice slowly recovered but by the end of January 1939, it was Issy's turn for a hospital visit. He was admitted again to Repatriation Hospital for treatment for arteriosclerosis, where a Dr Garrett noted he was not sleeping and was very nervy and depressed. Among the tests ordered was another eye examination for his headaches. On 8 and 9 February, a Sir James Barrett, renowned opthamologist, provided his findings for the eye examination. He concluded there was no evidence of arteriosclerosis in them.

For a further two weeks, Issy remained in hospital where his breathless attacks were observed. His lungs were noted as emphysematous and his blood pressure was again recorded as high, but a new report advised that his heart was not clinically enlarged. He was said to be easily depressed and a bit emotional.

Upon discharge, he was requested to return for another x-ray and an electrocardiogram (ECG): a month later he duly attended the clinic. The ECG machine, one of the first pieces of medical technology available, was not new. Although it had been in existence for some 30 years and had provided some useful results, it was only in the last ten years that it had been recognised as being able to differentiate between cardiac and non-cardiac chest pain. The device was still basic and used just three limb leads (known as electrodes) to gather some information about the heart's function. What it detected was the best on offer.[13]

The results were very concerning. The x-ray showed a marked cardiac enlargement, while the ECG reported 'myocardial irritability with some degeneration' – the heart muscle was inflamed and becoming damaged. This had the hallmarks of coronary heart disease and indeed Issy had all the symptoms: high blood pressure, light-headedness, sweating, anxiety, shortness of breath and pains in his chest and legs. What also came with it was a sedentary and short future – the prevailing view of the time.

Issy's war pension was adjusted to 75% and in April 1939 he returned to see Dr Maxwell, who warned his patient to avoid excitement and emotion.

After he left, the doctor noted on his files that the prognosis was grave.

Chapter 36

Grim Resolve

Australia observed Anzac Day 1939 like no other.
Just two months earlier, the British Prime Minister, Neville Chamberlain, was still unconvinced of the inevitability of war, accusing the Opposition 'of taking the worst possible view of the motives and intentions of the leaders of the Totalitarian states and of frightening themselves by feeding their imaginations on improbable hypotheses, as well as exaggerating the deficiencies in the British strength'.[1] But by early April, Britain and France had agreed to come to Poland's aid if it was attacked by Germany. The Commonwealth had come to appreciate the reality of the menacing threats and had begun to ready itself when on 7 April, Italy invaded Albania. On the same day, the Australian Prime Minister, Joseph Lyons, died suddenly while in office.

The Anzac Day atmosphere in Melbourne was thick with a mixture of shock, grim inevitability and grave anxiety. Crowds gathered in huge numbers in and around the city and were so tightly packed that 123 people collapsed during the service and had to be treated at nearby first aid posts.

On the day before, groups of diggers from every unit, including the 1914 Imperial Reservists with Issy at the helm, had gathered in the cafes and restaurants of the city, sharing vivid memories of the previous war and contemplating the uncertain future. Defence preparations were lacking, it was agreed, but not a great deal was being done. Australia was feared to be at least a year behind overseas countries in its rearmament.

The Minister of Defence, Brigadier Street, outlined a potential system of A class and B class reserves formed from ex-servicemen, with the latter being older men guarding vulnerable places such as power stations. Major General Sir John Gellibrand, the leader of the Anzac Day march, was scathing of the efforts. 'True, we have made our first plane, but one plane is little better than a promise of more to come. We could have completed national registration. We could have organised a reserve force. We could have had uniforms and equipment ready, not only for present recruits, but for mobilising requirements ...' he said. 'Australia needs to wake up, or within three weeks men could be fighting clad merely in their civilian clothes ...'[2]

But Issy could do little more than provide moral support. Within a week he was sent home from work: Elsie phoned Dr Maxwell and the Repatriation Clinic to warn he was very sick due to his high blood pressure. Dr Maxwell advised that he knew of his condition, which was arteriosclerosis, and agreed that Issy had been going downhill lately. A taxi was ordered and he was delivered to hospital, again for treatment of arteriosclerosis and this time bronchitis as well. Approval was given for a small amount of medical sustenance allowance.

The hospital stay lasted nearly a month, with Dr Garrett, who had seen him previously, visiting his bedside every very few days. Issy complained of chest pain, heart palpitations and dizzy attacks. By 27 May the doctor reported that Issy had improved a good deal but was very emotional and full of vague subjective symptoms of pains and trembling. He recorded his pulse at 96 and his blood pressure at 174/100 mm Hg. He agreed with the assessment of disability at 75 per cent and advised that 'there was no evidence of retrogression in the patient's condition and no indication at present for further hospital treatment'.

Issy was discharged two days later. A request for further medical sustenance and a medical certificate to cover the time away was refused and he was told to see his lodge doctor for any such help.

On his next monthly visit to the clinic, Issy saw Dr Maxwell, who observed that his patient seemed very dissatisfied with himself. By the end of June Issy reported that he had had several attacks and had been sent home three times from work, but had managed to lose no time. He was now trying Hutawai tonic and raw carrots.[3]

Hutawai tonic was one of a range of tonics available at the time and sold with the claim 'helps to drive out injurious acids and poisons from the body'. Advertised as a medicine for 'after the flu', it was promoted widely as the solution for almost everything from exhaustion, nervous prostration, insomnia, early old age, duodenal ulcers, depression, rheumatism, arthritis, backache, sciatica, skin disorders, high blood pressure and even kidney trouble. Although it was claimed to be a natural remedy made from the live juice of herbal plants, it appeared to be a stimulant similar to other tonics that were designed as a pep-me-up and to increase energy levels.

Many of these stimulants contained quinine and strychnine, the latter drug being used as a performance enhancer. Bidomak, a competitor's product, spruiked that their tonic would reduce fatigue and provide 'a markedly increased capacity for work'. It helped record breakers and athletes to succeed, the claims continued, including Harry 'Jimmy' Broadbent, an air-racing pilot, and Hubert Opperman, the long-distance cyclist.

While the quinine in the mixture might have helped Issy's leg cramps and any remains of malaria if he still had it, the strychnine or other stimulants were the last thing he needed. These chemicals caused rapid heartbeats, high blood pressure, sweating and hurried breathing – all of which he had already.

Issy continued on as best he could; on 14 July, on duty as control officer at the airport, he was featured in the papers collecting the autograph of Wing Commander Lachal who, along with another flight-lieutenant, was departing from Essendon en route to London, from where they would bring back the first of the new Sunderland Flying Fortress planes – 22-ton flying-boats – for the Royal Australia

Air Force.⁴ It was clear now, with further deterioration in the international state of affairs, that war was a given.⁵

By the end of July, Issy's health seemed to have improved a little: he had had no dizziness attacks while on the tonic; however he still had pains in his back and Dr Maxwell noted his joints were swollen. But on 7 August 1939, a manager from Essendon Aerodrome rang the clinic to state that Issy was white and unable to walk and had been sent home. The following day he attempted to return to work but was overcome with another attack – a taxi was ordered and he was once again sent to hospital.

In the ward, Issy was visited by the same Dr Garrett, who recorded on his new admission notes that his patient was a 'ruddy, robust-looking man' with a clear heart, blood pressure of 180/100 mm Hg and no chest, abdomen or nervous system issues, despite Issy complaining of pain and indigestion. He visited his bedside every few days as he had done on Issy's last stay and provided him with some pain relief. On 29 August, he deemed him to be fit for discharge, writing: 'Patient does have some mild syncopal attacks associated with extra systoles, but the degree of prostration is grossly hysterical. No indication for further hospital treatment at present.'

Issy left the hospital on 1 September 1939, unaware of the drama unfolding on the other side of the world with an invasion of Poland by Hitler's troops. Yet it wasn't long before he and the rest of the country would hear of it, along with the declaration that Britain, and therefore Australia, was once again at war. The announcement made by the new Australian Prime Minister, Robert Menzies, on the evening of 3 September left no doubt. The news spread like wildfire throughout the country.

All militia men were called up. This time, however, Issy was in no position to rush to the barracks and make himself available for service. On the day of his birthday, 18 September, he had two bad turns and had to attend the Repatriation Clinic, where his symptoms were noted as usual.

The following month he made the eighth pilgrimage to Sir John

Monash's grave without issue, but on 2 November he had an attack while sitting on a fire engine at the aerodrome and had to be helped down and sent back to the clinic.

Upon returning home that evening, he found a letter from the Repatriation Commission waiting for him. There was an overpayment on his medical sustenance, owing to the exchange supplement on his British pension not having been taken into account. He owed them money, and a form for signing for an adjustment to his pension was enclosed. Issy duly replied, his handwriting shaky and reflective of a man in poor health.

> Dear Sir
>
> I beg to acknowledge with thanks the receipt of your letter with enclosure. I regret to have caused you any unnecessary work but I was not aware that I have overdrawn. However I agree with your recommendation. I enclose herein the receipt duly signed.
>
> Thanking you once again
> I am yours obediently
> Issy Smith 4 November [6]

A few days later, Issy wrote requesting a payment plan from his Commonwealth War Pension to repay the money.

On Armistice Day 1939, the mood was overly subdued – the breakout of another war having robbed much of the usual reverence and introspection. Nevertheless, Issy attended the march to St Paul's Cathedral, led by the Hawthorn City Band and followed by various brigades, including his own 1914 Imperial Reservists. The next day he was part of the regular service conducted by the Jewish Returned Soldiers' Circle at the obelisk at the Melbourne General Cemetery, a memorial to the 61 Jews from Victoria who had served and paid the ultimate sacrifice in WWI.[7]

Always willing to help, he joined an appeal to all sportsmen to contribute sporting material for troops in camp. On 29 November, his letter was included in an article published by the *Sporting Globe* newspaper:

> I would like to congratulate Captain Bob Grieve V.C. and your paper on the way you are sponsoring the appeal to sportsmen for the supply of sporting material to the troops. We must also thank the president, committee and members of the Victorian Club for their wonderful support.
>
> I would like to draw to your attention that we have in camps the old A.I.F. still doing duty in Australia's defence in many a remote place. These men are getting on in years and have to do duty in very heavy uniforms during the summer averaging 36 hours on and 24 off.
>
> Sometimes the accommodation and food is far from the best. There is a great need for sporting goods and comforts among these men. I have already distributed cards given (to) me by the Victorian Club.[8]

The day after the letter was published, Issy attended the clinic. His fingers were blue and he had trouble sleeping. In late December, following treatment for a persistent cough and severe pain in his back, he spent a month at Hampton on Melbourne's Port Philip Bay, perhaps on his lodge doctor's advice.

At his monthly clinic appointment in January 1940, he was feeling better and advised the clinic that he thought he might shortly be transferred to the Censorship Office at Victoria Barracks.[9] On 20 February, he wrote to the 2nd AIF making application to join them. Three days later, however, he had a turn and woke one night in fright, fearing his heart would stop.

This kind of fear was not an uncommon phenomenon – documented as it was in the condition known as Da Costa's Syndrome which dated as far back as the American Civil War. Soldiers who experienced dizziness, heart palpitations, shortness of breath and insomnia frequently shared the same growing conviction that their heart was to blame for all their symptoms. They feared that if they applied any effort, they would face a sudden death.[10]

Understandably for Issy, a racing heartbeat and difficulty breathing could easily create panic, especially if it appeared abruptly from sleep and he knew that his lodge doctor was neither readily available nor could he be called upon for every such occurrence.

On 28 February, a reply was received from a Major JE Barrett, Deputy Assistant Adjutant General of 6 Australia Division, 2nd AIF 6th division, acknowledging his application.[11] At present, he advised, there were no suitable vacancies where Issy's services could be utilised; however, it would be appreciated if the details of Issy's age and service could be forwarded for future guidance. The letter concluded that the General Officer Commanding appreciated his offer of service.

Issy responded promptly. He advised, for the very first time, that he was born on 18 September 1890, 'thus making my age 50 in September next.' He followed with a summary of his service, beginning with his enlistment in the army on 2 September 1904 but leaving out his earlier six months in the Militia. He explained that he had transferred to the 1st Class Army Reserve on 12 November 1912 after serving eight years and 44 days with the colours and, with permission, had come out to Australia and lived here ever since. He gave brief details of his postings, award of his VC and other decorations before signing off:

> Trusting the following is the information you require,
> I beg to remain, Dear Sir,
> Your obedient servant,
> Issy Smith.[12]

If Issy had hoped to present for infantry duty, he simply couldn't. On his visit to the clinic two weeks later, his blood pressure was high, his cough was still plaguing him and the attending physician noted that he had a peculiar sensitiveness in his finger tips and toes.[13] During the next two months he was dizzy, slept badly, had a fainting moment while shaving one morning and struggled to breathe for nearly an hour one evening when reading the paper in bed.

The Censorship position he had applied for did not eventuate; nor did any roles for military service in the new war. But Issy did not let this, nor his declining health, stop him: he continued on with his involvement in the various organisations and charities of which he was an active and valued member. As Anzac Day approached, he joined his colleagues, still as president, at the 1914 Imperial Reservists reunion dinner at The Palms in Melbourne. A photo of him seated alongside the Archbishop of Melbourne, Frederick Head, was printed in the papers.[14]

Anzac Day 1940, the 25th anniversary of the landing by Australian troops at Gallipoli, was the most solemn since WWI. Issy marched with over 20,000 former members of the AIF, New Zealand troops and Imperial Forces past a huge crowd of spectators to the Shrine. Prayers were held for all the soldiers who, many felt, had died so valiantly and in vain. This war had to end, they murmured, and not with another, uneasy armistice. There had to be an imperishable peace.

Six weeks later, Issy told a packed audience at Monash House that 'Australia was facing a bigger task than in 1914–1918, but Nazism must be crushed'. A local councillor in a subsequent address added more. 'Great Britain was not fighting for conquest, but for life itself,' he said. After the speeches, members of the patriotic meeting, which was held by the Judean League of Victoria, decided to form an Auxiliary to work in conjunction with the Red Cross.[15] A session was convened to discuss the formation of this and Issy immediately joined.[16] The first goal, it was decided, would be to raise £200 to equip a ward in a convalescent hospital in Melbourne.

Within a week, the new Auxiliary had raised half the money. Given great progress had been made so quickly, larger plans were put in motion: a Hosts' Ball would be held on Saturday, 7 September, under the patronage of the Lord Mayor and Lady Mayoress of Melbourne, Councillor and Mrs AW Coles, for the equipping and maintaining of a ward at Stonnington Convalescent Hospital.[17] Gentlemen could volunteer to become a host at the ball and take on a specific function such as organising the floor show, preparing the buffets or managing a fundraising stall. Issy chose the chocolate stand in light of his various employments over the years as a chocolate sales representative. A Grand Bazaar with similar stalls was also organised for the following week, 14 September.

In the meantime, after four days in bed with sleep issues and a bad headache, Issy pulled himself together and travelled in mid-July to Maryborough and made an address in the Town Hall in one of the many Win-The-War rallies being held all over the State. Several young men volunteered for the AIF as a result.[18]

The Hosts' Ball on Saturday 7 September 1940 was a huge success. Being the warmest September day since 1928, a pleasant 79 degrees (26ºC), it was attended by over 500 people at Earl's Court in St Kilda. Issy ran the chocolate stall and Mr Michals, the vice-chair, took charge of the toy stall nearby. It was a wonderful evening enjoyed by all, and to the delight of the committee, the tidy sum of £170 was raised.

Chapter 37

The Final Salute

In the early hours of Tuesday, 10 September 1940, Issy died.[1] Just one week shy of his 50th birthday and after a busy weekend of fundraising activities with more to come, he passed away unexpectedly at his home in Derby Street, Moonee Ponds. He had been at work at Essendon aerodrome the previous day.

Elsie was overwhelmed. Sedated in one of the back rooms, it was left to Olive, now 20, to take charge.

Olive phoned the Repatriation Clinic, the rabbi and Issy's employer to advise of her father's death. Then she called her Aunt Rachel, Issy's sister. It was agreed that after the funeral, Issy's son Maurice, just seven years old, would go to stay with Rachel and her husband, Colonel George Wall, for a few weeks at their home in Randwick, NSW. Rachel caught the first available train to Melbourne.

Sometime that morning Dr Park, Issy's lodge doctor, who also worked for the Repatriation Clinic, came to the house. He had last seen Issy on 28 August. The immediate cause of death, he determined, was coronary thrombosis, with arteriosclerosis a contributing factor. Shortly after he completed his findings, members of the Chevra Kadisha (Jewish Burial Society) arrived and prayed by his bedside.[2]

Then, according to Olive, as she told me a half century later, an extraordinary sequence of events unfolded.

They began innocently enough. In accordance with Jewish

customs, a plain wooden coffin without adornment or polished handles was brought in and her father's body, having been slowly and carefully washed and wrapped in a simple shroud, was lowered into it. The mourners, perhaps a dozen or so, began making arrangements, speaking in Hebrew which Olive could not understand. Much discussion took place, but before details could be finalised, the occupants of the room were taken aback when an assembly from the military marched in unannounced. Several soldiers carrying an elaborate casket with brass handles squeezed in after them.

Firm words began between the two parties about the timing and format of the service. When Issy was suddenly hoisted from the pine box and deposited into to the fancy casket by the soldiers, the dispute immediately escalated and the men began wildly gesticulating at each other. Olive shrank into the corner and watched in disbelief as the feud continued. An officer guarded the coffin as if it was a prized treasure chest.

Eventually, after fervent debate, the apoplectic atmosphere lost its charge and Issy was passed back again to the pine box.

A compromise had been reached.

A State funeral with full military honours would be held and Issy would be buried in the Jewish section of the Fawkner Cemetery. In keeping with Jewish tradition the funeral, to be held in two days' time, would commence from his house and proceed to the cemetery, after which a detachment of the 12th Garrison Battalion would meet the cortege at the Hebrew gates.[3] From that point, all would march together to the grave where a salute would be fired.

Over the next few days, news of Issy's death spread across Australia and across the world.[4] 'Sergeant Issy Smith VC, who held the War Crosses of three nations – Britain, France and Russia – has died suddenly at his home,' the media reported.

Curiously, for a man so revered during his time in the UK, one brief article appeared to be the only recognition in the British papers. 'Sergeant Issy Smith, VC, who won the decoration for conspicuous gallantry near Ypres on April 20, 1915, has died in Melbourne, states Reuter,' it said.[5]

But as usual, the details in the papers were a mixture of truths and inaccuracies. With the public none the wiser, all was accepted without question. Issy, an Englishman and a tiny fellow who didn't look as if he had the physique to perform the deeds that earned him the VC (various papers said), was born in London on 13 (or 18) September 1886 (or 1888) and had died suddenly on 11 (or 12) September) aged 52 (or 54). He was part of the King's coronation (or was chosen as a member of the late King's personal bodyguard) when he was posted for services in India (or visited India for the Durbar). He came to Australia in 1912 (or 1913 or 1914) and transferred (or was debarred) from the AIF when war broke out. He was the first Jew to win the VC ever (or the first Jew in the last 1914–1918 war, or the second Jew ever) on 26 (or 20) April 1915 and was wounded four (or five) times. He returned to Australia in 1925 (or 1927 or 1929).[6] *The Daily Telegraph* in Sydney reported Issy as being 'one of the best-known Australian soldiers in the last war'.

The Melbourne communities in which he was well known were shocked, and the loss was keenly felt. Most knew nothing of his ill health and word of his passing came out of the blue. The Judean General War Auxiliary, where he had volunteered just a few days prior, noted that he was a staunch worker who had been active right up to the moment of his death.

The sad news was passed on to Alf and Flora in England. With Alf being Issy's closest friend from his war days and Flora being Elsie's dearest sister, both would have wished to attend, but with the distance and a war on this was impossible.

Hundreds lined the streets to watch the solemn procession, which left his house at 2 pm on Thursday, 12 September. The coffin travelled through the streets of Essendon and Coburg, with Elsie and Olive walking behind at some distance to a mixture of cheering and, alas, to some jeering.[7] Eventually it arrived at the gates of Fawkner Cemetery, where it was met by the military escort, the 12th

Garrison, who formed a military guard of honour.

Members of the Defence Force, the Jewish community, the film industry and various charities attended, along with returned soldiers, including Captain Dunstan, another VC awardee, and officials from the Civil Aviation Department.

The family gathered near the grave as the service began. Rachel tore at her clothes (a Jewish custom) although the story was told that she also tried to throw herself into the grave and had to be pulled away.

A service was conducted by Rabbi Freedman from the Toorak Synagogue, supported by Rabbi Danglow, the senior Hebrew chaplain for the Commonwealth. A soldier's service by the president of the RSL Essendon branch, Counsellor Alexander, followed before a final salute of three volleys was given and *The Last Post* was played.[8] A minyan (Jewish prayer service) was held at his synagogue that evening.[9]

Two days later Olive, who had had little time to grieve, went alone to the grave to quietly mourn her father's death. But when she arrived, the scene took her breath away.

The top of the grave, which had been adorned with tributes, had been ransacked and destroyed. Broken earth and rubbish were strewn across it and the large floral wreath that had been the centrepiece lay against the headstone as a large circle of wire with just the remnants of ivy sticking out. Olive broke down and cried.[10]

There was more bad news to come.

Over in Britain, an intense bombing campaign had begun on 7 September 1940 and had continued every day and night since. The basement of Dame Alice Owen's School, where Alf and Flora worked and lived, had become one of many public air-raid shelters in London.

On 15 October, the moon was bright and flying conditions were good when 400 bombers launched an attack. About 150 people who had come to sleep in the basement were settling in when a large parachute high-explosive bomb hit the school directly. Most of the building collapsed and a major water main burst, filling the basement with water. Rescues began immediately, and miraculously Flora was pulled from the rubble seventeen hours later – injured but alive. The last of the bodies arrived at the mortuary after three weeks of recovery work; sadly, 109 people died, with seventeen not formally identified. Initially it was thought that Alf was lost in the attack. He survived the bombing but unfortunately died six months later, with Flora by his side, from lung cancer that had spread. He was 52. Now it was Elsie who was unable to attend her brother-in-law's funeral and support her sister.[11]

Life could have been very difficult for Issy's family. Issy left no will and had in fact no assets to provide for his wife and two children – there was only a small widow's pension to rely on. Yet a steady stream of people began knocking at the door, giving 'bobs and quids'. Olive recalled that her father always had a soft spot for a returned soldier down on his luck, and now they were back to give their thanks. 'Issy lent me this money,' the visitors would say. 'Here it is back.' The family survived on these contributions, along with donations from the Hebrew congregation.

The Australian Jewish Herald began a public appeal, printing a request for donations in the paper every week. The vice-chair of the Judean League and chairman of the Victorian Jewish Advisory Board, Issy's colleague Mr Michals who worked alongside him at the Hosts' Ball, led the charge with a bequest and writing several appeals. *The Herald* also got on board, with the mayor of Essendon, Counsellor Elder, forwarding a cheque for £25.[12]

Yet donations were slow. It might have been the lack of funds in households generally due to the Great Depression, or the tide of antisemitism, or the many other appeals running consecutively – namely the victims of the Great Famine in Greece, the Red Cross war effort and the Australian Comforts Fund.[13] After four months, *The Australian Jewish Herald* reported that just £100 had been raised. *The Herald*, advertising to a significantly larger community, had raised £328.

Issy's old friend, Henry Lubransky, called on members of the Victoria Club to assist. 'Issy was a great worker for charity,' he wrote. 'He was asked to handle deserving appeals, and his untiring efforts helped to bring joy to many in needy circumstances.'[14]

Money trickled in, and by May 1941, seven months after his death, the two fundraising efforts were able to combine donations, resulting in a total of £575. A permanent committee was set up to purchase a house for the family and administer the funds. With the land already acquired in a new estate in Essendon North, building work could begin almost at once, but as the total outlay was just over £900, more money was needed. The problem was solved when a mortgage was established with Messrs Oswald Murray and Charles and John Wentworth Fenton, which Elsie could pay back. Elsie and Maurice moved into a small, two-bedroom home at 45 Bulla Road on 8 May 1941 – Olive having already moved out on her own.[15] Many years later, the mortgage was transferred to an Ethel Hadley, where it remained until the house was sold on Elsie's death.

✣

Issy's memory slipped quickly and quietly into the shadows. With another war in full swing, there was much to be done with little time for retrospect. Air-raid shelters popped up across town: Olive became an air-raid warden, and once a week Maurice attended practice drills – traipsing off at the sound of the siren to the trenches at the back of the school grounds and waiting with the other children in pools of stagnant water full of tadpoles and frogs.

To help make ends meet, Elsie made her own clothes, but instead of resuming her previous occupation she took a job as a cook at the local pub. Maurice secured various odd jobs, just like his father did – but this time fixing radios rather than gas fittings, and selling valve caps instead of fish. There was little money left over and, apart from the occasional trip into town for a treat of chicken and ham croquettes at the Myer cafeteria, the earlier staples of bread, dripping, specks and matzos continued.[16]

And as he became a teenager, Maurice's antics grew bolder – the pattern a mirror of Issy's tomfoolery a generation before. With all the young teachers off at war and only the elderly retired ones remaining to fill the gaps, there was plenty of room for daring escapades. The setting off of a firecracker under the teacher's table when the poor woman dozed off was a prime example. No doubt his endless pranks were the very reason Elsie's hair turned prematurely white!

On Anzac Day 1945, Issy was remembered once again when several photos were taken of Maurice at the Shrine, proudly wearing his father's medals. One of these photographs was displayed for some time, decades later, in the Australian War Museum in Canberra.[17]

In February 1954 Elsie celebrated a day at the Melbourne Cricket Ground with the Queen and the Duke of Edinburgh and a gathering of ex-servicemen and women, and then in April 1956 she joined three other VC widows and the mother of a VC recipient to take part in the centenary celebrations of the famous award in London. Despite several applications for her son to go with her, her request was denied. Likely unable to raise his fare, she attended alone. During her visit she was able to reunite with two of her sisters: Flora, who had recovered from her war injuries, and Myra. A happy snap was taken of the three of them together.[18]

In later years, Elsie recounted some of her memories of Issy. She noted that he struggled to sleep and there wasn't one night in which he didn't have nightmares. He told her that had they made a film about the way the war really was, there would never have been another war. This sentiment has been sadly shared by many other survivors.

Elsie often suffered from nose bleeds but rarely went to the doctor. On 31 January 1958, Maurice arrived home from work one evening to find his mother unresponsive on the kitchen floor. He called an ambulance but Elsie died the following morning at the Royal General Hospital in Heidelberg. Her death, just one week short of her wedding anniversary, was reported to be from arteriosclerosis, hypertension and a stroke.[19]

Chapter 38

In Memoriam

Issy's life, to this day, remains an intriguing mix of fact and fiction. The real facts surrounding some of the areas of confusion are now clearer; although with many records lost, nothing can be certain. It is believed he was born on *18 September 1890*, most likely in *Turkey*, and joined the 1st Manchester Regiment after he stowed away to England. He arrived in Australia before the war *in 1914* and was *recalled* to his regiment as an Imperial Reservist. He was the *first Jewish non-commissioned officer* to win the VC and was the *first (and for a time only) living Jew to win it*. He was awarded the decoration for honourable actions on *26 April 1915* and during his army career was wounded *four* times. He spent the rest of his life in Australia from *1927*.

A memorial stone, organised by the Jewish Returned Soldiers' Circle, was erected on his grave, and a consecration of his tombstone, a Jewish custom, was held there on 21 June 1942. The service was officiated by Rabbi Danglow.[1]

Many years passed with just an occasional reference to him – the most significant being by Enid Lyons in May 1953, in her recollection of that bitter political evening in December 1931.[2] Then, over 35 years later, Issy was remembered by the Manchester branch of the Association of Jewish Ex-Servicemen (AJEX) at a special service of the King's and Manchester Regiments at Manchester Cathedral.[3]

However, a story broke in 1991 which would have everlasting repercussions.

Early that year, Maurice and his sister Olive found themselves once again in need of funds. Olive and her husband Bill were having financial troubles with their business and Maurice had just bought a business of his own that was not making any money. The solution appeared to be to sell their father's medals.

A renowned auction house was happy to trade them on their behalf but advised that the best they would get was in the order of $20,000–$30,000. A valuation was produced from London as assurance.

Maurice and Olive reluctantly agreed to sell the seven medals, including the VC, along with a copy of the scrapbook and an original photograph of Issy, signed by seven other VC recipients. The total haul fetched $23,100 (approximately £10,000) at auction. In April 1995, a permit was obtained for permanent export and Issy's medals were sold in London on 10 October 1995 for a hammer price of £35,288 (approximately $75,000). They are now believed to be in the hands of a private collector. Maurice regretted ever parting with his father's medals for the rest of his life.

Interestingly, the following year, a case was heard by the Administrative Appeals Tribunal from an applicant who wished to sell another group of medals, including a VC awarded to a Major Edgar Towner in WWI, but had been refused a permit as the medals were deemed to be of 'substantial cultural significance' to the nation and to Queensland, where the soldier was born. The applicant argued that a permit had been given for Issy Smith's medals, but the Tribunal found that although Issy's medals were important, they did not have the degree of importance in Australia's history.[4]

Once again, Issy slipped out of the memories of most, and if it wasn't for a chosen few, would have been forgotten altogether.

In 2013, a decision was made by the British Government for Jewish VC winners to be commemorated with paving stones in Britain the following year, marking the centenary of the war's outbreak. However, only four Jewish VCs – Frank de Pass, Leonard Keysor, Jack White and Robert Gee – were to have stones laid outside their places of birth. Issy was to be denied the tribute; even though he had lived in Manchester and fought for Britain, he had not been born in the country. Following pressure from the community to remember him, the decision was reversed and in 2015 a stone was laid for him in London's East End in the Ropewalk Gardens. A Victoria Cross Commemorative paving stone was also placed at the National Memorial Arboretum in Staffordshire.

In Australia, there has been and still is debate about his recognition. As surprising as this may appear to be, looking back through his life, it is not. Having no obvious birthplace and no nationality, various countries have struggled to find a place for him. He is not on the honour roll in the Australian War Memorial, nor the Jewish War Memorial in Canberra either, not from lack of consideration but because he does not meet the criteria. Although he was in Australia before the war began, fought for the Imperial Forces as part of the Commonwealth, returned and lived a large part of his life in Australia and contributed in an extraordinary number of ways to the community, he is not deemed to be Australian. He has therefore slipped through the cracks because he did not (more correctly, *could not*) wear an Australian uniform. No doubt had he been able to, he would have proudly done so. He called Australia home.

Yet there are organisations that have done their best to help him be remembered.

On 12 September 2010, on the 70th anniversary of his passing, a special memorial service arranged by the Victorian Association of Jewish Ex-Servicemen and Women (VAJEX Australia) was held for him. More than 100 people attended, including VAJEX Australia President Ben Hirsh, Captain Rabbi Gutnick, members of the military, community and our family. Maurice, then 78, spoke as the guest of honour. Major General J Rosenfeld laid a wreath and The Last Post was played in a moving salute. Three trees were planted in his memory and a plaque was unveiled commemorating the event.[5]

And in May 2018, the Returned Services League, Essendon Branch, coordinated by the president, Mr Ange Kenos, laid a memorial stone for him in Victory Park, Ascot Vale, alongside the suburb's War Memorial.

Today, Issy is included in the guide to the history and heritage of Victoria's cemeteries, and in the *Australian Dictionary of Biography*.[6]

Hopefully now his story is told, this incredible man will not be forgotten.

Addendum 1

Brief account of the action between HMAS *Sydney* and SMS *Emden* off Cocos Islands on 9 November 1914.

BRIEF ACCOUNT OF THE ACTION BETWEEN H.M.A.S. "SYDNEY"

AND S.M.S. "EMDEN" OFF COCOS ISLANDS ON 9TH NOV: 1914.

On Sunday, 1st November, H.M.A.S. "Sydney" together with H.M.A.S. "Melbourne" and H.M.S. "Minotaur" left Albany with a convoy of 34 transports containing Australian and New Zealand troops. Bad weather was experienced off the Leuwin and up to the latitude of Fremantle off which place the Japanese armoured cruiser "Ibuki" joined the escort.

The convoy was very orderly, and nothing of any interest occurred until Sunday the 8th, when H.M.S. Minotaur received orders from the Admiralty to leave the escort and proceed upon some other service which was not made known to the remaining ships of the escort, but was guessed to be in connection with the "Scharnhorst" and "Gneisnau" which was still in Eastern Waters.

On the night of Sunday the 8th, the escort and convoy passed about 40 miles to the eastward of the Cocos Islands and extra vigilance was imposed; the night, in fact, was considered by the captain of the "Sydney" to be the most important night of all. In actual fact, the German cruiser "Emden", must, during the night, have passed within 30 or 40 miles of the convoy, in total ignorance of its presence. No high powered wireless had been used by the escort during the preceeding 7 days and during the 48 hours before reaching the CocosIslands even the short range wireless had been prohibited, and to this precaution is largely attributed the success which followed.

On Monday 9th November, at daybreak, a very disconnected wireless message was heard from Cocos to the effect that a strange cruiser was off the entrance. The "Melbourne was Senior Officer Ship and the "Ibuki" was on the left flank of the escort; it therefore fell to the lot of the "Sydney" to investigate, and the Senior Officer ordered her to proceed accordingly.

At 7.a.m. she parted company and proceeded at full speed towards the Cocos Islands which were then distant about 50 miles. There was ample time for the Officers and men to have breakfast and to complete the necessary preparations.

At 9.15 the land and the strange cruiser, which was easily recognised as the "Emden" were sighted almost simultaneously, and for a few minutes the "Sydney" eased her speed in order to complete the necessary preparations. She then proceeded at full speed, all ready to open fire. The two ships closed fast and at 9.40, much to the surprise of the "SYDNEY" the "Emden" opened fire at a range of 10,500 yds, having made no attempt to run away. Her opening fire at this range was a surprise because it had been previously thought that the extreme range of guns was only 9,500 yds. The "Sydney" at once opened fire upon the enemy and very soon the firing became general, each ship firing in salvoes(Volleys).

The "Emden's" first shots all fell within 200 yds of the "Sydney", they were well placed for range but were spread out for direction. It was thought by all on board the "Sydney" that the "Emden" possessed very accurate rangefinders or that she had great luck in picking up the range so quickly. The "Emden" continued to fire very rapidly in salvoes and with great accuracy during the first 10 minutes of the action; a hail of projectiles were falling all round the "Sydney" just short and over, the spray from the splashes often coming on board; very few projectiles, however, actually hit and those which did hit anywhere on the armour of the ship or the armour of the gun shields did no damage at all.

During the first 5 or 10 minutes of the action, all the casualties on board the "Sydney" occurred. Two shells hit a platform in the after part of the ship, the first did not burst but knocked down all the men who were there; then the second one came in while all the men were on their hands and knees, burst, and wounded them all in various degrees, none being killed or really seriously injured.

At almost the same time, a shell hit the rangefinder on the upper bridge killed the operator and completely wrecked the instrument and mounting. Luckily, it did not burst and so passed on without further harm, out thro' the screen and over the side.

Two other shells burst between the two forward guns killing the gun layer and one man of the guns crew and wounding 5 others besides setting fire to a quantity of gun charges which were very pluckily thrown over the side by the other men. The only other casualty was caused by the splinter of a shell under fore bridge which mortally wounded the gun layer of the forward gun. There were altogether 15 hits of which only 5 burst; the others either broke up on impact with the ship or passed harmlessly over the side.

To return to the moment of opening fire, the "Sydney"'s first salvo fell about 300 yds beyond the enemy, the next fell short and the next produced two hits. From then onwards, the "Sydney" continued to hit with fair frequency, and after about 15 minutes opening fire, the enemy's forward funnel went over the side to the accompaniement of much cheering from the "Sydney's" men. Almost at once the "Emden" caught fire badly aft and was seen to be burning there and in other places until the end.

The next part of the "Emden" to go was the foremast which was carried away close down by the shell which also wrecked her fore bridge & the superstructure around it. Her control station (from which fire was being directed) was aloft on the foremast and all the men stationed there were lost as well as those in another control position further aft.

At one time during the action, when the range had closed to 5,500 yds the shortest distance reached during the action, the "Sydney" fired a torpedo which unfortunately did not hit.

The two remaining funnels of the "Emden" disappeared soon after the first one had been shot away and more fires broke out. On one occasion she disappeared for about 5 minutes in the smoke caused by the fires, and most of the "Sydney"'s men, thinking she was sunk, cheered heartily, but soon got back to their guns when she appeared out of the smoke and started firing again. After the first 15 minutes of the action the "Sydney" was not hit again altho' shells were still heard to be whist-ling overhead.

Within an hour and twenty minutes of the commencement of the action, the "Emden" was to be seen to be sinking fast and making for North Keeling Island. The "Sydney" therefore went off at full speed to cut her off but the "Emden" was there first and ran up hard on th the reef with her colours still flying and having fought most gallantly for one hour and 40 minutes.

It was subsequently discovered that, after the first 30 minutes, the "Emden" had her steering gear completely wrecked, and had to steer with her screws; her torpedo flat was also put out of action so that she could not fire a torpedo, even if she could have got within range of the "Sydney" which she continually tried to do at the commencement.

On board the "Sydney", the men behaved splendidly throughout the action. Many of her crew were only 16½ years old and just out of the training ship.

---------------oOo---------------

Addendum 2

Talk by Issy Smith at Portland, 17 October 1927

Comrades, it would please me to have five minutes of your time to give you a few instances and facts in connection with the all-British production which is about to be screened for your approval. First of all I would ask you not to be too critical, but to remember the rest of the world has had a long start on our Empire in the production of pictures. However, being Britishers and of the Bulldog breed, I feel certain we will be there at the finish. When Colonel Broadhurst, of the British Army, and Morris Elvey decided to produce *Mademoiselle from Armentieres*, all sorts of obstacles were encountered, the principal being finance, location and, last, but not least, suitable characters. The good old British Government came to the rescue, however, and gave us some valuable assistance in allowing us, first of all, to use His Majesty's residence, Buckingham Palace. You will see some of these scenes at the commencement of the picture when the Guards change. Again, through the cooperation of the Government, permission was granted for the use of the greatest military camp in the world, Aldershot, also the Military College at Sandhurst. At Aldershot 11,000 British soldiers were put into camp for three weeks. You will have scenes shown you of an aeroplane over Armentières village. This proved one of the most difficult problems of the picture, and the services of the senior instructor at the Andover aerodrome were acquired. For days this scene was rehearsed before it was perfect, and to get the right effect the plane came within thirty feet of the village and dropped bombs, each containing 100 pounds of gunpowder. The terrific havoc wrought may be gauged when you see the explosions in the picture. You can take it from me that a picture producer's lot is beset with disappointments. At Aldershot, with over 10,000 men being paid daily, the weather was so fearfully bad that for six days it was impossible to produce a scene. Then, after two days' work, the scene was not to the satisfaction of the British military authorities, with the result that it has to be done again. I forgot to mention that the uniforms, evolutions etc. of the troops, both behind and in the line, had to be up to British military standard, and not even the story was allowed to be exaggerated. This embargo alone would have frightened most producers. Of course, some of the scenes were actually taken during the Great War, and the majority around Bullecourt. These have been included in the picture by permission of the British Government.

You will have to excuse me for calling you all comrades, but I consider women and all are comrades when it comes to talking of the recent big war. In fact, my personal opinion is that women of the British Empire did service equal to that of the soldier himself. If you think this picture worthy of your recommendation, we would esteem it a favour if you would tell your friends to see it before the season closes, as it rests with the public to show their appreciation, and thus inspire British producers to further efforts.

Acknowledgements

This book could not have been completed without the wonderful assistance of many. First and foremost, however, are four people who deserve special mentions. These are:

- my father's partner Nola, whose idea I am sure it was to inspire me to write this book;
- my father Maurice, for his help throughout and for the funny little scraps of information that were recovered from the depths of nowhere when the right memory buttons were pressed;
- my husband Warren for hearing endlessly about World War I and the Great Depression, particularly when he least felt like it; and
- my good friend Chris Gray, for his keen eye and tireless editing of the story as well as his brilliant restoration of torn and faded photographs.

Also a big thank you to the following people for their advice and guidance:

Neil Humphreys and Michelle Deray, son and daughter of Olive

Claire Coleman, granddaughter of Olive

Adrian Smith, my brother

Neila Smith-Dorfman, granddaughter of Morris, Issy's brother

Jean-Jacques Chamla, grandson of Fanny, Issy's sister

Didier Vignard, grandson of Fanny

Fanny Walberg, granddaughter of Fanny

Serge Walberg, grandson of Fanny

Jeannette Solomon, granddaughter of Jeannette, Issy's sister

Marion Rothman, granddaughter of Jeannette

Maurice Smith, longstanding friend of my father

Tim Fricker, Major, Department of Defence

Drew Fotheringham, cousin of my husband Warren (for assistance in writing to Queen Elizabeth II)

Miles Templeton, British Boxing historian

Paul Knight, British historian, co-editor of 'Away from the Western Front' website and author of *The British Army in Mesopotamia, 1914–1918*

Captain Robert Bonner MBE, Manchester Regiment

Laura Smyth and other staff from Tameside Metropolitan Borough and the Museum of the Manchester Regiment

Various staff from Australian National Archives

Dr Andrew Peacock, general practitioner

Dr Ian Hodges, Historian, Department of Veterans Affairs

Robert Winther, Austin Health

Peter Allen, Centenary of Anzac Jewish Program, Australian Jewish Historical Society (AJHS)

Ange Kenos, President of the Essendon RSL

Harry Lubansky, Past President of VAJEX (Victorian Association of Jewish Ex and Servicemen and Women Australia)

Nerrida Blashki Pohl, VAJEX

Dr Judy Landau, Past President of VAJEX

Ben Hirsh, Past President of VAJEX

Melbourne and St Kilda Hebrew Congregations

Rabbi John Levi

Peter Kohn, *Australian Jewish News*

Andrew Pittaway, Families and Friends of the First AIF Inc.

Various staff from Naval History Section of the Royal Australian Navy

Hybrid Publishers, for their support, patience and dedication.

There are also many others from Ancestry.com as well as libraries and historical societies across England who have contributed in various ways to the finer detail.

I thank you all.

Endnotes

Introduction
1   *Dublin Evening Telegraph*, 17 September 1915, 'Corporal Issy Smith V.C., Message to the Lord Mayor, your Great and Ancient City'.

Chapter 1
1   The Great War is referred to more commonly now as World War I, or WWI. The term 'Great War' was used then because it was literally greater than any waged before. A second world war was not envisaged and hence there was no need for differentiation. Later, it was referred to as 'the war that never ended'. The Second World War is abbreviated to WWII or WW2.

2   The re-establishment was sometimes referred to as the Second Polish Republic, with the First Polish Republic applied in hindsight to the Polish–Lithuanian Commonwealth (1569–1795). This lasted until 1939 when Poland was invaded by Nazi Germany, the Soviet Union and the Slovak Republic, the beginning of World War II. It is therefore also commonly referred to as Interwar Poland, being the period between the two World Wars.

3   Moldavia existed from the 14th century until 1859. The eastern side of Moldavia now belongs to the Republic of Moldova, the western half forms part of Romania and the northern and south-eastern parts are territories of Ukraine.

4   The Romanov family began their rule in 1613, with Michael I becoming the first Romanov Czar of Russia. Eighteen Romanovs took the throne for the next three centuries until the death of Nicholas II in 1918.

5   The Pale of Settlement also included eastern Poland, Lithuania, parts of eastern Latvia, Belarus and some parts of western Russia, roughly corresponding to the modern-day western border of Russia. The term 'Pale' is derived from the Latin word 'Palus', a stake, and has been adopted to mean the area enclosed by a fence or boundary.

6   The coup became known as the Decembrist Uprising. It arose after Russian soldiers became aware, during Russia's occupation of France,

Ratbag, Soldier, Saint

7 The boys were known as cantonists, which came from the term 'canton' meaning the 'military camps' to which they were sent.
8 Verst is an obsolete Russian unit of length, equivalent to 1.07 kilometres. The children therefore walked at least 107 kilometres and quite possibly through long and bitter winters – depending on where they were.
9 Herzen, A., *My Past and Thoughts*, 1 (1968), 219–20.

Chapter 2

1 The association between gangrene and diabetes was not recognised until 1852, and it wasn't until 1893 that a distinction was made between gangrene caused by infection and a good blood supply (which develops quickly), and gangrene caused by poor blood supply (which develops slowly). Regardless, surgery was extremely hazardous for diabetes-related gangrene until the discovery of insulin in 1921.
2 The Caucasian War of 1817–64 was an invasion by the Russian Empire of the Caucasus (between the Black Sea and the Caspian Sea).
3 The Crimean War ended in 1856.
4 The Long (or Great) Depression of the nineteenth century was a worldwide recession that began in 1873 and endured until either 1879 or 1896, depending on how it was measured. It was worst in Europe and the United States. Russia experienced three separate recessions in 1874–77, 1881–86 and 1891–1992.
5 Strangely, this was the German rather than the Yiddish spelling of the name, which was Feigele. We don't know why.

Chapter 3

1 Constantinople was the capital of the Ottoman Empire until 1923, when the Treaty of Lausanne established the Republic of Turkey and moved the capital to Ankara.
2 Ellis Island was formally established in 1892.
3 I made many attempts to view Turkish records, but even with access via a Turkish passport, the information must be extremely accurate to get results. Unlike Ancestry.com or other genealogy sites (where guesses can be provided plus or minus a certain number of years), exact names, dates of birth and places of residence are required. We don't have this.
4 Hamidiye were well-armed cavalry consisting of mainly Sunni Kurdish, but also Turkish, Circassian, Turkmen and Arabs that operated in the eastern provinces of the Ottoman Empire.

Endnotes

Chapter 4

1. The de facto protectorate stemmed from loans Britain and France had provided to build the Suez Canal and other projects. In 1875, Egypt's share of the canal was sold to the British government, giving them greater financial control. This led to tension and a revolt by the Egyptian Army in 1881 which was quashed the following year.
2. During interviews for this book, my father Maurice recalled that as an eight-year-old boy, he had been visited in February 1941 by Glen McKechnie, believed to be a relative of his mother Elsie's side of the family. Glen, then eighteen, had been training at the Flinders Naval Depot in Victoria and was on his way to service on the Royal Australian Navy cruiser HMAS *Sydney* (II), where he was later promoted to Able Seaman. Glen gave him a naval duffle coat with wooden toggles which he wore everywhere. Nine months after the visit, the HMAS *Sydney* (II), in a battle with the German raider *Kormoran*, was sunk on 20 November 1941 off the West Australian coast with the loss of all 645 crew.
3. The naming of children after living relatives is not allowed under Jewish Ashkenazi (Rhineland Valley and Slavic lands) traditions, where the family is believed to have originated. It is, however, acceptable under Sephardic (Modern Spain and Portugal) traditions and is not uncommon.

Chapter 5

1. In the late nineteenth century, the Greeks of Constantinople constituted the largest Greek urban population east of the Mediterranean Sea.
2. This appears to be the case but can't be proved.
3. In 1729 during the reign of George II, a new parish was approved. The church that was built was dedicated to St George as a compliment to the King; consequently, the parish became St George. To distinguish it from other places of the same name, it became known as 'St George's in the East', however it is often written as 'St George in the East.'
4. *The Nautical Gazette*, Vol. 100. No. 2, Whole No. 1578, Saturday, 8 January 1911, New York, '2392 Stowaways Reached U.S. Ports During Last Fiscal Year', pp. 38-9.
5. Issy initially spoke Yiddish, Russian and Turkish. He later added English and some Indian dialects from his army days in India.
6. While the school was co-educational, the earliest surviving records of admission and discharges are for girls only, commencing from 1898. Records for boys are from 1914, and show temporary accommodation continuing. The school was significantly damaged during WWII and rebuilt: https://www.british-history.ac.uk/vch/middx/vol10/ pp. 148-65; *Healesville and Yarra Glen Guardian*, 5 November 1927; Alderman, Geoffrey, *London Jewry and London Politics*, 1889-1986; London

Ratbag, Soldier, Saint

Metropolitan Archives, Notes p. 155.

7   Early industry included tanning, rope and lead making, slaughtering, fish farms, breweries, bone processing, tallow works and gunpowder production. Setting up in the East meant that these dangerous trades and the by-products from production didn't affect the city.

8   Years later, in 1915, a newspaper reported, apparently from the headmaster, that Issy had been born in Cable Street, St George's in the East, and as a child went with his parents to Constantinople. He returned at about twelve years old and went to Berner Street School, speaking no English but knowledgeable in French, German and Turkish. Due to his skill in picking up languages he was placed in 'Standard V' and in less than two years had a good knowledge of English. In order to be distinguished from another Issy Smith who attended, he was known as 'Constantinople Smith'. One day, each boy was asked to write a letter to somebody in the language they were most used to. Issy wrote his in German, said the headmaster, and little did he realise that he was to win such a great honour while fighting against the nation in whose language he was then writing. (Perhaps the headmaster's memory was lapsing, or he was muddling his students. Issy did not speak French or German, and would have chosen Yiddish, given it was the language spoken at home. If Issy had spun the yarn about returning from Constantinople, why would he lay claim to languages he could not speak?) *The Hebrew Standard*, 8 October 1915, 'Dublin and London Receptions for a Jewish Hero'.

Chapter 6

1   When militia units were called for service, they were attached to units of the regular army and took on the new regiment's name. In 1906 the 5th and 6th Militias were disbanded and became the Special Reserve.

2   *Attestation For The Militia*, Form E 504, 'Issy Smith: Regulations for Army Medical Services', War Office 1894, para 702.

3   Stanley, Peter, *Digger Smith and Australia's Great War*, Pier 9.

4   'Short Service Attestation Form [corners of form damaged, losing actual form number], Issy Smith'.

5   The term 'Glasshouse' originated from the military prison at Aldershot, which had a glazed roof. Gradually, the word 'Glasshouse' came to be applied to all military prisons.

6   Most British infantry regiments had two active battalions. Each contained about 1000 soldiers. There was also a part time territorial battalion. A battalion was made up of four companies, and each company consisted of four platoons of approximately 30 to 40 soldiers, headed by a lieutenant or second-lieutenant and supported by a sergeant. A platoon consisted of four sections, each of seven to twelve men.

7   The officer certifying his punishment was Lieutenant Philip Holberton, a distinguished regular army officer of the Manchesters. In 1918 he was a Lieutenant-Colonel and commanded the 1/5th Lancashire Fusiliers. He was killed by a stray bullet on 26 March 1918, aged 38. Interestingly, Issy's medical records list a contusion with 'doubtful history of blow in left rib'.

Chapter 7

1. Being abandoned or an orphan in a workhouse was not uncommon. A Royal Commission in 1909 found that approximately half the children were without parents or close relatives.
2. Ague, an old medical term, was used to describe intermittent fever and chills, usually, but not always associated with malaria.
3. It was just ten years earlier that Sir Ronald Ross, a British Army surgeon working in Secunderabad, proved that malaria is transmitted by mosquitos. Issy received quinine treatment but what effect it had is unknown. Scientists were only learning in 1907 that a biological resistance to quinine could occur, which much later partially explained why major outbreaks in WWI could not be adequately controlled. Synthetic antimalarial drugs were not available until after WWI and antibiotics, sometimes used in combination with them, not until the 1930s.
4. In 1887, around 40 per cent of soldiers could not obtain the fourth-class certificate, which was equivalent to a standard that children of eight years old were expected to pass. By the time of the decade preceding WWI, not a lot had improved with roughly the same percentage still unable to progress to the next level.

    To meet the new third-class level set in 1906, soldiers were required to work examples of addition, subtraction, multiplication and division, calculate reductions of weights and money, write a simple letter to a parent or friend (of no less than 70 words) and write from dictation of a relatively easy narrative. Skelley, A.R., *The Victorian Army At Home: The Recruitment and Terms and Conditions of the British Regular, 1859–1899*. Mc Gill-Queen's University Press, Montreal, 1977, pp. 94, 95, and 311; Smith, Elaine A., *The Army Schoolmaster and the Development of Elementary Education in the Army, 1812–1920*.
5. From the Scrapbook prepared by Sister Gertrude Wood, 'Issy Smith VC 1915', undated newspaper clipping; *The Sporting Judge*, 11 Sep 1915.
6. A rabbit punch, from a method used to kill rabbits, is a sharp blow to the back of the neck. It is dangerous because it can lead to serious and irreparable spinal cord injury, or instant death.
7. An extensive review and discussion with UK boxing historian Miles Templeton suggests this is the case. Both 'Jack Daniels' were of similar age with 'origins' from St George's in the East. This was easily confused.

Chapter 8

1. Now known as Jalandhar.
2. Pathans are an Iranic-speaking group native to South Asia, historically known as ethnic Afghans and now known as Pashtuns. Sikhs are people associated with the Sikhism religion. Dogras are an Indo-Aryan ethic group in India and Pakistan.
3. Wylly, Colonel H.C., *History of the Manchester Regiment (regular battalions)*' Volume II, pp. 68–70, provided by Tameside Archives.
4. Issy's transfer Army Form D. 426 is signed 15 October 1912. In a letter written by him to a Major J.E. Barrett in March 1940, he gives his release date as 15 November 1912.
5. Noted in Elsie's handwritten memoirs in the family's possession.
6. Australia's prospects were indeed on the up. Following a severe depression in the 1890s that lasted into the next century, the country incurred a period of instability resulting in nine changes of prime minister between 1901 and 1914. Now with a semblance of order, the government was investing in infrastructure and encouraging manufacturing and population growth. Issy and Elsie were part of a solid stream of immigrants, mostly from the British Isles, who arrived between 1911 and 1914.
7. According to his niece-in-law Dorothy Tallents, kind Uncle Joe was still offering his home to boarders 26 years later.

Chapter 9

1. Some newspapers also claimed that he was the first to enter the Broadmeadows camp. *The Daily News*, Perth, 12 January 1927, 'Izzy Smith, V.C. Returns to Australia, Five Years Abroad'.
2. *The Sydney Morning Herald*, 18 August 1914, 'Imperial Reservists'.
3. Of the 1509 men called up as Imperial Reservists, 111 managed to join the AIF. These were mostly men classed as 'time expired' (had served their time on the Reserve list) or who were medically unfit. Still wanting to serve, they were accepted into the AIF. There is no record of Issy achieving this.
4. National Archives of Australia, MT1487/1, pp. 8 and 1.
5. Not all the Imperial Reservists were able to embark with the first contingent, and some left with the 2nd AIF contingent on HMAS *Berrima* from Melbourne on 22 December 1914. One record suggests he was on the SS *Miltiades*. If Issy had been on this ship, he should have arrived in England on 22 December 1914. According to a letter he wrote to Major J.E. Barrett in 1940, which does contain other anomalies, he arrived in January 1915.
6. Merchantmen (ships carrying merchandise) were the largest ships in Australian ports at the time. They included passenger liners and great meat, wool and butter carriers. Once converted for the first transport,

they carried 30,000 men and thousands of horses.
7   *Manilla Express*, 29 August 1915, 'Rumours'.
8   Of the 38 ships, 36 left from Albany and two left from Fremantle, Western Australia.
9   The SS *Geelong* sank the following year, shortly after disembarking soldiers in Egypt in November 1915. On 1 January 1916, steaming with her lights off to avoid submarine detection, the lookout failed to see oncoming traffic and she collided with the SS *Bonvilston*, an Admiralty store ship that had just taken part in the evacuation of soldiers from Gallipoli. Thankfully there was no loss of life.
10 NAJEX (NSW Association of Jewish Service and Ex-Service Men and Women). Jack Epstein, co-author of *Australian Jewry's Book of Honour WWII*, also wrote a short life story on Issy. He noted that in an interview recorded in 1915 with Sergeant Rooke, one of the men whose life Issy saved, Rooke stated that Issy, at the outbreak of war in 1914, went with the Australian Army to assist in the capture of German New Guinea. The two men formed a close friendship while waiting to be sent to the front line, and on this basis, Epstein assumed that Rooke's account was correct. Epstein, Jack, 'The Life and Times of Issy Smith V.C. 1888–1940 for contribution to The Australian Jewry's Book of Honour', early undated draft given to the family.
11 The name 'HMAS *Sydney*' has been used for several ships. These events relate to the first *Sydney*, a light cruiser ordered in 1910 and now known as HMAS *Sydney* (1). Cruisers were a versatile tool for the Navy, being designed to go anywhere and do almost anything. During this period they were commonly used for trade protection and scouting.
12 *Larne Times*, Belfast, 22 January 1916, 'The First Jewish VC Arrival in Belfast'.
13 The newspaper story reports that at the time of the attack, the SS *Emden* was replenishing her bunkers from the SS *Berwick* captained by German Grand Admiral and Secretary of State of the Imperial Naval Office, Alfred von Tirpitz; according to the story, after the sinking of the SS *Emden*, the SS *Berwick* was chased down, the crew rescued and the ship sunk with Von Tirpitz onboard. It was actually the SS *Buresk*, a British steamship that the SS *Emden* captured and used as a prison ship and collier, not the HMS *Berwick* (the correct ship name – there was no such ship as the SS Berwick.). Although SS *Buresk* was indeed chased and sunk, it does not appear that she was replenishing SS *Emden* when the battle began and she was not captained by Von Tirpitz. He was in Europe managing the country's affairs and was never drowned (he died in 1930, aged 80). The article reads as if it was written to enthral readers with the new thrills of war rather than be an accurate record of the event.
14 The typed account has been included in an addendum to this book.

15   The National Archives of Australia lists Issy as departing on the SS *Miltiades* on 21 October 1914 (NAA: MT1487/1), but the passenger list cannot be located. Just prior to their departure, the Imperial Reservists were presented with a red flag of stars and the Union Jack by the then Attorney General, Honourable W.M. 'Billy' Hughes. Some 60 soldiers signed it, along with a few from the AIF, and the troop ship '*Miltiades*' was inscribed, although it was misspelt. Later, when he became Prime Minister, the flag was marked with the words 'W.M. Hughes P.M. 1914'. With the passage of time many of the signatures are illegible and it is difficult to tell if Issy's is one of them. Australian War Memorial, 'Australian red ensign presented to Imperial Reservists by W.M. "Billy" Hughes in 1914: Corporal E D Watson, East Lancashire Regiment', RELAWM0819.001.

Chapter 10

1   Pittaway, A., Digger, *Magazine of the Family and Friends of the First AIF Inc*, September 2011, 'Imperial Reservists from Australia'.
2   Bonner, Robert, *Issy Smith VC, The Manchester Regiment, A Soldier of the Jullundur Brigade, for most conspicuous bravery on 26 April 1915*, 2014, p. 6.
3   With the high attrition rate, more Allied troops were desperately needed for the Western Front. The Indian Army, a force of 161,000, was a great asset to be utilised. The two infantry divisions of 3rd (Lahore) and 7th (Meerut) in India were chosen and sent as reinforcements to the British Expeditionary Force (BEF) already fighting in France.
4   Soldiers sometimes succumbed to disease or minor unattended injuries from previous battles – not just the immediate enemy fire.
5   Trench foot is an infection of the feet caused by standing in cold, wet and unsanitary conditions. During the war, soldiers stood for many, many hours in waterlogged trenches without being able to dry their feet. In the worst cases, if treated too late, feet became gangrenous and had to be amputated. Trench fever and trench nephritis (inflammation of the kidneys) were other potential problems.
6   The 'original' brigade now consisted of 1st Battalion Manchester Regiment, 4th Battalion Suffolk Regiment (Territorials), 47th Sikhs and 59th Scinde Rifles.
7   Stewart, Herbert A., *Mons to Loos, Being the Diary of a Supply Officer* (1916).
8   Garrod, Heathcote William, www.hughboyle.com

Chapter 11

1   The First Battle of Ypres had three phases and ran from 19 October to 22 November 2014.
2   The gas was chlorine, which damages the eyes, nose and throat, and

3   causes death by stimulating an excess production of fluid in the lungs, resulting in 'drowning'.
3   *Dublin Daily Express*, 25 August 1915, 'Jewish VC in Dublin, Corporal Smith Describes Thrilling Moments on the Battlefield'.
4   Allied soldiers used various slang names to describe enemy weapons. A Jack Johnson, named after the first African-American heavyweight boxing champion, was the largest shell used by the Germans. It was between 16 and 17 inches in diameter (40-43cm), and when it exploded it left a shell crater about 20 feet deep (6m), along with a cloud of black smoke. It was also sometimes called the Ypres Express.
5   Issy's son Maurice had another account of what his father actually said about the brandy – told to him many years later. Apparently, Issy waved away the brandy, saying to the officer, 'I don't drink, and I'm not about to start.'
6   From the Scrapbook prepared by Sister Gertrude Wood, 'Issy Smith VC 1915', various undated newspaper clippings.
7   Ibid.
8   *The Guardian*, London, 'Manchester's Jewish VC', 27 August 1915.
9   From the Scrapbook prepared by Sister Gertrude Wood, 'Issy Smith VC 1915', undated newspaper clippings.

Chapter 12

1   Scientific studies have since suggested that cigarette smoking can worsen the long-term effects of chlorine gas.
2   Shell shock is an obsolete term associated with and deemed the primary war disorder of WWI, although Disordered Action of the Heart (DAH), also known by many other names such as 'soldier's heart', 'irritable heart' and 'effort syndrome' was just as common. Shell shock, now with the modern definition of post-traumatic stress disorder (PTSD), was considered an acute trauma of combat but was also seen outside war, such as in prisoners awaiting capital punishment.
3   *North China Herald*, Shanghai, 28 August 2021, 'Acting Corporal Issy Smith'.
4   A short bit of footage (barely 20 seconds in length) was made of Issy being told the good news. It was loaded onto the internet for the first time on 20 October 2021, the day before Issy's son Maurice passed away. Had it been loaded two days before, Maurice could have watched it. YouTube: 'Corporal Issy Smith wins the VC' (1915). In 1922, Issy was officially listed in the *British Jewry Book of Honour*, Adler, Rev. M. DSO, S.C.F., B.A., London, Caxton Publishing Company Ltd, 1922.
5   There are many press releases of the day which refer to Issy having 'won' his VC – Issy even uses these words himself. Views and perceptions have changed over time and many now argue that it is offensive to claim a medal as 'won', as it implies it is a competition. Instead, a VC is

	awarded for honourable actions. The historical references to 'winning a VC' have been retained and the prevailing views are now acknowledged. From the Scrapbook prepared by Sister Gertrude Wood, 'Issy Smith VC 1915', undated newspaper clippings; *The Hebrew Standard*, 8 October 1915, News from England.
6	The Cross of St George was awarded to non-commissioned officers and men. The 4th class was given for the first brave act, the 3rd class for a second brave act, etc. The 3rd and 4th classes were made in silver, the 1st and 2nd in gold. From the Scrapbook, loose article included from the *Official Gazette*, undated.
7	There is no information to substantiate a Russian rescue, however internet details claiming that it occurred while Issy was in Mesopotamia are clearly incorrect. The medal was awarded in 1915. Issy was not posted to Mesopotamia until late 1916.
8	According to various published articles, Nicholas II wrote a letter to his mother in 1917 which said, 'One thing is clear: it is that as long as the Yids are in charge everything will get worse.'
9	*International Encyclopedia of the First World War*, 'Antisemitism and Pogroms in the Military (Russian Empire)'.
10	If this was a disguise, it failed. Western governments and financiers were well aware of Russian ill-treatment and demanded an easing of it as a condition for extending monetary aid. The people of Great Britain were also cognisant, and by August 1915 a Russian Jews Relief Fund was well established and regularly advertised in public notices. The Russian army's treatment of Jews damaged its status and international financial position, and hampered their war efforts.
11	*The Jewish Ledger*, 1 October 1915, 'The Difference'.
12	In many articles, an example being: *Maryborough Chronicle, Wide Bay and Burnett Advertiser*, QLD, 26 August 1915.
13	In more than 30 articles, an example being *The Ballarat Star*, 7 September 1915, 'Modest V.C. Hero "I did nothing much"'.
14	From the Scrapbook prepared by Sister Gertrude Wood, 'Issy Smith VC 1915', various undated newspaper clippings.
15	*The Sporting World*, 29 October 1917, 'Boxing', from Papers Past, https://paperspast.natlib.govt.nz
16	*The Sun*, Sydney, 17 October 1915, 'Boxer wins the VC'; *El Paso*, Texas, 9 January 1916, 'Another highly honored Soldier Boxer'; *Sporting Judge*, Melbourne, 11 September 1915, 'Boxing'; *Sydney Sportsman*, Surry Hills, 6 October 1915, 'Fixtures'; *The Express* and *Telegraph*, Adelaide, 4 November 1915, 'From the Ring to the Arena'.
17	Jim Hagerty, a well-known New Zealand horseman and boxer, was sadly killed in action in the Dardanelles on 25 August 1915, just two days after Issy's award was announced. *Referee*, Sydney, 27 October 1915, 'Issy Smith – "Jack Daniels"'.

18 *Evening Echo*, Ballarat, 27 October 1915, 'Teetotal VC's'; *The Argus*, Melbourne, 27 October 1915, 'WCTU Convention, Women's part in War, The Liquor question'; *Barrier Miner*, Broken Hill, 27 October 1915, 'Temperance V.C. Heroes'; *The Herald*, Melbourne, 26 October 1915, 'Non Drinkers win V.C.'; *Heidelberg News and Greensborough and Diamond Creek Chronicle*, 30 October 1915, 'From the papers'.
19 New Zealand was keen to report that 'Now that it has been cabled out that "Issy" Smith is the first Jew to win the V.C., it seems only fair to record that the first Jewish boy to bear wounds nobly … is Bugler Abraham Wachner. He went to the front with the field ambulance, and such is the dangerous nature of the work of these ambulance men that it is feared that [he] will lose an arm as the result of his wounds.' *Papers Past*, Free Lance, Volume XV, Issue 794, 17 September 1915, p. 4.
20 Issy later signed one of the postcards: 'To my Darling Wife Elsie from your loving husband Issy' and framed it for her. This image frequently features in historical records.
21 Cigarette card, The Great War, Victoria Cross Heroes, 3rd series of 25, Issued by Gallaher Ltd Belfast & London.
22 Issy was the second Smith in the present war and the tenth Smith since VC awards began. Previous Smith heroes were Philip (Crimean War 1855), Henry and two John's (Indian Mutiny 1857), Frederick (Tauranga Campaign, New Zealand War 1864), Alfred (Battle of Abu Klea, Sudan 1885), another John (Hunza-Naga Campaign 1891), Clement (Fourth Somaliland Expedition 1904) and James (WWI, 21 December 1914).
23 Looking back further to when VC awards first began in 1856, two other boys who received it were even younger – Thomas Flynn in 1857 and Andrew Fitzgibbon in 1860, both aged fifteen at the time.
24 Commissioned officers receive their positions of authority through a commission – a formal document of appointment signed by the monarch. They may progress through a military academy or obtain a university degree. Non-commissioned officers receive promotions through the ranks. De Pass was commissioned into the Royal Horse Artillery in 1906 and transferred into the 34th Prince Albert Victor's Own Poona Horse in 1909.
25 In 1920, the policy was reversed and the official warrant amended to consider all acts by soldiers, still living or deceased.
26 Sir Eliot Arthur de Pass KBE was an English merchant in the West Indies who traded in sugar and coffee from Jamaica. The family's original surname, Shalom, was translated to the Spanish word for 'Peace' and became 'Paz'. It was anglicised to 'Pass' in the mid-1600s. He was appointed a Knight Commander of the Order of the British Empire (KBE). The silver cup, a little battered and worn from its travels, is still intact and is in the family's possession.
27 Three other Jewish recipients were Leonard Keysor, Jack White (born

Jacob Weiss) and Robert Gee. These five (including Issy and Frank de Pass) became household names by the end of the war and their photographs were regularly featured in the press. A sixth man, and in fact the fourth winner by date, was Captain David Hirsch. As his parents had converted from Judaism, he was not included in the British Jewry Book of Honour published in 1922, but was later recognised as having Jewish heritage (Hirsch's father had apparently converted for business purposes due to the anti-Jewish sentiment in commerce at the time. It is not known whether the young David, who was killed aged 20 during the deed which earned him his VC, still considered himself Jewish or not.) During WWI, the VC was awarded 628 times to 627 soldiers. Noel Chavasse, an English doctor and former Olympic athlete, won the VC twice for saving many badly wounded men while being injured himself. On the second occasion, in the Third Battle of Ypres, he was very seriously hurt and died a few days later. The Bar to his VC was presented privately to his father. Kitching, Paula, *Britain's Jews in the First World War*, Jewish Museum, UK; Lloyd, Anna Patricia, BA (Hons), MA, *Jews under Fire: the Jewish Community and Military Service in World War I Britain*, University of Southhampton Research Repository ePrints Soton, p. 73.

28   Burgess, Peter. Wartime, *Australian War Memorial magazine*, Issue 48, 2009, 'Our First VC! We all know it was Jacka, wasn't it?' Peter Burgess, a senior historian at the Australian War Memorial (AWM) noted in 2009 that 'Issy is not regarded as one of the 97 Australians to have received the Victoria Cross. That number represents men who won the award while in Australian uniform or who had earlier been in the local colonial or Commonwealth forces. Had he been so recognised he, not Jacka, would have to be regarded as the first Australian to get the VC in the First World War. Instead, Smith remains a reminder that there were several others who won the VC while serving in the British forces who had a strong association with Australia, either through their birth or later residency.'

29   The medal could also be awarded to military units. In a reply from the French Military of Defence to a request for information on the reason for Issy's award, written by a descendant in 2003, it was confirmed that a review of the archives did not find any evidence of an award to his battalion, 1st Battalion Manchester Regiment, and that the medal pertained to his distinguished actions.

30   Reply letter from the Ministère de la Défense, to Jean-Jacques Chamla, descendant of Fanny, Issy's sister, 26 September 2003.

31   Hugo Hercules – first hero of the twentieth century, created in 1902. Superman hadn't yet been invented.

Chapter 13

1. *Dublin Evening Telegraph*, 25 August 1915; *Dublin Daily Express*, 25 August 1915, Theatre Royal, 'Corporal Issy Smith to visit both theatre houses this evening'; *Irish Independent*, 25 August 1915, Empire Theatre, 'Corporal Issy Smith will attend the first performance tonight'.
2. Henry Ford started mass production of the Model T Ford in 1908.
3. Irish Motor Directory 1915–16, Department of Transport, Tourism and Sport, Department of the Environment Northern Ireland. www.cso.ie/en/releasesandpublications/ep/p-1916/1916irl/economy/tp/
4. *Dublin Daily Express*, 26 August 1915, 'Speech by Corporal Issy Smith VC'.
5. *Dublin Daily Express*, 28 August 1915, 'Corporal Issy Smith Reception at Mansion House'; From the Scrapbook prepared by Sister Gertrude Wood, 'Issy Smith VC 1915', various undated newspaper clippings.
6. *The Truth*, 7 February 1926, 'A Modern Prodigal Son, A True Story'.
7. Invitations abounded. On 3 September, a Reverend Lipson wrote to a P. Orstein, secretary of the United Synagogue in London, requesting that the United Synagogue host a dinner in Issy's honour. The secretary wrote internally that he thought the idea was ridiculous. A formal reply was sent to Reverend Lipson on 7 September, advising that the recommendation did not commend itself and would be unwise. If it was done for Smith, it would have to be done on every other occasion of a like or even lesser honour and sooner or later offence would be given in some quarters. If Issy was in town, he would be highly welcomed at the reception for Jewish soldiers on the first day of the New Year (Jewish Museum UK, JMM T2013.311.7).
8. Traditionally, the abbreviation for 'Victoria Cross' was written as 'V.C.' – as noted in nearly all excerpts from newspaper articles. Over time, this has been shortened to 'VC' and is therefore referred to this way unless in quoted material.
9. Various articles including *The Guardian*, London, 6 September 1915, 'The Jewish V.C. Presentation to Corporal Issy Smith'; *The Scotsman*, 6 September 1915, 'Presentation by Berner's Old Boys Club'; *The Star-Phoenix*, Saskatoon, Canada, 9 October 1915, 'Jewish V.C.'
10. *East London Observer*, 11 September 1915, 'Corp. I. Smith V.C. Great Reception at Berner Street School', Presentation by the Mayor of Stepney; Scrapbook newspaper clipping undated, Berner Old Boy's club, Annual re-union.
11. *Birmingham Mail*, 10 September 1915, 'Jewish V.C.'s modesty'; *The Graphic*, 11 September 1915, 'The first Jewish V.C.' (photo); *Dublin Evening Telegraph*, 14 September 1915, 'Corporal Smith V.C. Being Welcomed by Mr P. Sayers JP' (photo); *Illustrated War News*, 1 September 1915, 'For Valor' (photo).
12. Later Major General Sir Lovick Friend, KBE CB PC.

13   *The Irish Independent*, 16 September 1915, 'Corporal Smith V.C. A Hebrew Presentation'.
14   This was the third home rule bill, the previous two being defeated in 1886 and 1893 respectively. The new bill was intended to provide self-government for Ireland within the United Kingdom, but continuous postponements during the war led to a sense of betrayal and the armed insurrection known as the Easter Rising. The third bill never took effect. It was superseded by a fourth bill in 1920, resulting in the partitioning of Northern and Southern Ireland.
15   Now renamed Pearse Station.
16   *Dublin Daily Express*, 17 and 21 September 1915, 'Jewish V.C. Leaves Dublin, An enthusiastic send off'; *Dublin Daily Express*, 18 September 1915, 'V.C.'s Departure: Coliseum Film'; *Dublin Daily Express*, 18 September 1915, 'Corporal Issy Smith V.C.' [sends wire]; *Yorkshire Evening Post*, 20 September 1915, 'Issy's arrival'; *Leeds Mercury*, 21 September 1915, 'Jewish V.C.'s visit, Corporal Smith's recruiting campaign in Leeds'.
17   Renamed St James' Hospital in 1925 and later (present day) to St James' University Hospital.
18   Although it was a habit once frowned upon, attitudes to smoking moved favourably during the war, with soldiers given cigarettes in their ration kits and sent more through volunteer drives. Cigarettes were promoted as building mateship, boosting morale and providing calming effects. Protection of the lungs was also touted.
19   A 'house' is the audience chamber of a performance space. Larger theatres often had more than one and these were referred to as 'first house, second house, etc.'
20   *Leeds Mercury*, 22 September 1915, 'Recruiting in Leeds'; *Leeds Mercury*, 24 September 1915, 'V.C.'s Busy Day'; *Yorkshire Evening News*, 23 September 1915, 'Lord Mayor receives Jewish V.C. at Town Hall'; *Dublin Daily Express*, 25 September 1915, 'Jewish V.C. in Leeds Received by the Mayor'; *Manchester Evening News*, 25 September 1915, 'The Jewish V.C. Corporal Smith's Surprise Visit to Manchester'.
21   The Palace theatre was reconstructed in 1913, and the first artist to perform there was Harry Houdini. As an interesting side note, Houdini had appeared at the nearby Blackburn New Palace theatre some years earlier and challenged the public that he could escape from any lock they chose to manacle him with. A man named Hodgeson, who knew a thing or two about the human body, brought a suite of irons, chains and padlocks and tied him up tightly. Houdini, who was suspicious that some of the locks had been tampered with, reluctantly accepted the challenge and took almost two hours to escape. Furious, he described Blackburn as a 'Town of Hoodlums', and vowed never to return.

22 *The Guardian*, London, 27 September 1915, 'Corporal Issy Smith V.C. does a "turn"'.
23 *Manchester Evening News*, 27 September 1915, 'Call for 10,000 Men, Recruiting Agents' Strenuous Weekend, Slackers Indifferent'.
24 Newspaper clipping from unknown paper, 2 October 1915, 'Today's Grand Effort', speaks of the biggest recruiting demonstration being held at Ashton Barracks with Issy as one of the key speakers.
25 It is unclear why the position was unpaid. It is possible it was to fill an acting position. Extreme losses meant that many were promoted very quickly to fill gap positions. The appropriate remuneration was dealt with later.
26 Hill 60 was a battle that took place south of Ypres, roughly seven kms away and over the same period as the one in which Issy won the VC. *Yorkshire Evening News*, 8 October 1915, 'Jewish V.C. again visits Leeds'; *Yorkshire Evening Post*, Saturday 8 October, 'Jewish Recruiting Campaign in Leeds'.
27 By 1911, Harry Lauder was the highest paid performer in the world. After losing his only son in 1916 in WWI, he became heavily involved, singing to soldiers at the front and giving many concerts for war charities, raising considerable amounts for the war effort and for wounded soldiers. He was knighted in 1919.
28 *Manchester Evening News*, Saturday 9 October 1915, 'How the V.C. was won, Sergeant Issy Smith at Leeds'.
29 *Leeds Mercury*, 12 October 1915, 'Jewish V.C. at Bradford Powerful appeal to men "hiding behind war badges"'; *Bradford Weekly Telegraph*, 15 October 1915, 'Visit of a Jewish Hero to Bradford'.
30 From the Scrapbook prepared by Sister Gertrude Wood, 'Issy Smith VC 1915', undated newspaper clipping; *Hull Daily Mail*, 18 October 1915.
31 At the beginning of the war, men shorter than the normal minimum height requirement of 5 foot 3 inches (160cm) were turned away. Following public outrage, the British Army reduced the height to 5 foot (150 cm). 'Bantam' battalions were formed and so named after they evoked an image of a bantam chicken – a miniature version of a regular chicken but with the same pluckiness.
32 *Yorkshire Post and Leeds Intelligencer*, 18 October 1915, 'Big Rally At Hull'.
33 *The Guardian*, 19 October 1915, photo of Issy at the Town Hall presentation; *Manchester Evening News*, 19 October 1915, 'Recruiting at Ashton'.

Chapter 14

1 *Münchner Neueste Nachrichten*, Munich, 21 November 1915; 'Des Antisemitismus in England'; *Judishe Korrespondenz*, 11 November 1915,

Vienna; *L'aurore*, 26 November 1915; *Westungarischer Grenzbote*, 3 December 1915.

2. On the other side of the world and written ten years after the incident, a bizarre chronicle of the event appeared in a Perth newspaper. Upon being told to leave by the manager and without further ado (the story claimed), 'the Jewish VC grabbed him by the scruff of the neck, violently ejected him and proceeded to test the bouncing capabilities of all the crockery in the place. It is understood that he received a few days 'C.B.' [Confined to Barracks] for his recklessness but business people in Leeds placed no further ban on Jewish customers.' There is nothing in any other newspaper article that supports this tale. The article went on to say, 'Sergeant Smith visited Australia a few years ago. The writer had the pleasure of meeting him and found him to be a likeable, nuggety little chap with a determined eye that explained the Leeds incident.' *Yorkshire Post* and *Leeds Intelligencer*, 26 March 1920, 'Is Leeds Anti-Semitic?'.

3. 'John Bull' was a political caricature. Reflected as an affable and honest Englishman bringing 'action', it became a symbol of England. The character first appeared in a series of pamphlets in 1712 and became widely known by the late nineteenth century in books, plays and even trademarks for goods. Caricatures were often drawn of a portly man in a Union Jack waistcoat with a bulldog by his side.

4. From the Scrapbook prepared by Sister Gertrude Wood, 'Issy Smith VC 1915', undated article, 'To the Proprietor, Grand Restaurant, Leeds'.

5. One paper wrote that Issy should return his V.C. and start all over again, having missed his chance to demonstrate with his fists what the V.C. stood for. Papers Past, *Free Lance*, Volume XV, Issue 808, 23 December 1915, p. 11, 'Entre Nous'; *The Sentinel*, 12 November 1915, 'A V.C. who missed his chance'.

6. Captain Bowen-Colthurst was deemed to have 'cracked' under the pressure of the armed insurrection occurring in Ireland at the time. Incredibly, after killing at least four – maybe six – and injuring two (he took a third man along with the two editors, and attacked others in the street), he spent just over one year in an asylum before he was declared recovered and released. He moved to Canada on a full British military pension, dying in British Columbia in 1965. Mcnally, Frank, The *Irish Times*, 'Open and Shut – An Irishman's Diary about a short-lived newspaper of 1916'; *An Phoblacht*, 26 April 2016, 'On this day 1916 – The Portobellow Barracks Murders'.

7. Dominy, G., 30 March 2018, The first Jewish Governor in the British Empire, Sir Matthew Nathan: An 'outsider' in Africa and Ireland, Jewish Historical studies.

8. Henry Beamish (the journalist who Issy referred to) wrote numerous articles that were widely published. In 1918 he founded The Britons,

an organisation publicly espousing anti-Semitic and anti-immigration propaganda and rhetoric which, aside from a brief lull during World War II, was distributed right up until the late 1940s. Many denounced the prejudice and pleaded for cultural homogeny, but the calls went unheeded. From the Scrapbook prepared by Sister Gertrude Wood, 'Issy Smith VC 1915', undated article, 'Berner Old Boy's Club'.

9 Including but not limited to *Bradford Weekly Telegraph*, 15 October 1915, 'Visit of a Jewish V.C. Hero to Bradford'; *Yorkshire Post and Leeds Intelligencer*, 21 September 1915, 'Corporal Smith's visit to Leeds'.

10 *Yorkshire Post and Leeds Intelligencer,* 21 September 1915, 'Corporal "Issy" Smith's Visit to Leeds'.

11 This caused great offense due to the underlying and reprehensible assumption that Jews, the only religion singled out, were supposedly at risk of acting treacherously. *Manchester Courier and Lancashire General Advertiser*, 27 December 1915, 'Jews and Recruiting'.

12 From the Scrapbook prepared by Sister Gertrude Wood, 'Issy Smith VC 1915', undated article, 'Jewish V.C. welcomed in Bradford'; Multiple newspapers, for example *Belfast Telegraph*, 14 March 1916, 'VC's Arrest and its Sequel'; *Newcastle Journal*, 14 March 1915, 'V.C. Hero and Taxi Driver'.

13 *Dublin Daily Express*, 16 September 1915, 'Jews and the War, Presentation to Corporal Smith'.

14 *East Kent Gazette*, 5 January 1918, 'The Bogus V.C.'

Chapter 15

1 From the Scrapbook prepared by Sister Gertrude Wood, 'Issy Smith VC 1915' undated article, *The Herald*, Melbourne, 6 October 1915 'War's Wedding Present'; *The Sun*, Sydney, 8 October 1915, plus numerous other articles.

2 Additional proficiency pay of between 3d and 6d was payable if a soldier fulfilled certain conditions regarding service and qualifications. It is not known if Issy received any. From the Royal Army Pay Corps https://rapc-association.org.uk/ as defined by War Office Instruction 166 (1914).

3 *The Argus* and *The Age*, Melbourne, 18 October 1915 – two examples of 20 printed.

4 Just some of the newspapers reporting the romance include *Melbourne Herald*, 6 October 1915; *Sydney Evening News* (Date Unknown); *Barrier Miner*, 17 October 1915; *The Newsletter*, Sydney, 16 October 1915; *The Inverell Times*, 19 October 1915; *Dubbo Dispatch and Wellington Independent*, 22 October 1915; *Western Mail*, 22 October 1915; *Sunday Times*, 24 October 1915; *The Farmer and the Settler*, 19 November 1915.

5 *Jewish Herald*, 5 November 1915, 'Our V.C.'S Fiancée'; *Hebrew Standard*, 19 November 1915.

6   *The Australian Jewish Herald*, 27 June 1935, 'Mr Hyman Cohen, A Note of Appreciation'.
7   The UK issued its first interest-bearing war bonds (securities for the public to purchase to fund the war) in November 1914. The likely assumption was that these would mature in ten years, hence the reference to 1924. A catch, however, was that they were non-transferable, so it is unclear how they could have been given to Issy as a gift. It suggests that the whole story was indeed just that ... a story.

Chapter 16

1   The Ring opened in 1910 and became renowned for hosting the finest boxers. The Prince of Wales (later to become King Edward VIII) attended in 1928. The venue was unfortunately destroyed by an air raid in 1940. 'Asquithian' refers to Herbert Asquith, the British Prime Minister at the time. *Referee*, 19 January 1916, 'Issy Smith'.
2   *Coventry Evening Telegraph*, Tuesday 14 December 1915, 'Drill Hall Queen Victoria Road Grand Boxing Tournament Sgt. Issy Smith V.C. v. Ted Broadribb'; *The Sportsman*, 20 December 1915, 'V.C. Hero spars at Coventry'; *Birmingham Daily Gazette*, 6 December 1915, 'Big display at Coventry, Boxer's successful effort for charity, V.C.'s appeal'.
3   *Coventry Herald*, Friday 24 December, 'Canon Baille on Boxing, Tournament at Coventry'; *El Paso Times*, Texas, 9 January 1916, 'Another Highly Honored Soldier Boxer'.
4   Despite its popularity, boxing was significantly curtailed during the war, possibly to ensure focus remained on the war effort.
5   *Winner*, Melbourne, 26 January 1916, 'Sheffield bars boxing in exhibition of bigotry'.
6   *The Guardian*, London, 27 December 1915, 'Jew and the War, what the enlistments show'; *Manchester Evening News*, 27 December 1915, 'Fighting Jews, Honouring men who have joined the colours'.
7   Defence of the Realm Act (DORA) was a piece of emergency legislation passed by British parliament a few days after Great Britain entered the war. Its purpose was to provide greater powers to the military during the war for protection of the Kingdom, however, its capability was frighteningly far-reaching. The first Act meant those who breached regulations preventing communication with the enemy would be court-martialled rather than face civil court. Many more Defence of the Realm Regulations (DORRs) followed, curtailing a range of activities from censorship of war news to flying a kite and even to buying a set of binoculars. Interestingly, the wife of Herbert Cole (who used Issy's name to obtain charity by false pretences) was charged under DORA for spreading false reports likely to prejudice recruiting and was sentenced to three months imprisonment. After her internment, she released a book of poems with Herbert's illustrations called *Prison Impressions*.

8 *The Era*, 19 January 1916, 'Sergeant Issy Smith'.
9 *Northern Whig*, 14 January 1916, 'Sergeant Issy Smith, V.C. in Belfast'.
10 *Irish Independent* and *Dublin Daily Express*, 15 January 1916, 'Recruiting meetings'.
11 *Irish Independent*, 17 January 1916, 'V.C. and his hecklers'; *Belfast News-Letter*, 17 January 1916, 'Sergeant Issy Smith, V.C. Heckled'; *Northern Whig*, 17 January 1916, 'Sergeant Issy Smith V.C.'.

Chapter 17

1 Including but not limited to *Western Daily Press*, 4 February 1916, 'Court Circular'; *Yorkshire Evening Post*, 3 February 1916, 'The King's tribute to Piper Laidlaw and Sergeant Issy Smith decorated by His Majesty'; *Manchester Evening News*, 3 February 1916, 'Decorated by the King'; *Globe*, 3 February 1916, 'The King Presents V.C.s'; *Dublin Daily Express*, 4 February 1916, 'Officers Decorated, King holds an Investiture'; *Sheffield Daily Telegraph*, 4 February 1916, 'King and Heroes, His Majesty meets three new V.C.s'; *Belfast News*, 4 February 1916.
2 Eva, Issy's mother, never went to England. In 1916 she was 71 years old – the woman in the photograph is in her twenties or thirties. She could be Joseph's wife Hilda or one of Elsie's sisters. *Illustrated War News*, 9 February 1916, 'Decorated by the King, Sergeant Issy Smith with his mother and sister'.
3 *The Daily News*, Perth, 11 February 1916, 'V.C. Heroes, Gallant Jew honored'; From the Scrapbook prepared by Sister Gertrude Wood, 'Issy Smith VC 1915', undated newspaper clipping.

Chapter 18

1 Modern Iraq was created after the war from three provinces of the Ottoman (Turkish) Empire – Basra, Baghdad and Mosul. Persia became Iran in 1935.
2 Arab independence was promised in October 1915 by the high commissioner of Egypt, Britain's Sir Henry McMahon.
3 Since 1914 the Allies had held secret discussions regarding the future of the Ottoman Empire, or 'the sick man of Europe' as it was known. In particular, under what became the Sykes-Picot agreement of May 1916, Britain would acquire Southern Mesopotamia including Baghdad, along with other selected areas. The UK and France ultimately reneged on the agreement to recognise Arab independence.
4 The propaganda campaign was not limited to just Britain. France and Russia were also colonial powers in WWI which the German-Ottoman alliance wanted to break.
5 'Attack' included the sinking of boats in the river by the enemy to impede progress.

6   At the beginning of the siege there were approximately 11,600 British and Indian officers and other ranks, and 3500 followers, close to 15,100 in total. At the surrender, the numbers were reduced to just over 10,000 soldiers and 3200 followers, roughly 13,200. Followers were non-combatant support who provided essential services such as water carrying, cooking, laundering and labour but they also needed to be clothed, fed and protected. They were both a valuable resource and a drain on the army (drawn from *Official History Mesopotamia*, Vol. 11, courtesy of Major Paul Knight, British historian).

7   In all, there were eight divisions known as III Indian Army. They consisted of the Cavalry Division, 3rd (Lahore) Division, 6th (Poona) Division, 7th (Meerut) Division, and 12th, 14th 17th and 18th Divisions. The divisions were split and fought on both sides of the river. The 3rd (Lahore) and the 7th (Meerut) Divisions were withdrawn from France, despite Lord Kitchener's objections. This chapter follows Issy's division, the 3rd (Lahore), up the River Tigris.

8   Selected hospital ships were willing to receive a quota of wounded Turks, depending on available space. National Army Museum, First World War Mesopotamia Campaign; *Staffordshire Sentinel*, 28 June 1917, 'Mesopotamia Scandal, Sufferings of the Sick and Wounded'.

9   A 'redoubt', meaning 'place of retreat', is an enclosed fort or fort system, generally temporary and often situated outside a larger fort; it is made to protect solders outside the main defence line.

10 *Daily Mirror*, 7 April 1916, 'General Townshend, defender of Kut'.

11 The number surrendered was only surpassed by the Battle of Singapore in 1942, when roughly 80,000 British, Indian and Australian troops were captured by the Japanese in Singapore and became prisoners of war.

12 Attempts were made to bribe the Ottomans to release the garrison (first £1,000,000, then £2,000,000 was offered) to no avail. After Gallipoli, they were confident and in no mood to back down.

13 *Leeds Mercury*, 1 May 1916, 'A sunny street scene in Surrendered Kut'.

14 *Bath Chronicle and Weekly Gazette*, 19 August 1916, 'Wounded in Mesopotamia'.

15 Knight, Major Paul PhD, VR, Military historian and author of *The British Army in Mesopotamia, 1914–1918*; email communications arising from https://awayfromthewesternfront.org

16 Advice from Knight, Major Paul PhD, VR: British historian; Crowley, PT, Lieutenant Colonel British Army, Operational Lessons of the Mesopotamia Campaign, 1914-1918; British War Diary of 1st Manchester Regiment, Jan 1916–Mar 1918.

17 http://vconline.org.uk/issy-smith-vc/4588267016

18 The strategy was ambitious as a fleet of 200 boats was estimated to be required to achieve this. With less than 15 per cent of this number

	available, it would take time to fully implement, with the risk of inducing the US to become involved. In March 1917, three American merchant vessels were sunk and the tipping point was reached – America declared war on Germany in April 1917. Livesey, Anthony, *The Viking Atlas of World War I*, Penguin Books, London, 1994.
19	Issy's military attestation lists him as joining the Egyptian Expeditionary Force (EEF) from 16 September 1916 to 11 February 1919. The British Ministry of Defence records Issy's service as part of the 1st Battalion Manchester Regiment from 4 September 1916 until he transferred to the Royal Engineers on 1 April 1917. Malaria was a significant problem. The First World War exposed large gaps in the understanding of tropical diseases and how to deal with them. Major epidemics of malaria broke out in several locations in the Middle East, including Mesopotamia and Palestine.
20	British War Diary of 1st Manchester Regiment, Jan 1916–Mar 1918.
21	A Lewis gun was an automatic machine gun designed privately in America but not initially adopted there, instead being used extensively by British troops. It took seven men to operate it. Part of the training in its use was to strip the gun down completely and then put the 104 pieces back together while blindfolded – in less than one minute.
22	Known as Gharraf Canal, Shatt al-Gharraf or the Hai River, it was an important canal for both sides as it allowed the transport of troops from the Tigris to the Euphrates and vice versa.
23	The recapture became known as the Second Battle of Kut.
24	A picquet is the old name for a picket, and refers to the use of one or more soldiers making a line forward of a position to provide warning of any enemy advance. The Arabs could be friendly or hostile, depending on their view of the war. They may also have been opportunistic.
25	Now referred to as Diyala River.
26	War Diary of Commander Royal Engineers 3rd (Lahore) January 1917 to March 1918.
27	*Derry Journal*, 12 March 1917, 'Captured by British, Remarkable Advance'.
28	*Western Times*, 27 March 1917, 'How Baghdad fell, Dramatic Scenes told of British Valour'.
29	Specifically, the part of the 38th Lancashire Brigade selected to force the crossing were the 6th (Service) Battalions of the East Lancashire, South Lancashire, Loyal North Lancashire and King's Own Lancashire Regiments.

Chapter 19

1	The date recorded in Russia at the time of the event was 2 March. Many countries had moved from the Julian calendar to the Gregorian calendar over the previous centuries but Russia only adopted the new

style dates in 1918. Some history books record both dates. Nicholas II, his wife and five children and several servants were later assassinated in July 1918, ending a 300-year Russian imperial dynasty.

2   *The Scotsman*, 20 March 1917; *Western Mail*, 16 March 1917, 'Revolution in Russia'.

3   Second Lieutenant Benjamin Butterworth is officially listed in the Commonwealth War Graves as having died on 25 March 1917.

4   Departments consisted of Transport, Dockyards, Construction, Up-River Works, Personnel, Vessels, Marine Engineering, Accounts, Stores, Buoyage and Pilotage and Native Craft. In September 1916, staff employed were 214 Officers, 212 British NCOs and men and 6735 'Eastern races'. Aside from all of the activities surrounding boat and dock construction, men were employed (or had to be trained) as crane drivers, clerks, motor boat drivers or crews of ships.

5   There were also a few that foundered at sea and one that was stranded, but these were insignificant in the total number of boats acquired.

6   Now referred to as Tikrit.

7   Caldwell, Sir C.E, *The Life of Sir Stanley Maude, Lieutenant-General, K.C.B., C.M.G., D.S.O.*, Constable and Company Ltd 1920; *Globe*, 13 November 1917, 'Haig congratulates Maude'; *Globe*, 16 November 1917, 'Maude congratulates Haig'; *Edinburgh Evening News*, 16 November 1917, 'A well-managed campaign'.

8   A Colour Sergeant was responsible for the company stores as well as the accommodation and meals for men when they were detached from the battalion.

9   Anzac is an acronym for Australian and New Zealand Army Corps.

10   The Institute of Royal Engineers, Chatham 1952, *The History of the Corps of Royal Engineers*, Volume VI, Gallipoli, Macedonia, Egypt and Palestine 1914–1918, courtesy of MaxD from RootsChat.com

11   Letter in family files to Major Barrett from Issy dated 4 March 1940.

12   With the absence of detail in the letter, various matters are unclear. Aside from where Issy served in Palestine, it would appear from his words that after being demobilised in 1919, he returned to Australia immediately after the war. While he did make a fleeting visit to Australia in 1921, he did not resettle in the country until 1927.

13   National Archives Memorandum Former Reference GT 2103 Sir R. Winsgate's letter to Sir William Robertson, Chief of the Imperial General Staff, War Office, London. CAB 24/27/3.

14   National Archives of Australia, Ministry of Pensions records BP18330.

15   *Northhampton Chronicle and Echo*, 4 June 1917, 'Not Mesopotamia'.

16   In May 1920 C Company and the Battalion band of which Alf was part were detached and moved to Karind in Persia (now Iran) for six months. For this service Alf received the 'North West Persia' clasp.

17 Hall, Lieut.-Col L.J., *The Inland Water Transport in Mesopotamia*, London, Constable and Company Ltd, 1921; Battle, A.E., The University of Melbourne, *Inland waterways and docks, royal engineers in war time* (lecture and discussion), 1924; British Library, Untold Lives blog, 'The Chinese Labour Corps in Basra'; *Linlithgowshire Gazette*, 22 November 1918, 'War Casualties'.

Chapter 20

1 It would seem that only Joseph remained in England with whom Issy could readily keep in contact with. Morris had moved to America and the fate of brother Jacob has never been known.

2 The United Synagogue London, also known as the Hallam Street Synagogue, is still an Orthodox congregation. National Archives of Australia, Extract of Marriage Certificate, United Synagogue London.

3 Baron Nathan Rothschild and other philanthropists founded The Four Per Cent Industrial Dwellings Company in 1885, the purpose of which was to provide improved dwellings for the Jewish poor in the East End, although occupation was open to all. Navarino Mansions consists of 300 flats in four blocks, each of five stories, arranged in pairs. The buildings were completed in 1905.

4 https://www.defence.gov.au/Medals/Imperial/WWI

5 The three medals became affectionately known as Pip, Squeak and Wilfred respectively, the names coinciding with a popular comic strip published at the time. Pip (1914–1915 Star) was the dog, Squeak (British War Medal) was the penguin and Wilfred (British Victory Medal) was the rabbit. They are worn together and in that order from left to right. The Allied Victory Medals are similar in design and wording and have an identical ribbon. Australians were awarded the medal issued by Great Britain.

6 Elsie's brother Norman McKechnie listed with the 29th Battalion of the Middlesex Regiment in 1915, but was discharged in November 1916 with Phthisis of the lungs, (a wasting disease, especially relating to pulmonary tuberculosis; the term is no longer in use). He died in May the following year.

7 Doctors initially called it the three-day fever due to the quick recovery of many. The French called it 'La Grippe', because once in its grip, it took all the energy a person could muster to pull through. It was later named the Spanish flu, not because it originated there but owing to the press in neutral Spain, which was free from war censorship.

8 'A pneumonia blouse' was made of sheer material with a low neckline that exposed a woman's neck. This display in day wear, which had appeared as early as 1905, was scandalous and believed to be a catalyst for the flu. Munition factories made everything from guns, bullets and shells to tanks and gas masks. A significant proportion of the workforce

Ratbag, Soldier, Saint

    was women. Demand for munition was so high they could not afford to lose staff.

9   www.nottsheritagegateway.org.uk/events/influenza.htm

10   At a conference in February 1919 in London, eminent doctors discussed the epidemic. Sir St Clair Thomson said that people coughing in public without putting up their hands or sneezing without using a handkerchief should be prosecuted for indecency. *Sheffield Daily Telegraph*, 1 March 1919, 'Conference on the Flu'.

Chapter 21

1   From the Scrapbook prepared by Sister Gertrude Wood, 'Issy Smith VC 1915', 8 February 1919, 'Stranded Leave Men, Stringent Inquiry into an official blunder'.

2   The truncheon, which feels as if it has a core of lead, is now a family heirloom.

3   The United States was also experiencing violent racial riots at the time. James Weldon Johnson, a civil rights leader, referred to it as a 'Red Summer' for the blood that it shed.

4   Letter in family possession.

5   Olive's memoirs, 27 April 1991.

6   From the Scrapbook prepared by Sister Gertrude Wood, 'Issy Smith VC 1915', undated clipping.

7   www.ons.gov.uk, Office for National Statistics Long Term Trends in UK Employment: 1861 to 2018, Figure 1, Employment rate (of working age population), UK 1861 to 2018.

8   In February 1917, the British Government made a fundamental change to its pension legislation, shifting it from being based on 'loss of earning capacity' to 'degree of disablement by war service.' War pension entitlements were now essentially a medical problem.

9   The document on which Issy's details are recorded is both an Assisted and Unassisted Passenger List. Unassisted passengers paid their own way. Assisted passengers had their journey paid for by another party such as a government immigration scheme or an employer. Not yet ready to immigrate and with no employer to provide funds, Issy most likely paid for the journey himself. Ancestry.com, Victoria Australia Assisted and Unassisted Passenger Lists, 1839–1922.

10   *The Herald*, Melbourne, 28 April 1921, 'Sergeant Issy Smith VC, Pastime on voyage, trains boys in boxing'; *The Daily Mail*, Brisbane, 22 April 1921, 'On the Orsova, number of celebrities'.

11   *The Sun*, Sydney, 22 April 1921, 'First Jewish VC Receives £11,000 in Gifts'; *The Daily Telegraph*, 22 April 1921, 'High Reward, First Jewish Victoria Cross Winner, Baron Rothschild's Gift'; plus many other articles.

12	*Darling Downs Gazette*, 2 May 1921; *The Herald*, Melbourne, 28 April 1927, 'Sergeant Issy Smith V.C. Pastime on Voyage, Trains boys in boxing'.
13	*The Truth*, Sydney, 8 May 1921.
14	*Pall Mall Gazette*, 25 June 1921.
15	*The Hebrew Standard*, 17 December 1922.
16	*Yorkshire Post and Leeds Intellgencer*, 18 January 1922; *Hull Daily Mail*, 18 January 1922, *The Hebrew Standard*, 10 March 1922.
17	*The Stage*, 26 October 1922, 'The London, Shoreditch'.
18	Copy of the London Music Hall Xmas Fund Matinee Programme, in aid of poor children of the district, held in family records.
19	The Maudsley Hospital had only just been finished in 1915 when it was immediately requisitioned for the war. Originally built as a mental health hospital on the offer from renowned psychiatrist Henry Maudsley who provided £30,000, it did not open to the public until February 1923. Unfortunately, none of the medical records prior to that time have been retained. *Sydney Morning Herald*, 10 September 1935, 'War recalled, V.C. Greets Surgeon'; *The Mercury*, Hobart, 10 September 1935, 'A War-time Memory'; *Courier Mail*, Brisbane, 10 September 1935, 'V.C. Pays Tribute'; *The Age*, Melbourne, 10 September 1935, 'First Visitor – A doctor'; *The Sun*, Sydney, 9 September 1935, 'Doctors Meet, Delegation Lands'; *The Herald*, Melbourne, 9 September 1935, 'V.C. Meets Man Who Saved His Life'; *News*, Adelaide, '150 USA Doctors'.

Chapter 22

1	*Sheffield Daily Telegraph*, 24 June 1920, 'V.C's Party Arrangements'; *Portsmouth Evening News*, 28 June 1920, 'The V.C's Garden Party'; *Charters Towers QLD*, 2 September 1920, 'V.C's Pageant at the Palace, The King's Jolly Tea-Party'; *Nothingham Journal*, 28 June 1920, photo of Colonel E.D. Brown Synge Hutchinson V.C. giving his autograph to Sergeant Issy Smith V.C.
2	*Smith's Weekly*, 29 October 1927, 'The Royal Smack'.
3	*News*, Adelaide SA, 30 September 1927, 'Victoria Cross Hero Welcomed, Mr Issy Smith Arrives in Adelaide'. Although the incident occurred with Queen Mary, Princess Mary sent the gift.
4	On the 100th anniversary of the Royal Smack event, 20 June 2020, I wrote to Queen Elizabeth II with details of the amusing saga, sharing the newspaper article and attaching copies of both her family's wedding invitations, which Issy had been invited to. Having never seen the letter, I asked that if it did exist, could a copy be obtained? In due course I received a formal reply thanking me for telling the Queen of the biography and the story, and apologising that they had no record of any letter being sent, and due to the time elapsed no possibility of providing the confirmation.

5   From the Scrapbook prepared by Sister Gertrude Wood, 'Issy Smith VC 1915', Invitation card.

6   Invitation to the Memorial Service, 28 January 1936, in family's possession.

7   From the Scrapbook prepared by Sister Gertrude Wood, 'Issy Smith VC 1915', undated, 'Surprise for V.C.'.

8   There was a small hiccup at the Hackney Memorial service. Sergeant Kenny pulled the string but the flag failed to fall until someone fixed it. Later, a special unhindered service was also held in Issy's honour, where the Mayor of Hackney pinned his medals (successfully) to his chest. *Sheffield Daily Telegraph*, 1 November 1922, 'In memory of the great battle of Ypres'; *Birmingham Daily Gazette*, 1 November 1922, 'Ypres Day in London'; From the Scrapbook prepared by Sister Gertrude Wood, 'Issy Smith VC 1915', undated, 'Two V.C.s Join in Ypres Day Homage at the Cenotaph'.

9   The Returned Sailors and Soldiers Imperial League of Australia (RSSILA) was the precursor to The Returned & Services League of Australia Limited (RSL) that is known today. In the 1930s, the organisation was often referred to as the Returned Soldiers' League before officially changing its name, firstly in 1940 to Returned Sailors' Soldiers' and Airmens Imperial League of Australia (RSSAILA) and then to Returned Services League of Australia (RSL) in 1965, with a modification to Returned Services League of Australia Limited in 1983.

10   *The Herald*, Melbourne, 9 January 1930, 'Prince's Official Fails in Geography, V.C. Dinner Invitation Addressed to "Melbourne, New Zealand"'; *The Register News-Pictorial Adelaide*, 10 January 1930, 'Letter From Prince's Official Sent to V.C. In Melbourne, New Zealand'; *Advocate*, 14 January 1930, 'Off the Map'.

Chapter 23

1   Howard, RD, Journal of Neurology, Neurosurgery & Psychiatry, 19-21 September 2018, 'FM2-5 Shell Shock or Neurasthenia? The queen square experience in the First World War'.

2   University of Oxford, 'World War I Centenary: Continuations and Beginnings: Perspectives on "shell shock"', www.ox.ac.uk

3   The hospital purportedly had an old lady ghost who wore a long dress like a nurse's uniform and had her hair tied in a bun. She would sit on the bed in one of the rooms of the upstairs flat which was the accommodation for hospital staff.

4   No details can be found regarding the mission and principles of the London Lodge of the Wolves. A newspaper clipping notes that on 18 January 1924, several members of the lodge visited a children's hostel to check on the welfare of their subjects. No doubt Issy attended. *The Era*, 23 January 1924, 'The Wolves'.

5   National Archives of Australia, 'Evidence in the Appeal against the decision of the State Board 2 July 1937', p 10.
6   National Archives of Australia, BP18330, 'Final Award by Special Board Expiry of Current Award 12.12.1924'.
7   *Kalgoorlie Miner*, WA, 1 January 1925, 'Victoria Cross Winner Reduced to Poverty'; *Northampton Chronicle & Echo*, 1 January 1925, and at least 25 other papers.

Chapter 24

1   Her Majesty's Head of Treasury.
2   Bonner, Robert, *Issy Smith VC, The Manchester Regiment, A Soldier of the Jullundur Brigade, for most conspicuous bravery on 26 April 1915*, 2014, p. 18.
3   *Shields Daily News*, 9 June 1925, 'Two V.C. Actors'; *Gloucester Citizen*, 9 June 1925, 'Two V.C.s on the Stage'.
4   *Leeds Mercury*, 13 February, 'The Hippodrome'.
5   *Leeds Mercury*, 16 February 1926, 'The Hippodrome'; *Liverpool Echo*, 9 February 1926, 'Round the halls'.
6   The film *Citizen Kane*, made in 1941, was loosely based on Hearst's life. Hearst became the grandfather of Patty Hearst who was famously kidnapped in 1974 and then joined her kidnappers to commit several major crimes.
7   *Liverpool Echo*, 11 February 1926, 'Wedding Surprise at Theatre'.
8   *Westminster Gazette*, 11 February 1926, 'Trix Sister Married, Secret Kept even from her Stage Partner'.
9   Josephine (and likely Eddie) came to Australia in July 1931 for an initial performance at the Theatre Royal – Tivoli. Later Josephine starred in *The House That Jack Built* at Her Majesty's Theatre. No doubt while in Melbourne, the couple would have met up with Issy.
10 Miskell, Peter, Open Edition Books, *British responses to the cultural influence of American films, 1927–1948*. Notes: Board of Trade to Committee on Cinematograph Films (Lord Moyne's Committee), 1936, BT 55/3, PRO.
11 *Leed Mercury*, 4 November 1926, 'Empire market for films'.
12 *Shields Daily News*, 17 May 1927, 'Boro Theatre'; *The Herald*, 16 July 1927, 'Mademoiselle from Armentieres at Majestic'; *Market Harborough Advertiser and Midland Mail*, 2 July 1927; *Banbury Advertiser*, 3 November 1927, 'Mademoiselle from Armentieres'; *Portland Guardian*, 17 October 1927.
13 *The Register*, Adelaide, 30 September 1927 and 6 October 1927, 'Mons, Britain's Great Film Epic'; *News*, Adelaide, 3 October 1927, 'Mons, Epic of Great British Retreat'; *The Register*, Adelaide, 3 October 1927, 'Undying Glory, "Mons" at the York'.

14   *The Canberra Times*, 21 November 1928, 'Australian V.C. hurt in film acting'; *Hartlepool Northern Daily Mail*, 19 November 1928, 'V.C. injured in film scene re-enacting his exploit'.

Chapter 25

1   *Dover Express*, 30 April 1926, 'Lancashire Fusiliers Sports'; *East London Observer*, 18 December 1926, 'Berner Street Old Boys' Club'.

2   *The Register*, Adelaide, 8 October 1926, 'Issy Smith V.C. Repatriation Problem'; *Evening News*, Sydney, 7 October 1926, 'V.C. Shuttlecock, wants to come back', plus many other news articles; *The Mercury*, Hobart, 16 October 1926, 'The Case of Sergeant Smith, V.C.'; *The Age*, Melbourne, 16 October 1926, 'VC Winner Not Wanted, Turned down at Australia House', plus numerous other articles.

3   Stanley Bruce was not a man of the people. In *A History of Australia*, by Mark Peel and Christina Twomey, (2011), it was noted that 'Bruce's key political asset was his capacity to appear patrician and passionless in an era when it was important to give the impression of a firm hand.' According to the authors, Bruce reminisced in later life: 'My chief advantage as a politician was that I did not give a damn.' *The Daily Telegraph*, Sydney, 16 October 1926, 'Not for Australia'.

4   *The Bunbury Herald and Blackwood Express*, 26 October 1926, 'Passing Comment and People in Passing'.

5   All of the newspapers reported different amounts, ranging from £1000 to £11,000. *The Daily News*, Perth 13 January 1927 and 18 January 1927, 'Issy Smith V.C. Returning to Melbourne, Deed that won the Cross'; *Warwick Daily News*, Queensland, 20 January 1927; *The Hebrew Standard*, 21 January 1927; *The Manaro Mercury*, Local and General News, 17 January 1927.

6   Alf was not technically Issy's brother-in-law, being Elsie's sister Flora's husband. But he was family.

7   Rangoon is now known as Yangon and Burma as Myanmar. It is the largest city in the country and retains some of its British colonial architecture. Prior to Burma, Alf had returned to Mesopotamia in 1920 to deal with an insurgence there. On Boxing Day 1920, he had moved back to Kamptee with Flora. There, he sat his first-class certificate of education and was promoted to Acting Company Sergeant Major in December 1921. Flora became an assistant schoolmistress to the Battalion's children. When Alf retired from the Army in 1925, he received the 1914 Star with clasp, British War Medal, Allied Victory Medal, General Service Medal with clasps 'Iraq', 'N.W.Persia', Delhi Durbar 1911 Medal, Long Service and Good Conduct Medal. Bonner, Robert, *Issy Smith VC, The Manchester Regiment, A Soldier of the Jullundur Brigade, for most conspicuous bravery on 26 April 1915*, 2014, p. 6.

Endnotes

8   The 'Australasian Council of Trade Unions' was in the process of being established and was officially founded in May 1927. It was later renamed the Australian Council of Trade Unions (ACTU).
9   *Mademoiselle from Armentieres* was reportedly the most profitable British film of 1926.
10 Anzac Day was officially so named on 25 April 1916. On that day Australian and New Zealand soldiers formed part of the Allied expedition that landed on the Gallipoli peninsula, in an attempt to open up the narrow straits known as the Dardanelles. When the campaign ended, over 130,000 men from both sides had died, including more than 8700 Australians and 2700 New Zealanders. Over 21,200 from Great Britain and Ireland were also among the dead.
11 The photo is held by the Australian War Memorial. Issy is standing ninth from the right. 1927-04-25, 'Australian Victoria Cross Winners who took part in the Anzac Day march, Australian War Memorial', Accession number J03075; *The Argus*, Melbourne, 26 April 1927, 'V.C. Winners in Anzac Day March'; *The Mercury*, 3 May 1927, 'Anzac Commemoration'; *The Queenslander*, 3 May 1927, p. 23, 'Official group of Australian V.C's who took part in the march past on ANZAC Day in Melbourne' (photo); *Advocate*, Burnie, 6 May 1927, 'V.C.s on parade, Tasmania's proud position'; *Western Mail*, Perth, 12 May 1927, 'Anzac day commemorations in Melbourne'.
12 *The Argus*, Melbourne, 26 April 1927, 'Two Heroes'.
13 The Majestic Theatre, originally built in 1912, was near the corner of Flinders and Russell Streets. Over time it underwent several refurbishments, was renamed the Chelsea Cinema and was later demolished in 1986. It is now a car park.
14 *The Herald*, Melbourne, 14 July 1927, 'English V.C. Invited to See Himself Act'; *The Age*, Melbourne, 18 July 1927, 'Picture Theatres, Majestic'; *Everyones*, 17 August 1927, p. 56, 'New Moves in Victorian Country and Suburbs'; *Everyones*, 28 September 1927, p. 26, photo: 'Diggers See Mademoiselle'.
15 *The Herald*, 16 July 1927, 'Mademoiselle from Armentieres at Majestic'; *Everyones*, 20 July 1927, 'Leading "Armentieres" player found in Melbourne'; *The Bulletin*, 21 July 1927; *The Herald*, 25 July, 'Mademoiselle is British'; *Western Star* and ROMA *Advertiser*, 3 August 1927; *The Herald*, 1 August, 'Mademoiselle Again'; *The Richmond River Herald* and *Northern Districts Advertiser*, NSW, 26 August 1927, 'V.C. as Movie Lecturer'; *The Canberra Times*, 19 August 1927, 'Actor as Lecturer'; *The Kyogle Examiner*, NSW, 2 September 1927, 'V.C. As Movie Lecturer'; *The Bioscope*, 6 October 1927, 'Sergeant Issy's Appointment, V.C.'s Success in Australia'.
16 *Advertiser*, Adelaide, 1 October 1927, 'A modest hero'.
17 *The Riverine Herald*, 22 November 1927, 'V.C. Hero, Visit to Echuca'.

18 Over the years, Issy appeared in this magazine many times. *Everyones*, 17 August 1927, p. 3, 'Sergeant Issy Smith, V.C., Enters the Industry'.
19 *The Mirror*, Perth, 13 August 1927, 'Izzy's New Job'.
20 Due to the high cost of 35mm film stock in Australia, producers only made a certain number of copies of a film for distribution and released them usually via a rental arrangement. The film was carefully scheduled around the city, and then suburban and country theatres. By the time screenings ended, the quality was poor, the film having been subjected to many showings. In England, only fragments of *Mademoiselle from Armentieres* remain, around one-third in total, with the rest considered to be 'missing, believed lost'.
21 *The Geelong Advertiser*, 9 August 1927, 'Diggers' Re-union, A memorable function, Over 300 Returned men Attend Geelong Dinner'.
22 *News*, Adelaide, 30 September 1927, photo and news article, 'Victoria Cross Hero Welcomed, Mr Issy Smith Arrives in Adelaide'; *The Register*, Adelaide, 30 September 1927, 'Mons, Britain's Great Film Epic'; *Advertiser*, Adelaide, 1 October 1927, 'A Modest Hero'; *The Register*, Adelaide, '"Mons" Britain's Screen Epic'; *Everyones*, 12 October 1927, p. 27, '"Mons" Adelaide Season under Distinguished Patronage'.
23 *News*, Adelaide, 5 October 1927, 'Government Visit'.
24 Issy's speech at Portland is attached in Addendum 2. *Portland Guardian*, 17 October, 24 October 1927, 'Sergeant Issy Smith VC'.
25 *Healesville and Yarra Glen Guardian*, 22 October 1927.

Chapter 26

1 From the Scrapbook, loose article undated, 'V.C. Hero at Kooweerup'.
2 *The Argus*, Melbourne, 5 November 1927, Wonthaggi; *The Horsham Times*, 8 November 1927, 'V.C. Winner at Horsham'; *The Age*, 12 November 1927, 'Kooweerup'; *The Riverine Herald*, Echuca, 19 and 22 November 1927, 'V.C. Hero'; *The Riverine Herald*, 22 November 1927, 'School Notes Moama Public School'; *The Riverine Herald*, 23 November 1927, 'Sergeant Issy Smith V.C. Visit to Moama'; *Sunshine Advocate*, Vic, 3 December 1927 '*Mademoiselle from Armentieres*'; *Melton Express*, Vic, 10 and 17 December 1927, 'Mechanics Pictures'; *Gippsland Times*, 15 and 22 December 1927, 'Sergeant Issy Smith V.C.'; *Gippsland Times*, 15 December 1927, 'RSSILA Meeting of Sale Branch'; *West Gippsland Gazette*, Warragul, 27 December 1927, 'This week's pictures'; *Traralgon Record*, 30 December 1927, 'Soldier's Re-union, Serg. Smith V.C. honored'; *Traralgon Record*, 30 December 1927, 'Appreciation'.
3 *Everyones*, 8 February 1927, p. 28, 'For Original Stunting'; *Everyones*, 22 February 1928, p. 30, 'Sergeant Issy Smith V.C.'; *Murray Pioneer and Australian River Record*, Renmark, 2 March 1928, 'Wentworth Notes'; *The Independent*, Deniliquin, 6 March 1927, 'Issy any good?'.
4 A 'smoke social' was popular in Australia in the late nineteenth and

early twentieth century, where men met socially, sometimes to discuss local business and community affairs or otherwise purely for a relaxed evening. The evening was enjoyed smoking tobacco together.

5 *The Age*, Melbourne, 1 February 1928, 'Mildura'; *The Telegraph*, Brisbane, 8 February 1928, 'Mildura Soldier's motion'; *The Age*, Melbourne, 8 February 1928, 'Tactless Invitations, A Returned Soldier Function, Committeeman's Action Deplored'; *Toowoomba Chronicle and Darling Downs Gazette*, 17 February 1928, 'Tactless Invitations'; *Glen Innes Examiner*, 21 February 1928, 'Tactless Invitations, Mildura and German Swimmer'.

Chapter 27

1 Australasian Films was also involved in the management of theatres, and was known as 'Union Theatres and Australasian Films'.

2 *The Herald*, Melbourne, 28 June 1929, 'Industry Imperilled'; *Everyones*, 22 August 1928, p. 32, 'Issy Smith Leaves Australasian Films'.

3 *Smith's Weekly*, Sydney, 27 July 1929, 'All in the Game'.

4 *Brisbane Courier*, 27 July 1927, 'Film Merger, Companies Unite'.

5 NFSA Cinema Art Poster Collection, https://www.nfsa.gov.au/latest/cinema-art-poster-collection

6 *The Herald*, 13 June 1929, 'British Film Praised by U.S. Review Board, Put on "Exceptional" List'.

7 RCA stands for Radio Corporation of America. *The Herald*, 27 June 1929, 'Talkie Equipment Ban Ignored, British Firm's Lead, Interchangeability must be agreed upon'; *The Herald*, 28 June 1929, 'Talkie Firm Will See Minister, Fighting U.S. Monopoly'.

8 *The Herald*, 28 June 1929, 'Industry Imperilled'.

9 *The Herald*, 27 August 1929, 'Film Censorship Act Breaches'; *The Age*, 28 August 1929, 'Film Censorship Offences'; *Everyones*, 4 September 1929, p. 22, 'Hoyts fined for Censorship Breaches'.

10 *The Herald*, 21 October 1929, 'British Talkie Veto Surprise, Mystery Objection By Australian Censors, America will Benefit'.

11 DH Lawrence's book *Lady Chatterley's Lover* was banned as well in 1929 for being too sexually explicit. Eventually, after a court case, the book was released in Britain in 1960 – but the ban remained in Australia for another five years until a copy was smuggled into the country and published widely.

The Story of the Kelly Gang is considered by many to be the first feature-length film ever produced in the world. The film did cause controversy as it painted the gang's notoriety as legendary.

12 *The Sun*, 19 October 1929, 'Not For Us, Blackmail is Banned, Censor Shocked?'.

13 *The Herald*, 22 October 1929, '"Blackmail" ban, Film circles astonished, Slur on British-made'; *Hartlepool Northern Daily Mail*, 21 October

1929, 'Ban on "Blackmail", Australian Decision Causes Surprise'; *Coventry Evening Telegraph*, 21 October 1929, 'Blackmail Not To Be Shown in Australia'; *Hull Daily Mail*, 21 October 1929, '"Blackmail" Banned, Successful British "Talkie" Not To Be Screened in Australia'; *Staffordshier Sentinel*, 21 October 1929, 'The Banning of "Blackmail"'.

14 *Blackmail* was originally planned as a silent film, although Alfred Hitchcock commented that he always intended it to have a sound version. As sound was being introduced, parts of the film were shot as a 'talkie' and two versions of the film were released in the UK – one with sound and, some months later, one without for the theatres without sound equipment.

Chapter 28

1 *The Herald*, 7 November 1929, 'Governor's Dinner for V.C. Winners, Addresses sought'; *Table Talk*, 3 April 1930, 'Reveille Ball at St Kilda'.

2 *The Age*, 8 May 1930, 'Recruiting Campaign, Rally at Essendon'; *The Herald*, 7 May 1931, '58th Battalion Recruit Drive Begins, V.C. to Speak'.

3 A birth certificate for Issy hasn't ever been sighted, and it is highly possible that he never had one. National Archives of Australia, BP18330, Letter from Repatriation Commission, Melbourne, 15 May 1930; Reply from Issy, Cinema Art Films, 15 May 1930.

4 While interviewing my father Maurice for this book, he confirmed the number of the house as being 54 and having a laneway between it and 52 – where a murder of a child took place. He couldn't remember when it occurred as he was a child himself at the time, but he recalled a woman had put her head over the fence, possibly his mother Elsie, after hearing moaning. The child was rushed to hospital but sadly died. Ronald Morgan, a 24-year-old man who lived immediately behind the houses, was caught and sentenced to death for the murder of seven-year-old Janice Maree Baul, whom he attacked with an exploded mortar bomb. His sentence was commuted to 25 years at Pentridge prison and he was released in January 1969, only to be re-sent to jail in 1976 for multiple sexual offences for which he served another thirteen years. The murder was in fact in 1944, after Elsie and the family had moved to Bulla Road, so it was perhaps the new occupant who tried in vain to save the poor child's life.

5 *The Herald*, 1 July 1930, 'New Companies'; *The Herald*, 10 July 1930, 'Killing the Films'; *The Brisbane Courier*, 10 July 1930, 'The Most Crushing Budget in the History of Australia'.

6 Keystone was a US film company operating from 1912 until its bankruptcy in 1935. *The Girl in the Moon* was actually the movie *Woman in the Moon*, released in 1929. *Moulin Rouge* (1928) was another production released by Cinema Art.

7 *The Argus*, Melbourne, 18 September 1932, 'European Films'.

8   A constitution was drawn up with key objectives to do homage to the memory of fallen comrades and to provide services to Jewish ex-servicemen and their families. The association met annually and in later years, went on to work tirelessly for the Second World War, sending food parcels and other comforts to the troops and assisting with Jewish chaplaincy services. Issy took an active part from its formation until his death. Today, the association is known as Victorian Association of Jewish Ex & Servicemen & Women Australia Inc (VAJEX Australia).

9   Butler, AG, *Official History of the Australian Army Medical Services 1914-1918*, Volume III – Special Problems and Services (1st Edition), Section IV The Aftermath of War, Chapter XVI, 'The War Damaged Soldier', pp. 789, 794.

10 Amy Johnson, to whom Mr Brown referred, was an English pilot and the first woman to fly solo from London to Australia. Issy's thoughts on the donation of land to build homes for aged soldiers were also printed. *The Argus*, 25 July 1930, 'Soldier's Conference, Preference Question, Federal President's Part'; *The Argus*, 25 July 1930, 'Soldiers' Conference, Establishing Homes'; *Daily Pictorial*, Sydney, 25 July 1930, 'Are Memorials Exploited?'.

11 *The Age*, 4 October 1930, 'Public Service Dismissals, Protest Meeting at Essendon'.

12 Cinema Art began briefly again in 1939 but did not continue, most likely due to the start of WWII.

13 The Reichstag was the lower house of Germany's national legislature. 'Weimar system' referred to the Weimar Republic, the German federal state that existed between 1918 and 1933. Also known as the German Republic, 'Weimar' refers to the city where it was created and based. It ended when Hitler became Chancellor in 1933.

Chapter 29

1   *The Herald*, 28 April 1929, *The Argus*, 29 April 1929, 'Personal'; *The Bulletin*, 7 May 1930.

2   *The Age*, Melbourne, 8 December 1930, 'Children's Christmas Treat, Appeals for Assistance'.

3   Five Mile Press, 2004, *The Illustrated History of Australia*, page 315.

4   Issy was always well dressed. Never frugal with money and not one to accept charity for himself, he took the opportunity to ensure the family were suitably attired when times were good.

5   *Smith's Weekly*, 12 January 1929, 'Monster Punter who is beating the Victorian Ring'.

6   *Sporting Globe*, 15 September 1951, 'Frank Dummett's Mixed Luck in Riding for Fortunes'; *Smith's Weekly*, 21 December 1929, 'Tame Plungers Dominate Victorian Turf'.

7   *The Labour Daily*, 4 November 1930, 'Racing Men Sum Up for Today's Cup'.
8   That achievement still remains, more than 90 years later.
9   Issy was awarded his medal on 26 April 1915. Did the newspapers err in their reporting, did Issy forget the date or did he make a slight adjustment to put greater emphasis on the principles he was arguing?
10 *The Herald*, Melbourne, 4 April 1931, V.C. Urges Brighter Anzac Night Spirit, 'Open Amusements'.
11 *The Herald*, Melbourne, 10 April 1931, '"Hands Off Anzac Day", Cry Soldiers' Delegates, Theatre Threat Attacked'.
12 Not all of the Victorian Branch was united on this front. The Richmond Branch of the Returned Soldiers' League published in *The Age* on 21 April 1931 that they were in favour of everything opening after 6 pm. *The Herald*, Melbourne, 'Attack on Anzac Day Theatre Opening, League Makes Appeal'.
13 *The Argus*, May 18, Public Notices, 'Apology'; *The Herald*, Melbourne, 15 April 1931, 'A V.C. Winner's view'.
14 *The Bulletin*, 17 December 1930.
15 From the Scrapbook prepared by Sister Gertrude Wood, 'Issy Smith VC 1915', newspaper clipping.

Chapter 30

1   *The Herald*, Melbourne, 20 March 1931, 'The Moneylenders'.
2   Later Dame Enid Lyons AD, GBE. Enid went on to become the first woman elected to the House of Representatives and the first woman to serve in federal cabinet.
3   *The Herald*, 28 November 1931, 'V.C. A Candidate, Mr Issy Smith to oppose Dr Maloney'.
4   From *So We Take Comfort*, Dame Enid Lyons, Heinemann, 1965.
5   Lyons, Enid, *So We Take Comfort*, 1965; *The Courier-Mail*, Brisbane, 13 May 1953, 'Hatred, passion beat reason'; *The Advertiser*, Adelaide, 13 May 1953, Dame Enid Lyons, 'Unsuspected Political Feeling'.
6   *The Brisbane Courier*, 10 December 1931, 'Disgraceful scenes, V.C. Winner Refused Hearing'; *Advocate*, Burnie, 10 December 1931, 'Insulted, Hooted. V.C. Winner Not Allowed to Speak, Contemptible Larrikinism'; *The Mercury*, 10 December 1931, North Melbourne, 'Disgraceful Scenes'; *Examiner* Launceston, 10 December 1931, 'V.C. Howled Down Meeting has to be abandoned'; *The Daily News*, 10 December 1931, 'V.C Winner's Ordeal'; *Daily Standard*, Brisbane, 10 December 1931, 'Izzy Was Hooted So He Fled'.
7   *The Age*, 11 December 1931, 'Dr Maloney at Kensington'.
8   *The Herald*, 10 December 1931, 'Fair Play Plea Dr Maloney and Sgt Issy Smith V.C'.

9 *The Herald*, 10 December 1931, 'Flinders for Bruce'.
10 In Victoria, Members of the House of Representatives are sometimes referred to as MHRs.
11 *The Daily Telegraph*, Sydney, 'Dr Maloney has Savage Patients, Why Smith was Howled Down'.
12 *The Argus*, 12 December 1931, 'Interjector in Court, Threat to break up meeting'.
13 *The Argus*, 15 December 1931, Labour and Finance, 'Sergeant Smith at Kensington'.
14 *The Herald*, 17 December 1931, advertisement, 'Anzac Day Observance'.
15 *The Herald*, 'Dr Maloney at Poll Declaration'; *The Herald*, Melbourne, 24 December 1931, 'Melbourne Poll Declared'; *The Advertiser*, Adelaide, 21 December 1931, 'Melbourne Gossip'; *Numurkah Leader*, Vic, 22 December 1932, 'Federal Elections, Electors' Great Breakaway from Labor'.
16 *The Argus*, 19 December 1931, 'Posters altered'.
17 From the Scrapbook prepared by Sister Gertrude Wood, 'Issy Smith VC 1915', various undated newspaper clippings.
18 Maloney ran in the 1929 elections unopposed, ultimately serving as a member of the Australian Labor Party in the House of Representatives for 36 years. In 1939 he celebrated 50 years in politics, aged 85. He withdrew from the 1940 elections, and died one month before polling day and just thirteen days before Issy, on 29 August 1940.

Chapter 31

1 *The Herald*, Melbourne, 25 March 1931, 'Nation's Tribute to Great Soldier, Gen. Elliott Buried'.
2 *The Age*, 16 October 1939, 'Monash Pilgrimage', family newspaper clipping from unknown paper.
3 Jacka died from chronic nephritis, which may or may not have been caused by the war. In 1915, this previously unrecognised condition arose in the trenches and was subsequently classed as 'war nephritis' but was more commonly known as 'trench nephritis'. It was considered to be due to infection, exposure and poor diet.
4 *The Herald*, Melbourne, 18 January 1932, 'Burial of Capt. Jacka'; *The Riverine Herald*, Echuca, 19 January 1932, 'The Late Captain Jacka'; *The Advertiser and The Chronicle*, Adelaide, 20 January 1932, 'Thousands Mourn Jacka, V.C.'; *Riverina Recorder*, Balranald, 23 January 1932, 'Hero's Funeral' plus many other articles.
5 Just prior to Jacka's death, Issy had also put out a public appeal on behalf of another returned soldier. The man, who was the head of a family of seven, had been out of work for two years. One of his children had just passed away and another was still in the Children's Hospital. Issy advised that the burial costs were paid by the Essendon RSSILA and

Anzac House, and he made a plea for employers to find work for the father.

6   *The Argus*, Melbourne, 19 June 1931, 'Disagreements On Bench'.
7   *Advocate*, Burnie, 27 January 1932, 'Constable Shot in Head by Bandits'; *The Weekly Times*, 30 January 1932, 'Dramatic Hold-up Story Told in Court by Constable Derham'; *The Daily Telegraph*, Sydney, 28 January 1932, 'Had three guns, Hold-up Arrest like the movies'; *The Daily Telegraph*, Sydney, 30 Janueary 1932, 'Seven for Trial, Shooting and Hold up in Melbourne Lane'; *The Riverine Herald*, Echuca, 2 June 1932, 'Flinders Lane Hold-up, Three men receive floggings'.
8   It is not known if Issy knew Taylor through the cinema industry, perhaps as a former client, or whether this was an unrelated matter.
9   *The Herald*, Melbourne, 15 July 1932, 'Man Insults V.C.'; *Gippsland Times*, 18 July 1932, 'Insulting Behaviour, Former Gippsland Showman Fined'.
10   *The Herald*, Melbourne, 26 April 1932, 'Seven V.C.'s meet'; from the Scrapbook, 27 April 1932, 'Anniversary of Bravery'.
11   *The Herald*, Melbourne, 6 September 1932, 'Pensions Cut'.
12   The Melbourne Hebrew Congregation is the oldest Jewish congregation in Melbourne, having begun in 1841. It had just moved from Bourke Street to Toorak Road in 1930. *The Herald*, Melbourne, 10 October 1932, 'The Day of Atonement'.
13   *The Herald*, Melbourne, 8 November 1932, 'Woman Charged With Perjury, Sequel to Trial of Former Constable'.
14   Despite its name implying a welfare business, the 'Public Benefit Bootery' was merely a shoe shop, trading so successfully that it could afford upmarket retail frontage on the ground floor of a notable high rise building in Bourke Street. It became known to later generations as PB Shoes.
15   *The Herald*, Melbourne, 8 November 1932, 'Two Fined In Gaming Case, Bookmakers at City Court'; *The Sporting Globe*, Melbourne, 9 November 1932, 'Gaming Charges'.
16   *The Herald*, Melbourne, 28 January 1933, '£250 Jewel Theft, Sneak Thief Raids Bedroom'; *The Sun*, Melbourne, 29 January 1933, 'Haul of £250, Jewel Robbers, While Family Played'; *Warwick Daily News*, 30 January 1933, 'Dog Barks, Thief Leaves Job Unfinished'.

Chapter 32

1   National Archives of Australia, BP18330, Commonwealth of Australia Australian Soldier's Repatriation Act Record of Evidence.
2   The Company changed its name to Dunlop Perdriau in 1929 after a merger but was still known colloquially as Dunlop Rubber.
3   *The Herald*, Melbourne, 1 May 1935, '1914 Imperial Reservists of Australia'; *The Argus*, Melbourne, 3 May 1935, '1914 Imperial

Endnotes

Reservists'; *Smith's Weeekly*, Sydney, 20 May 1939, '1914 Imperial Reservists' Association'.

4   The Commercial Travellers' Association operated in Victoria for over 130 years, finally closing its doors in 2014. Services in the early days included lobbying the railway and steamship companies for better facilities, organising accident and sickness insurance schemes and providing scholarships to children of members.

5   *The Herald*, Melbourne, 20 June 1935, 'V.C. Injured in Car Smash in Carlton'; *The Herald* Evening, 20 June 1935, 'V.C. In Motor Smash'; *The Daily Telegraph* Sydney, 21 June 1935, 'V.C. Injured, Car Crash in Carlton, Victoria'; *The Argus* Melbourne, 'Victoria Cross Winner Injured in Collision'; *The Age*, Melbourne, 21 June 1935, 'Mr I. Smith V.C. Injured, involved in Car Collision'; *The Newcastle Sun*, 21 June 1935, 'V.C. Winner is injured'; articles from the Scrapbook prepared by Sister Gertrude Wood, 'Issy Smith VC 1915'.

6   *The Australasian*, Melbourne, 29 June 1935, 'Motoring by New Models, 1935 Willys "77"'.

7   *The Herald*, Melbourne, 20 July 1936, '36 to 38 M.P.G. In Willys 77'.

8   According to a local newspaper, the selectors were apparently unable to choose between two players, Plummer and Reynolds, and Issy's prize money of £2/2s was split equally between them. Football records, however, state that champion player Dick Reynolds was the sole winner. *The Argus*, Melbourne, 19 August 1936, 'Essendon Ready, Injured Men Recovering'.

9   The Sustenance scheme, or 'susso' as it became known, was no free ride. Under the legislation, receivers were obliged to work and anyone found to be making false statements in order to claim it faced heavy fines. Those who were unwilling to work or participated in stop-work meetings were immediately dismissed and their sustenance cancelled. Men found to be unfit due to disabilities were removed from the allowance and transferred to the benevolent society list. National Archives of Australia, BP18330, 27 May 1937, 'Issy's Treatment Allowance, Ex Imperial Soldier, Memorandum'.

10 'Matzah' is the traditional name. The food industry almost always spells it as 'matzo'.

11 Campbell was granted the honorary rank of major in 1945. He was one of few land speed record holders of the period who did not die in a crash.

12 Below this letter was a postscript. It read: '1911 Imperial Reservists of Australia, ["Snowy" Howell, V.C. admits that he was wrong regarding V.C. pension being £5. Ed., A.I.F.']. *Smith's Weekly*, Sydney, 27 November 1937, 'From Issy Smith V.C.'.

Chapter 33

1. Personal family items, letter to Issy from Government House, Canberra, 8 May 1937; *The Argus*, Melbourne, 12 May 1937, 'Coronation Medals, Honour for Leading Citizens'; *The Hebrew Standard Of Australasia*, Sydney, 20 May 1937, 'Coronation Medals'.
2. *The Argus*, Melbourne, 25 April 1936, 'Soldiers vote on Anzac Observance'; *The Age*, Melbourne, 9 November 1936, 'A Jewish Service'.
3. *The Australian Jewish Herald*, Melbourne, 6 May 1937, 'The Late Colonel Isaacson'.
4. *Record, Emerald Hill*, Victoria, 7 August 1937, 'Mr "Jock" Cameron'.
5. *Northern Star*, Lismore, 19 February 1938, 'War is not Imminent'.
6. *Barrier Miner*, Broken Hill, 7 December 1933, 'Training for Military, Recruiting work in Sydney, Colonel Wall is here'.

Chapter 34

1. *News*, Adelaide, 30 September 1927, 'Victoria Cross Hero Welcomed'.
2. The notes taken by the doctor stated that the dizziness made him lie down and take some brandy. Issy was a staunch teetotaller – this was clearly incorrect. Did the doctor mix up details from another patient or not listen seriously to his client's complaint?
3. Labyrinthitis is an inflammation of the inner ear.
4. Hyperpiesis, now referred to as Essential Hypertension, refers to a persistent high blood pressure with no specific cause. It is not a specific disease but a clinical sign that may manifest in a large number of other health disorders, including infections and nervous conditions. It is sometimes referred to as the 'silent killer', as it alone usually doesn't present any symptoms and the patient doesn't feel or notice it.
5. Different views exist as to what a high (and dangerous) blood pressure reading is. Some consider 160/105 mm Hg to be hyperpiesia, others believe 180/120 mm Hg indicates a serious health problem. Nonetheless, symptoms that are often present include chest pain, shortness of breath, headache, dizziness and eyesight changes. If not treated, this could lead to a sudden heart attack or stroke.
6. In arteriosclerosis, the blood pressure may or may not be high. Hypertension and arteriosclerosis are often found together but hypertension can occur without evidence of arterial disease.
7. The use of catheters was later to become the process called a coronary angiogram, used to evaluate heart function and cardiovascular conditions.
8. A lot of repatriation administration was devolved to State Boards. The Boards could accept a medical opinion but not act in contravention of it. If it disagreed or was in doubt, the case could be referred to the Commission for a decision.

9   In among the appeals and on one of Issy's regular declarations for pension payments, a captious administration clerk produced an Extract of Entry from the State of Victoria stating that Maurice was born on 8 October 1932, not 8 November as claimed. Issy recovered the original birth certificate to show this was an error.

10 Arteriosclerosis is now understood to be caused by a low grade, long-term inflammation of the arteries. While there are some genetic factors and diseases that have a bearing, it is believed that poor lifestyle habits are a major contributor – high stress, tobacco smoking, lack of exercise, poor diet and alcohol or drugs abuse being factors. Issy had the first three and possibly the fourth, given there were times that the family lived on bread and dripping. The high blood pressure could also have been caused by the stress of the war followed by two decades of severe economic depression, resulting in a continuous and exhausting battle to make ends meet. This constant state of severe hypertension could have led to pressure on the arteries and ultimately coronary artery disease. Additionally, the strain on his lungs (and in turn on his heart) from lung damage caused by gas could have contributed.

11 National Archives of Australia, BP18330, 6 December 1937, 'Memorandum for Hospital File'.

12 Butler, AG, *Official History of the Australian Army Medical Services 1914-1918*, Volume III – Special Problems and Services (1st Edition), Section IV, 'The Aftermath of War', Chapter XVI, 'The War Damaged Soldier', p. 838.

13 *Morwell Advertiser*, Morwell, 27 June 1935, 'Renewed Hope for Unaccepted T.B. Cases'.

Chapter 35

1   *The Argus*, Melbourne, 27 December 1937, 'The Flying Smiths'.

2   The young girl, Jean Burns, was reported to have been dragged along the ground by her parachute and was taken away in an ambulance with some facial abrasions but was not seriously injured. She made about a dozen jumps in total and nearly made it to her 100th birthday.

3   *The Herald*, Melbourne, 16 April 1938, '"Good Mixer" Is Colleagues Verdict on Bogus V.C.'; *News* Adelaide, 18 April 1938, '"Good Mixer" Is Colleagues Verdict on Bogus V.C.'; *Leader*, Melbourne, 2 February 1935, 'A Gruelling Voyage, Food Supplies Exhausted'; *Barrier Miner*, Broken Hill, 6 February 1935, 'War Veterans Comprise Crew of Freighter'; *La Crosse Tribune and Leader Press*, 15 July 1938, 'V.C. spots Bogus V.C.'

4   'Major Bloomfield VC', an Australian VC it was claimed, apparently arrived in Melbourne in February 1935 on the tiny cargo steamer *James Cook*, surviving 67 days of a cyclone and terrific seas and living on nothing but salt fish and black coffee without sugar – conditions not dissimilar to the bully beef and biscuits endured during his war time in 1916. He was quickly praised as one 'possessing the highest degree of

valour and endurance'. Not long after, perhaps realising that Australia had only a small population, he became a British Army VC, before changing again to be South African. Unfortunately for the major, the charade did not last. When he reappeared in mid-November 1938 at the Sydney offices of the Australian Broadcasting Commission for a talk show, the wary Board decided to check up on his credentials by contacting the Victoria Barracks. No sooner had he been identified as the impersonator previously employed with the Melbourne Civil Aviation branch than he disappeared, never to be heard from again.

5   Germany and Italy signed a formal alliance (known as the Rome–Berlin axis) in October 1936, forming a partnership of military aggression. Germany had also established an alliance with Japan, signing the Anti-Comintern Pact a month later. Italy also joined the pact in November 1937. *The Age*, Melbourne, 26 April 1938, 'Homage to the Heroes of Anzac'.

6   *The Age*, 29 June 1938, 'Box Hill Soldiers, Four V.C.s at Ball'.

7   National Archives of Australia, BP 18330, 27 January 1939, 'Memorandum for Hospital File', p. 2.

8   Prior to the establishment of government welfare, friendly societies or lodges provided support – this was essentially an organisation of working people cooperating together and providing their own welfare. By the turn of the century, many offered an inhouse doctor, whereby a physician provided care in exchange for an annual salary based on the size of the lodge membership. Eventually, doctors insisted on fee for service arrangements directly with patients, by-passing the lodges, and the custom of lodge doctors ceased.

9   Commercial Travellers' Club Melbourne, Programme 1 October 1938, personal family items.

10 *The Argus*, 20 October 1938, 'Names in the News'.

11 I often wonder what Issy made of his son's antics – after all, the apple hadn't fallen far from the tree.

12 The Black Friday fires, as they became known, resulted in 71 deaths, 1000 homes lost, five townships destroyed, huge numbers of sheep, cattle and horses killed and over 1,300,000 hectares of forest burnt. Massive amounts of smoke were generated, with reports claiming that ash fell as far away as New Zealand.

13 The ECG machine wasn't comprehensive and more electrodes were still being developed to pick up 'silent areas' in the heart. Yet it was an essential clinical tool. The American Heart Association recommended six chest leads be added in 1938 but this new model, which could better diagnose the extent of damage, was not commercially available until the 1940s. The 12-lead electrocardiogram that is used today was developed in 1942 and standardised for use in 1952 (Majd AlGhatrif MD and Joseph Lindsay MD, *A brief review: history to understand fundamentals*

of electrocardiography, 2012). Unfortunately, this was after Issy was gone.

Chapter 36

1. *The Sydney Morning Herald*, 2 February 1939, 'Efforts for Peace, Chamberlain's Speech, "Exaggerated Fears"'.
2. *The Age*, Melbourne, 25 April 1939, 'Diggers Meet Again'; *The Herald*, Melbourne, 25 April 1939, '"Wake Up Australia" call sounded by Leader of March'.
3. It is not known why Issy was trying this tonic or who recommended it. National Archives of Australia, M18330, Victorian Outpatient Clinic, BP10030, 2 June 1939 to 8 August 1939, 'Memorandum for Medical File'.
4. *The Herald*, Melbourne, 14 July 1939, 'England Bound for Warplanes'.
5. Although thoughts were now on the soldiers of the future, mention was made of previous heroes from time to time. On 12 August Issy was referred to in a story in the *Smith's Weekly*, Sydney, 'There Were Giants in the Past'.
6. National Archives of Australia, M18330, 4 November 1939.
7. *The Argus*, Melbourne, 13 November 1939, 'Spirit of 1914 Still Lives'; *The Australian Jewish Herald*, Melbourne, 16 November 1939, 'Armistice Day'.
8. *Sporting Globe*, Melbourne, 29 November 1939, 'Calling All Sportsmen! Help the Troops Who Will Help You'.
9. Strict censorship was applied in Australia in WWII, just as it had been in WWI. The Censorship Office was considered vital by the government to prevent valuable information falling into the hands of the enemy and also to protect the public from the brutalities of war. This helped maintain morale and encourage enlistments.
10. This chronic disorder was also later noted in civilians. Oglesby, Paul, *Review: Da Cos.ta's syndrome or neurocirculatory asthenia*, BR Heart, J, 1987; 58:306-15.
11. Despite extensive searching, Issy's original letter to Major JE Barrett has never been located and is presumed lost. Major JE Barrett, in his reply, states: 'I have been instructed by Lieut-Gen. Sir Thomas Blamey, to acknowledge receipt of your letter of 20th inst. in which you make application to join the 2nd A.I.F. At present, there are no suitable vacancies where your services could be utilised, but it would be appreciated if the details of your age and service could be forwarded for future guidance. I am to add that the General Officer Commanding appreciates your offer of service.'
12. Letter in family files from Major JE Barrett dated 28 February and to Major Barrett from Issy dated 4 March 1940.
13. Problems with extremities is a symptom consistent with poor blood

14   Archbishop Head held the Military Cross and Bar for his services in WWI and was also the chaplain to King George V from 1922 to 1929. He served as Archbishop of Melbourne from 1929 until his death on 18 December 1941, following serious injuries received in a car accident 11 days earlier. *Advocate*, Burnie, Tasmania, 29 April 1940, 'Anzac Day Revives Memories of First World War'.

15   The Judean League, which began in 1922, was formed to promote Judaism and Jewish understanding among Jewish youth but was also involved in various other humanitarian activities including the Red Cross and the war effort.

16   It was customary during this period for men's and women's committees to be formed separately. The association became known as the Judean General War Auxiliary (Men's Section).

17   Stonnington House was converted into a Convalescent Home and used by the Red Cross Society from 1940 until 1953.

18   At the end of August 1940, across the other side of the world, the *Belfast Newsletter* printed a memory of the reception given to Issy in Dublin 25 years previously. *The Age*, Melbourne, Maryborough; *Belfast News-Letter*, 31 August 1940.

Chapter 37

1   The exact date of death is noted on both the record of Olive's call to the Repatriation Clinic and the attendance by the doctor on the death certificate. The State of Victoria's Registry of Births, Deaths and Marriages incorrectly records the date as 11 September 1940.

2   No autopsy was ever carried out and therefore Issy may or may not have had arteriosclerosis. Similarly it was assumed, from his history of symptoms, that the primary cause of death was coronary thrombosis. Many of these symptoms also appeared in other illnesses. Issy could have died from the abrupt occurrence of something else, such as a stroke. We will never know.

3   Garrison battalions were part of the Australian Army Reserve, raised in each State to assist with Homeland Defence – that is, to man fixed defence and vulnerable locations. They were 'Class B' men who had seen service before the start of WWII, as the Minister of Defence, Brigadier Street had proposed, so were mostly WWI veterans. The 12th Battalion was based in Victoria.

4   A news article even appeared in *The Palestine Post* in Jerusalem; *The Herald*, Melbourne VIC, 11 September 1940, 'Sudden Death of Sergeant Issy Smith', and many more; *The Advertiser*, Adelaide SA, 'Jewish V.C. Holder Dies Suddenly' (and more); *The Sydney Morning Herald*, Sydney NSW, 12 September 1940, 'Death of Sergeant 'Issy' Smith V.C.' and many more; *The Examiner*, Launceston TAS, 'Jewish V.C. Winner Dies';

Endnotes

The Courier-Mail, Brisbane QLD, 'Izzy Smith, Last War V.C., Dead'; *Northern Standard*, Darwin, NT, 'Sgt I. Smith V.C. Dead'.

5   It is possible that this was not the only British announcement, and that there were many more newspaper articles advising of his death that are not yet digitised. However, given such a huge number have been, it is odd.

6   *The Hebrew Standard*, Sydney, 26 September 1940, 'Death of Sergeant 'Issy' Smith V.C.'; *The Bulletin*, Vol. 61 No. 3162, 18 September 1940, and many more.

7   A babysitter was found for Maurice – he was considered too young to attend. The jeering likely reflected the antisemitism that prevailed at the time.

8   *The Age*, Melbourne, 12 September 1940; *The Australian Jewish News*, Melbourne, 20 September 1940, 'Obituary Mr Issy Smith V.C.'; 13 September 1940, 'Funeral of V.C. Winner'; *The Herald*, 12 September 1940, 'Services Pay Last Honors to V.C. Hero'; *The Daily Telegraph*, Sydney, 12 September 1940, '1914–1918 War V.C. Dies, Aged 52'; *The Australian Jewish Herald*, 19 September 1940, 'Feat of Late V.C. Winner Outstanding in Great War, Judean General War Auxiliary – Mens' section' (and many more).

9   *The Argus*, Melbourne, 12 September 1940, Funeral Notices, 'Smith, Issy'; *The Age*, 12 September 1940, 'Smith'.

10   Leaving flowers is not a traditional Jewish practice, but if the flowers had to be removed then the wreath would have simply been put a distance away. The vandalism of the grave is indicative of the prejudiced views prevalent at the time.

11   The bombings, which became known as the Blitz, lasted for eight months. Approximately 43,000 people were killed – nearly half of Britain's total civilian deaths for the whole of the war. The photo of Flora being rescued was sent all over the world and became the graphic image of the Blitz. It is located on a panel in a memorial to the people who were lost, at Owen's Fields, City and Islington College, London. War Memorial to the Victims of the London Blitz, Dame Alice Owen's School, Dame Alice Owen's School, War Memorials, www.damealiceowens.herts.sch.uk

12   *The Australian Jewish Herald*, 2 October 1940, 'Appeal for Late V.C.'s family'; 19 December 1940, 'Issy Smith Appeal, More Support Urged' (and many more); *The Herald*, 10 December 1940, 'Appeal for V.C.'s Widow'.

13   The occupation of Greece by the Axis Powers resulted in mass starvation due to the plundering of food, raw materials and labour. The Australian Comforts Fund was set up in 1916 to send comforts to the troops and continued in the Second World War.

14   *Sporting Globe*, 18 December 1940, 'Members of the Victoria Club'.

15 *The Australian Jewish Herald*, 8 May 1941, 'Plans for Fund, Issy Smith Appeal'; Certificate of Title, Transfer of Land Act, Land Use Victoria.
16 Specks were second-grade fruit. As a child, Maurice was allowed to venture to the local fruiter by himself to fetch these – at a piece a penny.
17 *The Herald*, Melbourne, 25 April 1945, 'Morris Smith'; *The Age*, Melbourne, 26 April 1945, 'Proudly displaying their fathers' decorations', (photo).
18 *The Age*, Melbourne, 26 February 1954, 'Happy Scenes at Cricket Ground'; *The Argus*, Melbourne, 26 April 1956, 'What a time it will be!'; *The Age*, Melbourne, 24 May 1956, 'London Bound; and more'.
19 National Archives, Repatriation General Hospital, Heidelberg Victorian Branch records.

Chapter 38

1 *The Australian Jewish Herald*, 4 June and 18 June 1942, 'Consecration of Tombstone'.
2 *The Courier-Mail*, Brisbane, 13 May 1953, 'Hatred, Passion beat Reason'; *The Advertiser*, Adelaide, 13 May 1953, 'Unsuspected Political Feeling'.
3 *Jewish Telegraph*, 17 November 1989, 'AJEX Remembers Hero'.
4 1995 Annual Report of the protection of Movable Cultural Heritage permit for medals, Appendix II, Permits Issued in 1994–95; Email 26 May 2003 from Paul Oldfield, author of various books, including *Victoria Crosses on the Western Front*; *1995 1996 Annual Report Administrative Appeals Tribunal* Chapter 4, 'Decisions of Interest', p. 198.
5 *Parade*, Official Journal of the VAJEX, October 2010, 'Sgt Issy Smith VC JP, The World Forgot Him but VAJEX hasn't!', p. 17.
6 Hardie Grant Books in conjunction with the State of Victoria, 2014, *In Memoriam – a Guide to the History and Heritage of Victoria's Cemeteries*; Price, John E., Biography / Issy Smith / Australian Dictionary of Biography, https://adb.anu.edu.au/biography/smith-issy-8473

www.ingramcontent.com/pod-product-compliance
Lightning Source LLC
Chambersburg PA
CBHW030218170426
43201CB00006B/131